Late Pleistocene and Early Holocene Small Mammals in South West Britain

Environmental and taphonomic implications and their role in archaeological research

Catherine R. Price

BAR British Series 347
2003

Published in 2016 by
BAR Publishing, Oxford

BAR British Series 347

Late Pleistocene and Early Holocene Small Mammals in South West Britain

ISBN 978 1 84171 485 1

Typesetting and layout: Darko Jerko

BAR Publishing is the trading name of British Archaeological Reports (Oxford) Ltd.
British Archaeological Reports was first incorporated in 1974 to publish the BAR
Series, International and British. In 1992 Hadrian Books Ltd became part of the BAR
group. This volume was originally published by Archaeopress in conjunction with
British Archaeological Reports (Oxford) Ltd / Hadrian Books Ltd, the Series principal
publisher, in 2003. This present volume is published by BAR Publishing, 2016.

Printed in England

BAR
PUBLISHING

BAR titles are available from:

BAR Publishing
122 Banbury Rd, Oxford, OX2 7BP, UK
EMAIL   info@barpublishing.com
PHONE   +44 (0)1865 310431
FAX   +44 (0)1865 316916
www.barpublishing.com

'I should like you to see my house ... the only decorations on the door are the footmarks of various animals ... or the hideous regurgitations of owls'

Abélard to Héloise

Contents

List of Tables

List of figures

List of maps

List of plates

Abstract

This thesis examines small mammal faunas from cave sites in South-west England and South Wales. The aims are threefold:

- To examine the rapid environmental changes taking place in the Late Pleistocene and early Holocene:

- To understand the processes by which small mammal remains were deposited in the caves examined:

- To demonstrate the value of small mammal studies as an archaeological tool.

All identifiable small mammal remains from twelve selected sites are listed. Ten of the sites are new material. As the species examined here are seldom exploited by humans, their biostratigraphy provides a record of the past environment unaffected by human selection of particular species, as might be the case in larger mammal assemblages. An examination of possible agents of accumulation is provided for each site to identify any bias introduced by prey selection. Reconstructions of the environments local to each cave at the time of deposition are offered.

The evidence provided by the small mammals is related to the archaeological findings from each cave, to demonstrate the effect of human habitation of cave sites on the depositional and post-depositional processes shown by the microfauna. The environmental evidence provided by the study reflects a wider landscape rather than merely the immediate surroundings of the cave, and so gives a basis for human exploitation patterns in the area accessible from the cave.

Reconstructions of the ecological mosaics formed by the rapidly changing climate of the period and the topographic variation around the cave sites are provided, demonstrating the potential complexity of the environment in which the humans and other fauna of the period existed. It is hoped that this will encourage archaeologists to look beyond the general division of environmental boundaries in this period, and to examine the local variation in habitat availability and use.

Acknowledgements

This research was made possible by the funding provided by University of Wales College, Newport, and the facilities of SCARAB research department. Special thanks are due to my supervisor, Professor Stephen Aldhouse-Green for his unfailing support, patience and faith in me, and to the departmental head, Professor Miranda Aldhouse-Green for dealing instantly and efficiently with every problem I caused. UWCN also provided funding for my study tour of Sweden, for which I am grateful

I am greatly indebted to Andy Currant, for his supervision of this project, for the encouragement and education he provided from the early days of my interest in small mammal bones, and particularly for his unfailing friendship and good humour in the best and worst of times.

Dr Nick Barton and Alison Roberts deserve special thanks for encouraging me to embark on a PhD, and for providing the opportunity to learn small mammal identification from scratch whilst employed on their excavations and post-excavation programmes in Torbryan and the Wye Valley. Their friendship and support is beyond price.

For access to their collections and facilities to work on material, I would like to thank the Quaternary section of the Department of Prehistoric and Romano-British Antiquities at the British Museum, the Natural History Museum Department of Palaeontology, Cambridge University Museum of Archaeology and Anthropology, University of Oxford Donald Baden-Powell Research Centre, and Kent's Cavern Research Committee. Funding for the excavation of Priory Farm Cave was provided by the National Museum of Wales, and permission to excavate granted by CADW and the landowners Mr and Mrs Wyn Jenkins. I am grateful to the staff of the environmental archaeology laboratory, Umeå University, and particularly to Dr Roger Engelmark and Johan Olofsson for making me welcome and giving every assistance during my stay in Sweden. My thanks are also due to Tim Hipkiss of Umeå University, who provided the contents of many owls' nests.

Thanks are due to many friends who have assisted, supported and encouraged me in different aspects of my work. Drs Roger Jacobi and Chris Gleed-Owen gave valuable advice in the early stages of the project. Dr Martin Street provided much information on European mainland small mammal faunas in the Pleistocene. Dr Simon Parfitt risked life, limb and drowning in owl-guano to secure my first collection of owl pellets, providing essential reference material. Dominic Davis of the Financial Department, UWCN, has been a faithful collector of the victims of cats, adding many interesting comparative specimens to my collection, and my brother, Richard Price, has unstintingly scraped up road-kills and eaten strange species of fish for my benefit. My niece, Llinos, assisted enthusiastically in the preparation of skeletons. Peter Norman of the Dumfries and Galloway ranger service contributed otter spraints, and the voluntary wardens of Skomer Island (Wildlife Trust West Wales) owl and gull pellets. Lucy Gibbons provided invaluable moral support and shared the tribulations of postgraduate research with unfailing good-humour and elegance. Anne Leaver, UWCN Department of Archaeology and Prehistory, offered vital technical support, as well as friendship, company and innumerable cups of coffee.

The photographs are my own, with the exception of plates 2 and 3 which are reproduced by permission of Alison Roberts, and plates 6, 7 and 10 reproduced by permission of Dr R.N.E. Barton.

Especial thanks are due to my mother, Cathy Price, without whose unfailing support this work could not have been completed. She has put up with her garden being turned into a mortuary, her sink being filled with small mammal bones, and travelling many miles in the company of a decomposing stoat and a bag of otter spraints. Her unfailing common sense, good humour and sense of the ridiculous have been invaluable.

Finally, I am indebted to Joe Vole, who by surviving beyond his intended role as a comparative sample has provided valuable insight into the habits of *Microtus* voles, and a great deal of entertainment. I would like to put on record that no animals suffered during the course of this research, and all comparative specimens were obtained as road kill, owl pellets or cat kills.

Chapter 1
Introduction

1. Timescale

This research covers the closing phase of Oxygen Isotope Stage 2 and beginning of OIS 1, from the initial climatic improvement of the Lateglacial Interstadial, c.13,000 BP, to the development of full boreal conditions at around 9,000 BP. The end of the Pleistocene and beginning of the Holocene was a period of massive environmental change in Britain, with the climate swinging from sub-polar to temperate, back to polar or sub-polar, and then finally to temperate again, all within five thousand years. The effect of this climatic change on the vegetation, and so on the animals dependent on it right through the food chain to the large hunters including humans, was dramatic. The archaeological evidence for this period is divided into the Upper Palaeolithic from the Lateglacial Interstadial, and the Mesolithic from the early Holocene. The pre-agriculture hunter-gatherer human societies represented by the cultural material recovered from these periods operated within the existing environment, rather than changing it to serve their own purposes. The other mammals with which they co-existed were an important part of the living environment. Understanding the social and technological developments seen in the human cultural material retrieved in excavation is only possible by reconstructing the natural world in which the hunter-gatherer communities of the period existed, and the forces for change it generated. Studying the small mammals allows a reconstruction of the complete local environment, without the biases introduced into the large mammal assemblage by human hunting preference.

As most excavation on sites of this age is instigated with the aim of recovering evidence of human activity, small mammal remains have been seen as incidental to the research objectives of the fieldwork. However, with the modern perception of archaeological sites as a finite resource and the recognition of the destructive nature of excavation, the planning of fieldwork projects now has to include strategies for maximising the evidence recovered. The excavation team is now likely to include specialists, either on site for the duration of the dig or 'on call' to visit when their input is required. In this way, strategies for positioning trenches, sampling and recording can be developed while the excavation is in progress,

ensuring the retrieval of the maximum available data in the most useful form. This is particularly important for early prehistoric sites, because of their comparative rarity as well as the importance of the environmental evidence to the understanding of human behaviour in the area.

The background environmental evidence is presented in chapter 2, outlining the changes in climate and vegetation between 13,000 and 9,000 BP. This is taken from the available literature generated by a vast amount of research in various fields of environmental archaeology and geography over the past fifty years.

Dates given in the text are in uncalibrated radiocarbon years before present (BP), unless otherwise stated. There are problems inherent in this, as dendrochronology combined with AMS radiocarbon dating has shown two plateaux, at 9550 BP and 9950 BP, where the same radiocarbon age was obtained from tree ring samples covering nearly 400 years and 250 years respectively (Becker & Kromer 1991). The advantage of presenting uncalibrated radiocarbon ages is that it follows the international convention confirmed by the 1985 12th International Radiocarbon Conference, Trondheim (Kra & Stuiver 1986), and so allows the data presented here to be compared with other sources.

2. Geographical boundaries

The area studied in this thesis covers the southwestern peninsula of Great Britain, the Mendips, the Wye Valley and the south coast of Wales. All of the sites considered lie south of the maximum extent of the Devensian ice-sheet, though the South Wales sites, Cathole Cave and Priory Farm Cave would have been at its edge. The area is unlikely to have experienced early or short-term colonisation from the Continent. Sea level at the Devensian maximum has been calculated to have been around 100m lower than at present, and by tracing the –100m marine contour, a wide land-bridge joining mainland Britain to the Continent is reconstructed (Sparks & West 1972). Britain's south-west peninsula was directly linked to Brittany by a wide plain, which would have allowed easy access to mammalian colonisers as the ice retreated, and what is now the English Channel was a low-lying plain offering a corridor to the west. However, recent work on the mitochondrial DNA of temperate small mammal species (common shrew, pygmy shrew and bank vole) suggests that these species invaded the newly temperate Britain from refugia in central Europe and western Asia rather than the Mediterranean area (Bilton *et al.* 1998). This implies a westward colonisation route across the North Sea land-bridge. There is no genetic evidence for northward colonisation from Iberia, and 'Mediterranean refugial populations ... have apparently remained within the Mediterranean peninsulae as geographical isolates' (*op.cit.* p.1219). West England and Wales would therefore represent the furthest extent of east-west immigration. Ireland was isolated by St George's Channel, which at over 100m deep formed a water barrier as soon as the ice melted.

The geology of southern England and Wales played an important part in deciding the boundaries of the region studied. Whilst caves exist in a variety of rock formations, 'one above all others provides extensive integrated cave systems of a size which allows the biologist to study the life they contain with relative ease. It is the Carboniferous Limestone' (Chapman 1993, p.37). The same facility is required by the archaeologist in search of the remains of the dead. Four major areas of cave-bearing limestone exist in mainland Britain; the Northern Pennines, the Peak District of Derbyshire, the Mendip Hills in Somerset and South Wales. The Devonian Limestone exposed to the south-east of Dartmoor also contains extensive cave systems. This allowed the selection of a geographic limitation of the study which still contained adequate potential material. Limestone caves have two particular advantages to research into past faunas. First, the alkali environment is conducive to the preservation of bone, which in acid conditions would be degraded or destroyed. Second, the consolidation of sediment by brecciation may preserve the biostratigraphy, 'set in stone', as it were.

My involvement in the Torbryan Valley Research Project (1998-92), directed by Alison Roberts, and the Wye Valley Caves Project (1994-97), led by Dr Nick Barton, provided a basis for the current work, and to some extent defined the area of study. The selection of further sites relied upon the availability of a large enough collection of small mammal bone covering at least part of the time period under consideration. Sites with poorly defined stratigraphy were omitted, as were those with only small collections of relevant material.

3. Sites

3.1. South Devon

3.1.1. Torbryan Valley

The caves examined are situated in Dyer's Wood, an area of mixed deciduous woodland on the south-west side of a dry valley in the Devonian Limestone, running north-west to south-east.

a. Broken Cavern

NGR SX 8153 6747
Altitude c.70m OD, c.6m above valley floor, c. 9m below plateau level.
Aspect - north.
Description - A collapsed cave, now a rockshelter. Survey and excavation revealed an Early Neolithic occupation horizon (contexts 8, 13, 25) within red stony cave earth (context 7). Below this lies c. 2 metres of stony cave earth and talus material containing no cultural material but offering rich environmental evidence for the early Holocene (contexts Lower 7, 9, 11, 12). A Lateglacial horizon containing Final Palaeolithic flint artefacts underlies the early Holocene material (contexts 14, 21). At the rear of the cave a small deposit of tufaceous material (context 10) containing wolf remains and gnawed reindeer bones seems to show the use of the cave as a wolf den, activity dated by AMS radiocarbon at 10 950 ± 95 BP (OxA-3888), in the Younger Dryas Stadial (Roberts *et al.*, 1996). The collapse of a large part of the cave roof, apparently during the Younger Dryas, left large boulders and a great deal of angular limestone scree in the shelter, providing a loose, vacuous matrix through which subsequent deposits might percolate. See figure 6.1 for the stratigraphic relationships between the contexts, and figure 6.2 for a drawn section through the excavated deposits.

b. Three Holes Cave

NGR SX 8154 6747
Altitude 68m OD, c. 4m above valley floor, c. 11m below plateau level.
Aspect - north-north-east (10°).
Small mammal material was recovered from the excavation of deposits outside the west side of the cave mouth. A layer of stony talus was divided into Red Stony Talus (RST), Black Charcoal Rich Stony Talus (BCST), Dark Brown Stony Talus (DBST), Grey Tufaceous Stony Talus (GTST) and Light Brown Stony Talus (LBST). These cover the archaeological periods from Bronze Age (RST) to Later Mesolithic (LBST). Below the talus deposits were found Late Pleistocene sediments, an orange-brown horizon (OB), the Dark Grey/Black horizon which yielded Upper Palaeolithic artefacts, and an underlying Red Stony Cave Earth (RSCE) (Roberts *et al.* 1996). See figure 6.3 for a drawn section. The disturbance caused by human activity at this site is probably responsible for the poor small mammal evidence recovered. The proximity of Broken Cavern, with less human disturbance, more small mammal remains, but the problem of stratigraphic blurring (see above) allows the two caves to be considered together to provide an environmental reconstruction for the area.

c. Torbryan 6

NGR SX 8170 6738
Altitude 69m OD, 10m above valley floor, 7m below plateau.
Aspect - north.
Description - close to Tornewton Cave, which lies to the east of Torbryan 6. The only deposit of interest here is a shallow band of black-grey sediment adhering to the eastern wall of the cave, around 1.5m above the cave floor. This yielded

Upper Palaeolithic flint microdebitage, burnt bone, and a small amount of microfaunal remains, and may represent a hearth or relocated hearth material. The cave was excavated by J.L. Widger during the 1870s or '80s, after which he seems to have used it as a sort of garden shed during the excavation of Tornewton Cave, sorting through Pleistocene bones there (A.P. Currant, pers. comm.). Material from the floor of Torbryan 6 was therefore deemed unreliable as to its provenance, being as likely to be a discard from the Tornewton assemblage.

3.1.2. Kent's Cavern

NGR SX 9343 6418 - situated on the west side of the dry Ilsham Valley.
Altitude 58m OD, 18m above valley floor, 15m below plateau above.
Aspect - entrances face due east.
Description - A re-examination of this well-known complex cave site was undertaken by Chris Caseldine, Chris Proctor and Peter Berridge in 1991. The microfaunal remains were recovered from sieved samples taken from two areas particularly rich in small mammal remains - Wolf's Cave (Sample Point 1) and High Level Chamber (Sample Point 6). Wolf's Cave is located to the north-west of the cave entrance, adjoining the Cave of Rodentia, while High Level Chamber is at the south-western end of the cave system (see fig. 6.5). A narrow sample section was cut through the Loamy Cave Earth and Wash Facies in Wolf's Cave, in the side of a trench excavated by William Pengelly in 1884 (Proctor 1995). High Level Chamber was formerly the site of an entrance to the cave, now 'choked with Pleistocene sediments' (Proctor 1995, p.91). The samples recovered were not from excavation, but collected from the surface 0.6m beneath an overhang. *In situ* cave earth material containing small mammal remains was observed to be eroding from the underside of the overhang (P. Berridge, excavation field notebook 24/5/91).

3.2. Mendip area

3.2.1. Gough's Cave

NGR ST 4670 5391- on south east side of the deep Cheddar Gorge.
Altitude 30m OD, at base of gorge, 100m below immediate plateau.
Aspect - opens north-west, overshadowed by equally high face of gorge on opposite side.
Description - this is a large show cave, extensively excavated in the past. A large assemblage of Upper Palaeolithic flint artefacts and associated bone has been recovered, providing evidence of comparatively intensive human use of the site. Recent excavations were conducted for the Natural History Museum in 1986-87 and 1989 by Mr A. Currant, Dr R. Jacobi and Professor C. Stringer. These were restricted to a small area near the entrance of the cave. As the floor of the cave is concreted, digging was possible only immediately adjacent to the cave walls. The 1987-89 excavation concentrated on Area I, a trench approximately six metres long, on the north side of the cave from the 'Skeleton Pit' to the grille gate, and a maximum of two metres wide, extending below the overhang

of the cave wall. In 1989-90 Area III was opened outside the grille, roughly the same size as Area I and also running from the concrete edge to beneath the cave wall (see fig.7.1). Investigations of the south side of the cave were sterile. Two distinct bone-bearing sediments were observed, described as 'an upper fine gravel' and an 'underlying red silt' (Currant *et al.* 1989, p.132). The latter overlay the 'unfossiliferous conglomerate' (ibid.). The fine gravel is dated to the Younger Dryas, c.10,500 BP, while the red silt from which the small mammal remains examined here were extracted dates to the Lateglacial Interstadial, around 12,000 BP (see Chapter 7).

3.2.2. Bridged Pot

NGR ST 5260 4866 - situated in Ebbor Gorge, part way up the east side among cliffs
Altitude 175m OD, 33m above valley bottom, 74m below main plateau.
Aspect - west facing.
Description - excavated in 1958 by Charles McBurney. A large collection of small mammal bone (mostly teeth and mandibles) is preserved in the University of Cambridge Museum of Archaeology and Anthropology, where I was able to examine it. McBurney describes the cave as a 'small shelter' which 'consists of a funnel-shaped dissolution hole some 8-10 feet in diameter, only partially roofed' (McBurney 1959, p.262). Prior to excavation, the shelter was largely filled by the conical mound of debris forming beneath the hole. This was first excavated by H. Balch in 1926-29 (Barton & Collcutt 1986), who removed the top and inner slope of the cone, leaving the outer portion intact. McBurney cut trenches through the remaining deposits (see fig.7.3), exposing a stratigraphy including a wide band of reddish yellow thermoclastic gravel or scree (McBurney *op.cit.*) - layer B - which included large numbers of small mammal bones. This deposit was dated at 9090 ± 350 BP (BM-2102R) by radiocarbon analysis of fragments of large mammal limb bone shaft (Bowman *et al.* 1990).

3.3. Wye Valley Caves

3.3.1. King Arthur's Cave

NGR SO 5458 1558 - situated in a low cliff on Great Doward Hill, on the east side of a small dry valley running down to the Wye.
Altitude c.110m OD, above a gentle slope into the valley running down to the Wye at 18m OD. Great Doward Hill rises to 200m above the site.
Aspect - north-north-west (335°).
Description - The cave has a broad entrance platform, where much of the work of the recent excavation programme (1995 - 1996) was concentrated (fig. 8.1). The cave itself comprises two main chambers, which are thought to have been largely emptied by W.S. Symonds' excavations in 1870 - 71 (Barton & Collcutt 1986). The entrance platform was partially covered by the spoil-tips of previous excavations. To the west of the platform a 2m deep stratified sequence of undisturbed deposits was excavated, providing good microfaunal samples (see fig. 8.2). Of particular interest were the two scree deposits - the

upper Yellow Scree, a loose, angular clast deposit, and the lower Dark Scree, similar to the overlying yellow context but with more earth included (Barton *et al.* 1997). These proved to be of Younger Dryas and Lateglacial Interstadial age respectively. The deepest levels of excavation exposed an underlying orange stony earth, and below that, a clayey silt. These two basal contexts were largely sterile, with only fragmentary, very weathered bone (Barton *et al.*, 1997).

3.3.2. Merlin's Cave (Great Doward Cave)

NGR SO 5560 1525 - in south-west side of Great Doward Hill, on right bank of the Wye.
Altitude - 110m OD, 2.75m up vertical cliff face, above steep wooded slope (c. 45°) down to river at 20m OD. Cliff levels to more gentle slope c. 5m above cave entrance, with hilltop above site at 175m OD.
Aspect - faces south-south-west (208°) over River Wye.
Description -The cave is not easily accessible. There is a small platform outside the entrance, which comprises bedrock. The cave is around 14m long, and narrow. The Natural History Museum (London) holds collections of small mammal bone from excavations of the site by Dorothy Bate (1901) and T.F. Hewer & M. Hinton (1924-25), but the cave was disturbed prior to these scientific explorations by ochre or iron miners and bone-hunters (Barton & Collcutt 1986). A 2m x 1m test pit in the cave floor revealed no stratigraphy, the sediment being a homogenous red cave earth with frequent rock and breccia inclusions, and many microfaunal remains. A further deposit of the same sediment was located outside the cave at the foot of the cliff. It seems probable that Hewer, with the collaboration of Martin Hinton, excavated only in the floor of the cave, extracting complete crania and mandibles, and leaving the spoil *in situ*. This is reflected in the Hinton collection studied at the Natural History Museum, which includes no post-cranial material, and in the cave floor assemblage I collected myself, which included few complete skulls, but a great many post-cranial elements. Fossiliferous deposits remained on the cave walls, with a particularly good sequence of bone-rich breccias near the front of the cave on the west wall (see fig.8.4). These were sampled, together with similar concretions from elsewhere in the cave, after careful planning and recording to establish their locations as a form of ready-made section.

3.2.3. Madawg Rockshelter

NGR SO 5474 1527 - on north side of a limestone bluff, part of Seven Sisters' rocks.
Altitude c. 70m OD, above very steep slope down to river.
Aspect - faces almost due west, overlooking the Wye.
Description - the shelter is c. 30m long, 9m deep at maximum, with a roof height of 6m at the front, sloping down to the rear (see fig.8.7 for plan). A vertical rift at the rear is choked with rockfall debris (Barton *et al.* 1997). While only small quantities of fragmented small mammal bone was recovered from samples from this site, it is included in this study for reasons of taphonomic comparison. The sediments uncovered were divided into an upper Grey Tufaceous Earth and an underlying Brown Stony Cave Earth, with large amounts of charcoal and some Late Mesolithic cultural material recovered

from the latter. AMS dates of 8710 ± 70 BP (OxA-6081) and 6655 ± 65 BP (OxA-6082) were obtained on charred sloe stone and charred hazelnut shell respectively, from the lower levels of a feature of redeposited hearth material (see fig. 8.8 – drawn section).

3.2.4. Symonds Yat East Cave

NGR SO 5611 1555 - in cliffs on east bank of River Wye.
Altitude 95m OD, above river at 15m OD and below immediate plateau at 130m OD. High cliffs (>25m) above cave, and steep slope below.
Aspect - north (348°).
Description - a large rockshelter with a small cave leading off at the rear. Excavation was carried out on the narrow platform in front of the cave. Two trenches were opened (see fig. 8.11), locating the trench excavated by Rogers in 1980, and exposing sections through Final Palaeolithic to Late Bronze or Iron Age sediments (see fig. 8.10 – drawn section). Recent reassessment of the stratigraphy together with the small mammal fauna and the cultural material recovered shows that the basal level, containing an *in situ* Final Palaeolithic (c. 12-11,000 BP) assemblage of flint artefacts and knapping debris (Barton 1994), is overlain by a thick layer of red clays, probably from the Lateglacial Stadial (see fig. 8.12).

4. South Wales

4.1. Cathole Cave

NGR SS 5377 9002 - situated on NE side of a small dry valley in woodland.
Altitude 30m OD - 10m above valley bottom, 25m below plateau.
Aspect - main entrance facing west-south-west, smaller entrance facing south-west.
Description - extensively excavated, including work by McBurney in1958-59, and Campbell in 1968. The main entrance 'commands a good view of the valley, or would do if the trees were not there' (Campbell 1977 p.55). Both entrances open into the large main chamber (see fig.9.1). McBurney's excavations inside the cave and at the cave mouth recovered Upper Palaeolithic flint artefacts from layers B and C (McBurney 1959). The stratigraphy was re-investigated by Campbell and refined to five layers within the yellow-buff thermoclastic scree layer B (see fig.9.2 – drawn section). The overlying layer C is a reddish, weathered thermoclastic scree, from near the base of which Mesolithic artefacts were recovered. The majority of recorded finds are from McBurney's excavation, while Campbell's smaller trenches lie largely outside the main occupation area. However, the later work provided the refined stratigraphy and a large collection of small mammal remains. These were examined at the University of Oxford Baden-Powell Quaternary Research Centre. The small mammal material from McBurney's excavation was not examined in detail, as an adequate sample was available in Campbell's more finely stratified collection.

4.2. Priory Farm Cave, Pembroke

NGR SM 9789 0184

Altitude 16m OD. Valley bottom c.2m OD; plateau above, 19m OD. Cave situated at base of low cliff of Carboniferous Limestone, above steep slope down to Pembroke River - at this point tidal, with mudflats.

Aspect - cave entrance faces East-North-East over Pembroke River.

Description - There has been extensive quarrying of the limestone cliffs in the area, and so it is probable that the front part of the cave has been removed. Excavations were conducted at the site by Dr N. Barton (Oxford Brookes University) and myself, with a small team, in 1999 (Barton & Price 1999) and 2000. The cave comprises a narrow main passage leading back c. 30m from the c. 6m wide by 2.5m high entrance, and ending at a terminal choke. A low side passage branches off on the west side, turning to run north, almost parallel to the main passage, before ending in a small chamber and terminal choke. The side passage is extremely low and narrow, being in places no more than 30cm high and c. 45cm wide, allowing only the most grudging access. A full survey of the interior of the cave was completed (Fig.9.3), and remnants of in situ material sampled. Unfortunately, the cave interior was largely emptied by previous excavations by Dr A. Hurrell Style and Mr E.E.L. Dixon in 1906-7 (Barton & Collcutt 1986). The remaining sediment is a homogenous red clay, which appears to be distributed throughout the cave system. At the cave entrance, trenches were excavated to determine the extent of the previous digging and spoil tip, to uncover undisturbed material beyond and beneath these, and to sample in situ material for environmental evidence.

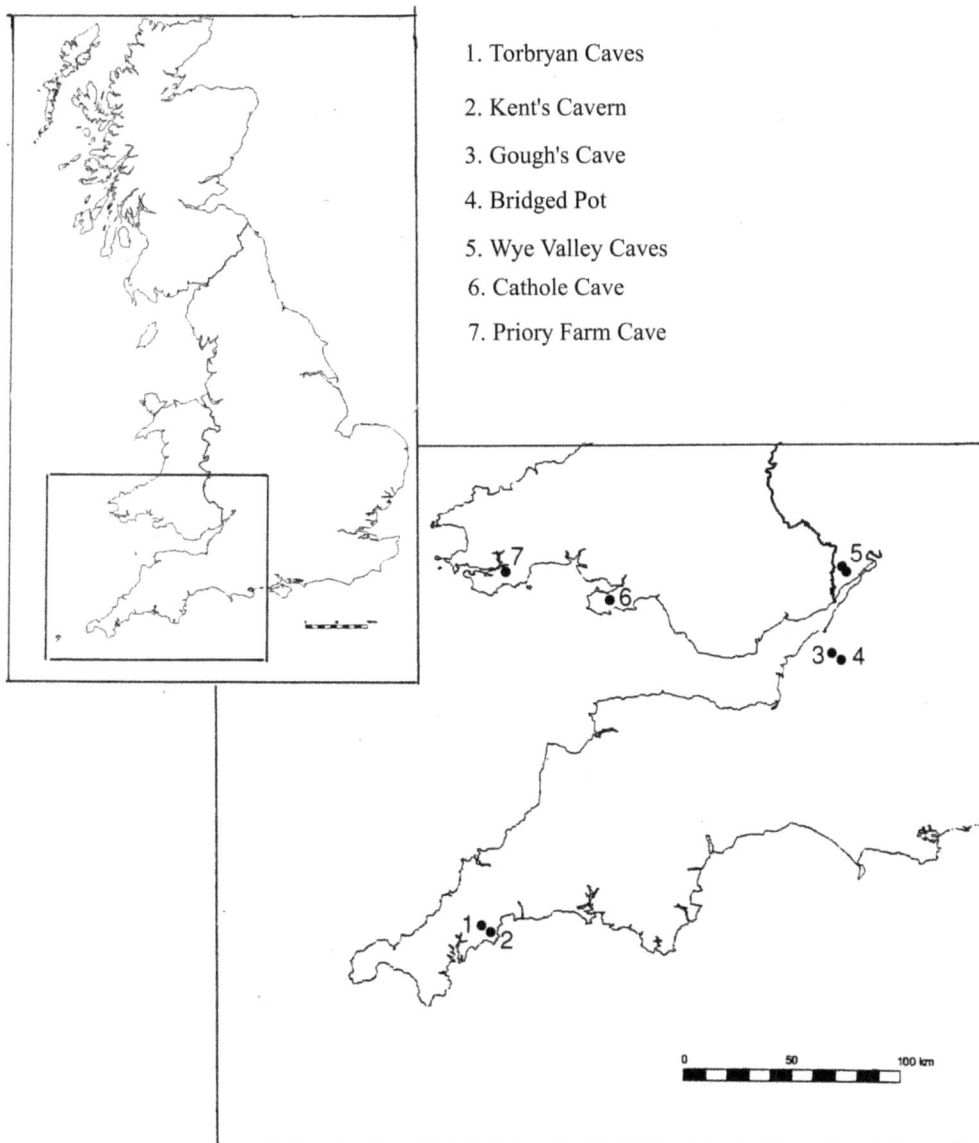

1. Torbryan Caves
2. Kent's Cavern
3. Gough's Cave
4. Bridged Pot
5. Wye Valley Caves
6. Cathole Cave
7. Priory Farm Cave

Map 1.1 – Map showing locations of sites examined

Chapter 2
Background Environmental Evidence

Overview: Environmental Background from 18,000 to 9,000 BP

The last major glaciation, in British terms the Devensian Main Stadial, reached its maximum extent between 22,000 and 18,000 BP in terms of maximum global ice volume (Bowen 2000), with ice sheets reaching as far south as Cardiff. Mean annual temperatures around 16-17° centigrade lower than present, with a mean July temperature of c.8°C, are conjectured throughout what is now Britain, then joined extensively to the European mainland as sea levels were up to 130m lower than present (Chappell & Shackleton 1986). The cold climate would have restricted the vegetation to mosses, sedges, and grasses, described as 'steppe-tundra' (Adams 1998) - a classification having no modern analogue, combining tundra elements in moister areas with typically steppe flora in the drier zones.

A steep rise in actual temperature at around 13,000 BP produced warm summers, at least 17°C, though winter temperatures remained comparatively cold (average1°C). This marked the beginning of the Lateglacial or Windermere interstadial, which is equivalent to the European Bølling and Allerød interstadials. There is little evidence in southern Britain of the Older Dryas cold phase between c. 12,000 and 11,800 dividing the two interstadial phases identified in sequences from continental Europe. The initial warming rapidly attained temperatures sufficient to support the growth of temperate woodland, but tree growth was delayed by other factors, such as the lack of stable ground and fertile soils in previously glaciated areas. Plant communities were dominated by coloniser species (*Rumex, Juniperus*) able to withstand poor soils and exploiting the rapidly changing conditions. Tree species were able to establish themselves in succession to these colonisers (Pennington 1977) but, by the time open birch woodland was spreading across Britain, the climate was

Table 2.1 – British and European subdivisions of the Late Glacial (Barton, Roberts & Roe 1991).

Radio-carbon years BP	Pollen zones (after Iversen 1954)	NW Europe chrono-zones (based on Mangerud et al 1974)	NW Europe climato-stratigraphic units (after Lowe & Gray 1980)	British biozones (based on Gray & Lowe 1977; Coope & Pennington 1977)
	IV	PREBOREAL	FLANDRIAN INTERGLACIAL	FLANDRIAN
10,000				
			TRANSITION	
10,500	III	YOUNGER DRYAS		LOCH LOMOND STADIAL
			YOUNGER DRYAS STADIAL	
11,000				
11,800	II	ALLERØD		WINDERMERE INTERSTADIAL
			TRANSITION	
	Ic	OLDER DRYAS		
12,000	Ib	BØLLING		
			LATE GLACIAL INTERSTADIAL	
13,000	Ia			
			TRANSITION	
14,000		WEICHSELIAN STAGE	LATE DEVENSIAN/MAIN STADIAL	LATE DEVENSIAN

cooling once more (Coope *et al.* 1998). The spread of tree birch was gradual across different areas of the country, and whilst there is pollen evidence of increasing birch at 12,500 - 12,000 BP in the southern Lake District, in North Wales this is not seen until 11,900 - 11,000 BP (Pennington1977). Altitude, aspect and edaphic factors all influence rates of plant immigration and colonisation. This will be examined more fully below. Coope *et al.* (1998) correlate the beginning of the Lateglacial interstadial with the GRIP Greenland ice-core GI-1e interstadial event, and the later part of the interstadial, as temperatures declined, with interstadial events GI-1d to GI-1a. The isotope record of interstadial events GI-1d to -1a reflects 'highly unstable climatic conditions' (Coope *et al.*1998 p.421) coinciding with the birch pollen maximum.

A rapid cooling episode at around 10,800 BP led to the regrowth of icesheets in Scotland and on high ground in the Lake District and Wales. This is termed the Loch Lomond Stadial in the British sequence, and equates with the Younger Dryas of the European records. While the cold must have been severe, particularly in areas of glacier development, there is evidence to suggest considerable local variation in the effects of this reversal of the climatic trend. This will be discussed in reference to regional environmental developments. It is quite possible that whilst exposed areas were once again deforested, clumps of tree birch might have survived in more sheltered locations amongst the juniper and dwarf shrub communities suggested by the pollen records. Generalised isotherms reconstructed by Coope *et al.* (1998) show the maximum temperature of the warmest month at less than 9°C in areas of Britain north east of a line between East Anglia and the Rhinns of Galloway, and at 9-11°C to the south, compared with post-glacial temperatures (10,000 – 9,000 BP) of 15-17°C over most of Britain, and 17-19°C south of a line between Strumble Head in Dyfed and the Thames estuary. The division between 'arctic' and 'sub-arctic' in climatic classification is drawn at the 10°C July isotherm (Köppen, 1933), placing at least the Devon, Mendip and Wye Valley sites in the sub-arctic rather than the arctic zone during the Younger Dryas.

Interpretation of Greenland ice-cores indicates that the Loch Lomond stadial ended very suddenly at around 10 000 BP. Within 75 years temperatures had risen to give temperate conditions. This warming phase marks the beginning of the Holocene. Birch woodland quickly expanded and was succeeded by more thermophilous tree species (oak, hazel etc) which formed closed forest by around 8,000 BP.

Regional Environmental Evidence

1. South Devon

Pollen stratigraphies have been studied from sites on Dartmoor - Black Ridge Brook (Caseldine & Maguire 1986), Shaugh Moor (Smith *et al.*1981); on Bodmin Moor - Hawks Tor, Parsons Park, Dozmary Pool (Brown 1977); and from marine deposits off south east Devon (Clarke 1970). Of these, the evidence from Hawks Tor (Brown, 1977) is potentially most useful, as the deposits span the whole of the late glacial and

early Holocene time range of this study, and radiocarbon dates were secured for each level. The site is also included by Coope in his investigation of coleopteran assemblages (Coope *et al*, 1998), providing estimates of actual temperature ranges for the area. However, it must be remembered that the Hawks Tor samples are from an elevation of 229m OD, compared with sites sampled for this study in Torbryan Valley, at around 80m OD, and that the Torbryan Valley is sheltered by much higher ground in every direction.

The record from Bodmin shows a slow response to the climatic amelioration of the Lateglacial Interstadial. The birch pollen maximum taken to indicate the Allerød (Godwin's pollen zone II) lies between c.11 500 and 11 000 BP. Even where birch colonised the hillsides, the continuing evidence of *Empetrum* (crowberry) suggests quite open conditions persisting. Pre-Allerød silts contain plant fossils similar to the modern Scottish highlands – 'a collection of snow-bed, flush and lichen/moss heath vegetation' (Brown 1977, p.282), suggesting raw, unstable ground. Edaphic conditions would have to improve considerably before tree birches could colonise and mature sufficiently to produce flowers. Juniper is present both before and after the rise in birch values, showing gradual warming from the semi-polar conditions of the full glacial. It is probable that juniper survived the Younger Dryas cold phase, insulated from severe cold by thick snow. Brown describes the pre- and post-Allerød assemblages as 'derived from communities frequently associated with solifluction phenomena' (*op.cit.* p.287), particularly the slumping of soils caused by saturation during the thaw of thick snow cover. This is seen as indicative of an oceanic climate, where humid air currents combined with decreasing temperatures in the Younger Dryas might produce snowfall of increasing frequency and depth. Vegetation would be limited to those species able to withstand the snow, and in some places, the renewed instability of the soliflucted soils.

Climatic amelioration after the Loch Lomond Stadial is first demonstrated by a peak in juniper levels at around 9500 BP as the species, having survived the cold period, responded to warmer conditions with increased flowering. On Dartmoor and Bodmin Moor, the development of birch/willow carr on wetter soils, and of open birch woodland on the drier hill slopes led to the disappearance of juniper, but not of crowberry. A steady development of temperate post-glacial vegetation followed, with full woodland conditions held back by the exposed upland locality. It seems likely that areas to the south east, sheltered by the higher ground now known as Bodmin Moor and Dartmoor, might have responded more promptly to the very rapid temperature rise shown by the Greenland ice cores, a change from almost glacial to temperate conditions in perhaps less than fifty years. It has been estimated that 'about half of the warming was concentrated into a single period of less than 15 years' (Adams 1997, p.5).

Maximum temperatures at Hawk's Tor (from Coope *et al.*1998) have been established by the mutual climatic range method applied to fossil coleopteran assemblages:

14.5 -13.0 kBP 11°C

13.0 - 12.5 kBP 19°C

12.5 - 12.2 kBP 13°C (much lower than expected for Allerød)

The coleoptera show a climatic deterioration at the horizon where *Betula* pollen curve rises in many sites in Britain.

For the Younger Dryas, no specific data is available for the SW peninsula, but generalised isotherms put temperatures at 9 - 11°C between 11.000 and 10.000 BP. Between 10,000 – 9,000 BP the general isotherm is 17 - 19°C. Recent records of climate in the region show that the Torbryan area is indeed relatively sheltered, with an average annual rainfall of between 1000 and 1200mm between 1941 and 1970, compared with 2000mm on the peaks of Dartmoor, and 1800mm on Bodmin Moor (Meteorological Office, 1990). Temperature records from Exmouth, on the sheltered south coast, show a greater number of days reaching very high temperatures than either Ilfracombe on the north coast of the peninsula or North Hessary Tor on Dartmoor. At Exmouth temperatures of over 25°C were attained on an average of 3.1 days per year, at Ilfracombe on an average of 1.8 days per year and at North Hessary Tor on an average of only 0.3 days per year during the period 1961 to 1980. In the colder months during the same period, temperatures of less than -5°C were recorded at Exmouth on an average 2.3 days per year, at Ilfracombe on an average 0.2 days per year, and on North Hessary Tor on an average 5.2 days per year (*op.cit.*, p.5). The south coast can thus be seen to show rather less Atlantic influence with warmer summer and colder winter climates than the north coast, but enjoying warmer winter conditions than the exposed upland Dartmoor. Generally drier conditions are indicated by the average rainfall isobars, with Exmouth suffering less than 800mm rain per year while Ilfracombe has between 1000 and 1200mm on average. The more inland Torbryan Valley exhibits a similar but slightly moderated climatic regime.

2. Mendip

Pollen analyses from Badger Hole, Gough's Cave and Hyaena Den (Campbell 1968) imply that there is a presence of *Pinus*, *Betula*, *Juniperus* and *Salix* through the late Pleistocene deposits. However, analyses by Leroi-Gourhan of thoroughly cleaned sediment block samples from Painter's 1949-50 excavations at Gough's Cave show Campbell's results to be heavily distorted by pollen introduced by later episodes of flooding, which contaminated the Lateglacial pollen spectra with quantities of willow and sedge. Instead, she shows that 'tree pollen does not exceed 10% in any sample' (Leroi-Gourhan 1985 p.142), and that tree species were limited to *Betula* (birch), *Juniperus* (juniper), *Alnus* (alder) and *Corylus* (hazel). The low frequency of pine pollen is considered to be windborne, possibly over long distances. The sheltered Cheddar Gorge may have supported a slightly more wooded environment during the Lateglacial Interstadial than is suggested for the previously mentioned exposed upland sites - 'Thanks to the humidity brought by springs and streams, and to the shelter provided by the cliffs, gallery woodlands, with alder, willow and hazel, were able to develop' (Leroi-Gourhan 1985, p.142). The surrounding upland area is seen to support a steppe-type vegetation. It should be noted that pollen evidence from cave deposits is rarely completely reliable, as water movement through the system may introduce pollen, especially of riparian species, from some distance

(Evans & O'Connor 1989). This can easily infiltrate earlier deposits, producing a completely false picture of the contemporary vegetation. Where possible, pollen evidence from sampling of peats, mires or lake deposits should be preferred, even where they are only available some distance away.

3. Southern Wye Valley/Forest of Dean

The climate and environment of the Southern Wye Valley, sheltered as it is from westerly winds, is more akin to Central England than Wales (Meteorological Office 1999). Particularly during the Younger Dryas, westerlies are seen to have dominated the weather system of western Britain, bringing with them the cold influence of offshore ice sheets, perhaps as far south as 52°N during winter (Isarin et al 1998). Unfortunately, no pollen profiles directly relating to the area are available, so reconstruction relies on extrapolation from sites further afield, invariably from more exposed, more elevated locations, such as Elan Valley Bog in Cardiganshire (Moore 1970), Llangorse Lake in the Brecon Beacons (Walker et al, 1993), Llyn Mire in the upper Wye Valley (Moore 1978), and Llanilid, Mid Glamorgan (Walker & Harkness 1990, Coope *et al.* 1998). At c. 60m OD, the site at Llanilid is slightly lower than the Wye Valley caves, and lies in a relatively sheltered position. It is probable that the pollen profile from Llanilid gives a more accurate indication of the environment in the Wye Valley than those from more exposed sites. The evidence will be examined below, in section 4 (Gower peninsula).

Similar sequences to those from Bodmin Moor are found in the Welsh sites. Dwarf shrub heath including *Betula nana* (dwarf birch) and *Dryas octopetala* (mountain avens), and taller herb communities including indicators of disturbed soils, give way to increasingly shrubby vegetation as the climate improved at the beginning of the Lateglacial Interstadial. Pollen of tree birches and juniper show rapidly increasing values, indicating the spread of birch carr in damper areas, and scrubby birch and juniper on the hillsides (Moore 1970).

The full development of the interstadial environment is marked by a peak in tree birch pollen, with juniper values still high. Tall herb communities from this zone (Godwin's pollen zone II) include new warmth-demanding species such as *Filipendula* (meadowsweet) and *Urtica* (nettle). The deterioration of the short-lived warm period is shown by decreasing tree birch values. While juniper values also decrease, the species continues to contribute pollen. Exposed montane grassland is indicated, especially by the appearence of *Artemisia norvegica* (Norwegian mugwort) and other indicators of short, dry turf communities. A mixture of thermophilous and non-thermophilous tall herbs shows that the prevailing conditions, while colder than previously, were not yet cold enough to eliminate species such as meadowsweet, and so present a transitional phase before the onset of the Loch Lomond Stadial (Younger Dryas) and the return of dwarf shrubs, montane and alpine communities, and indicators of disturbed soils, showing cold conditions and associated solifluction (Moore 1970). In the more sheltered southern Wye Valley it seems likely that a more transitional vegetation continued, with a progression from the valley floor to the more exposed high ground.

The transition from stadial to interstadial conditions marking the onset of the Holocene is shown first by a re-expansion of juniper (as in Devon, either the result of increased flowering or of reinvasion by the species), decreasing dwarf birch, and the disappearance of many of the species typical of alpine and montane grassland. The beginning of the post-glacial or Holocene *sensu stricto* (Godwin's zone IV) is shown by rapid expansion of birch (Moore 1970, Walker *et al.* 1993). Macrofossils from Elan Valley Bog are identified as *Betula pubescens* (downy birch), which 'generally replaces *B. pendula* [silver birch] on badly drained soils' (Blamey & Grey-Wilson 1989, p.54), indicating local carr development, which Moore admits 'may have exaggerated this expansion' (Moore 1970, p.373), but he goes on to point out that the gradual decrease in juniper pollen indicates that the hillside juniper scrub was also being replaced by birch. The stabilising influence of the birch cover, and its organic input into the soil, allowed the invasion of secondary coloniser tree species. At Llangorse Lake *Pinus sylvestris* (Scots pine) and *Corylus* (hazel) were established by c. 9300BP, followed rapidly by elm (*Ulmus*) and oak (*Quercus*), forming a dense mixed woodland over the pollen catchment area by c. 9000 BP (Walker *et al* 1993).

As in Devon and Cornwall, there is evidence from Llangorse Lake for a fairly arid climate during the Loch Lomond Stadial, continuing into the early Holocene, as high counts of *Artemesia* (mugwort) pollen are found throughout the period. Mollusc and ostracod evidence indicates the lake was becoming shallower in response to this relatively dry climate, a trend supported by the findings of Isarin *et al.* (1998), who suggest from multi-proxy analyses that the Loch Lomond stadial might be divided into an early phase of maximum cold and humidity, followed by a later phase of less cold and relatively dry conditions. Lower-lying, more sheltered areas such as the lower Wye Valley were probably to some extent buffered against the extremes of dryness, as they were against the extreme cold.

At Llangorse, many open ground herbaceous species were present for at least the first 500 years of the Holocene, some indicative of bare and unstable soils. These show soil instability and erosion continuing for the first few centuries of the Post-glacial, presumably until soil development processes had been underway for long enough to provide sufficient nutrients and stability to support the larger, longer-lived tree species.

Mean July temperatures, derived from beetle mutual climatic range data (Coope *et al.* 1998) from Llanilid, are given as

13,000 - 12,500 BP - 19°C
12,500 - 12,000 BP - 15°C
12,000 - 11,000 BP - 11.5°C
11,000 - 10,000 BP - 9°C
10,000 - 9,000 BP - 21°C

In the reconstructed isotherm diagrams of Coope et al (1998), all of the sites under consideration in this thesis are in same band, except between 12,000 and 11,800 BP when the SW peninsula and Pembroke are in the 13 - 15° C band, whilst the Wye Valley, Gower and Mendips sites are in the 11 - 13°C band. The largest difference is likely to have been caused by the degree of shelter and altitude at each site, and in this respect the various sites examined, with the exception of Priory Farm Cave in Pembroke, would have enjoyed temperatures at the upper end of the isotherm range.

4. Gower peninsula

Evidence presented by Campbell (1977) suggests that *Pinus* and *Betula* were present in the vicinity of Cathole Cave during the Lateglacial Interstadial. His percentage of trees and shrubs to non-arboreal pollen increases through the Lateglacial Interstadial with no Bølling/Allerød division until it drops in Younger Dryas (Campbell's layer USB). In his diagram (1977 vol.2, p.223), an increase in thermophilous tree species is seen before the arboreal pollen decline indicating the Younger Dryas, suggesting problems either of contamination of the samples or in interpreting and presenting the results. Bowen (1980) suggests that some of pollen may be derived, and Jacobi (1980) argues that most of it is Holocene. It should certainly be treated with caution.

The pollen analysis and detailed dating programme carried out on samples from Llanilid (see section 3, this chapter, for location) offer a detailed record of environmental fluctuations in the Late Glacial and early Holocene periods from 14,200 ± 75 to 9,320 ± 60 BP (Walker & Harkness, 1990). The beginning of the Lateglacial Interstadial, at 13,200 BP, is characterised by a high proportion of grass pollen, declining sedge values and high *Rumex* values (docks and sorrels), indicative of poor soils and open conditions. The juniper maximum, taken to indicate the warmest part of the Lateglacial (Lowe & Walker, 1986) lies between 12,400 and 12,500 BP, accompanied by lesser rises in birch and willow. At 12,200 BP, the marked decline in juniper common to pollen diagrams for this period, is seen as preceding the increase in birch. This suggests that, rather than the juniper decline resulting from the increasing birch shading it out, it was caused by climatic cooling (Walker & Harkness, 1990). At 11,700 'the abrupt increase in *Betula* pollen ... marks the establishment of closed birch woodland in lowland South Wales' (Walker & Harkness, *op. cit*, p.141). The continuation of high juniper values seen in the Llyn Mire diagram is absent at Llanilid, where the lower, more sheltered position was no doubt more favourable to woodland development. A decline in birch between c. 11,400 and 11,300 BP suggests a cooler period, recovering, with a second increase in birch, before the beginning of the Younger Dryas Stadial at around 11,000 BP. Birch continues to contribute around 20% of the total land pollen for most of the cold period, and there is a noticeable increase in sedge and *Artemisia* (mugwort) pollen, suggesting a fairly arid climate. Sedges do not necessarily indicate damp conditions. Many species thrive in waterlogged soils, but others colonise drier areas with poor, infertile soil (Fitter *et al.* 1984). The beginning of the Flandrian, marked by a rapid rise in birch pollen, is preceded by an increase in juniper, indicating the initial warming phase starting after 10,500 BP. Juniper reaches a maximum at 9,850

BP, at which point there is a fall in sedge pollen and a clear rise in the thermophilous *Filipendula* (meadowsweet). A sudden rise in birch values at 9,600 BP shows a return to closed birch woodland at an earlier date than is seen on Bodmin Moor (c. 9,200 BP - Brown 1977), once again demonstrating the effect of elevation and local topography on the vegetational reponse rate to climatic change. By 9,300 BP, hazel (*Corylus*) appeared for the first time in the pollen record for Llanilid, at a similar time as it colonised South-West Britain (Brown 1977, Walker & Harkness 1990). Information relating to the Llanilid pollen evidence is taken from Walker & Harkness (*op.cit*), including their interpretation of the radiocarbon dates of major biostratigraphic horizons. Interpretation of the environmental significance of particular species is based on my own experience, however, and does not necessarily reflect the opinions of others. The forthcoming publication of a further examination of the pollen and plant macrofossil material from Llanilid (Walker, pers. comm) is eagerly awaited.

5. Pembrokeshire

Irish Sea ice was present off both north and south Pembrokeshire during the last glacial maximum (18,000 BP). Isarin *et al.* (1998) indicate the winter sea ice margin during the Younger Dryas lying about level with the South Irish coast and Pembrokeshire at 52° North (just south of Strumble Head). The simulated westerly storm track hits Britain level with Pembrokeshire bringing strong westerly winds from the sea, air cooled by sea ice in winter. 'In the YD [Younger Dryas] simulation this [steepest] thermal gradient was located just south of the sea-ice edge and ... here the atmospheric instability was evident as an increase in cyclonic activity and an increase in jet-stream strength' (Isarin *et al.*1998, p.450). Isarin *et al.* postulate that though most precipitation would have fallen as snow, 'the combination of a sparse vegetation ... with very strong winds probably prevented a thick snow pack' (*op.cit.,* p. 451). This would mean that the insulating effect of a deep layer of snow would have been lacking. Exposed coastal areas of western Britain would have offered a bleak and unforgiving environment to living creatures.

The mean temperature of the warmest month in the coldest part of Younger Dryas lay between 13° and 14° C; the maximum mean temperature of the coldest month for same period was -15 to -20° C. (Isarin *et al.*, 1998).

Pollen evidence from Little Hoyle Cave, collected during Dr S. Green's excavations in 1984 (Green 1986), shows no major development of woodland during the Lateglacial. The context containing evidence of Upper Palaeolithic occupation, the Red Cave Earth (layer 12), appears only as a lens within the Upper Scree (layer 3). The scree deposit appears to have been devoid of pollen, as no record is given of its presence. The deposit underlying the scree, the Buff Grey Silt (layer 4) contained pollen interpreted by Coles as coming from 'a form of scrub or park tundra. Large open expanses of grassland with a varied herb flora, punctuated at intervals by thin stands of Pine, Birch and Juniper' (Coles 1986 p.117), in a relatively cold and wet climate. The overlying screes are expected to be the product of thermoclastic shatter during a very cold period, and appear to be very similar to the Younger Dryas scree deposits at King Arthur's Cave. The Red Cave Earth produced pollen showing 'a major decrease in the incidence of *Pinus* and *Juniperus*' (Coles *op.cit*, p.117), and only a single grain of *Betula*. Herbs of open or disturbed ground, grasses, sedges, mosses and ferns were common, suggesting 'open tree-less tundra'. Coles goes on to comment 'the low total pollen-count suggests low biological productivity in a very harsh environment' (*op.cit*, p.117). If, as he suggests and as the archaeological evidence would indicate, this is the Late Devensian oscillation, it shows none of the birch woodland development found at Llanilid, and implies that the western extremity of Wales rather missed out on the Lateglacial Interstadial. The absence of dates makes it difficult to present definite conclusions about the timing and nature of environmental changes shown by the pollen here. It is to be hoped that some future palynologist will locate and investigate sediments from an equally westerly site, preferably not in cave deposits, to prove or conclusively disprove the depressingly and unrelievedly cold and wet prehistory of Dyfed.

Chapter 3
Small Mammals as Environmental Indicators: Method of Reconstruction

The use of small mammals as proxy evidence for past environments depends entirely on an understanding of the way of life of the individual species under consideration and how they operate as members of what ecologists refer to as a 'guild' - that is, as common consumers of plant resources, or in the case of shrews, moles and hedgehogs, of invertebrates. Knowledge of their requirements for life - foodstuffs, shelter, climate range etc. - allows the student to mentally construct a suitable ecological niche into which the small mammals, represented by recovered bones from a site, might fit. Such knowledge is based primarily on the study of the current distribution and lifestyle of modern rodent and insectivore populations.

Dramatis Personae

Except where directly referenced, information in this section is taken from Corbet & Harris 1991.

Lepus timidus (arctic hare)

Size - head-body length 457-545mm, weight average 2.8kg.

Teeth - molars and pre-molars prismatic, unrooted. Molars divided into two prisms by deep infolding. Second pair of very small incisors immediately behind first large upper incisors (Hillson 1986). Dental formula 2/1, 0/0, 3/2, 3/3 = 28.

Habitat - tundra and boreal forest, heather moorland, montane grassland. Lowland grassland in absence of brown hare (*Lepus europaeus*). See map 3.1 for modern distribution.

Behaviour - nocturnal and crepuscular, but sometimes active in daylight. Feeds by grazing on grasses and herbs during summer, and browsing on more woody plant material when grass is poor. Breeding season February - August, 1-3 litters per year, 1-4 young per litter. A short burrow may be excavated to shelter young; adult hares use shallow scrapes during hard weather and burrow through deep snow for insulation. Moults from grey-brown summer pelt to white winter coat in response to shorter day length, but colour change may be incomplete or even absent particularly in lowland areas (eg. much of Ireland). Life-span maximum 9 years (Macdonald & Barrett 1993).

Predators - Foxes, wild cats, stoats, large owls (eg. eagle owl), eagles & hawks.

Ochotona pusilla (steppe pika)

Specific information on *O. pusilla* is scarce, more extensive research having been concentrated on the American pikas. Information given here is taken from Nowak 1999.

Size - head-body length average 200mm, weight c. 125-300g.

Teeth - molars and premolars prismatic, rootless. Large first incisors have infold in front enamel, molars divided by deep infolding into two prisms, three in M^2. Upper third molar absent, upper third premolar reduced. Dental formula 2/1, 0/0, 3/2, 2/3 = 26. (Hillson 1986).

Habitat - open plains, desert and steppes, especially in rocky areas. Confined now to the steppe region of Russia and Kazakhstan. See map 3.2 for modern distribution.

Behaviour - Active at all hours, particularly early morning and evening. Feeds on grasses, sedges and herbs, woody plant material. Collects grass into 'haystacks' as provision against winter, but also forage even in extremely cold weather. Do not hibernate - 'individuals have been observed sunning themselves on bright days when the temperature was -17°C' (Nowak 1999, p.1718). Breeding season spring & summer, 3-5 litters per year, average 8 or 9 young per litter. Excavates burrows for shelter. 'Reported to be gregarious, and to live in large colonies' (Nowak 1999, p.1718)

Predators - owls, hawks, foxes, mustelids.

Scuirus vulgaris (red squirrel)

Size – Head-body length 18-24cm. Weight 250-350g.

Teeth – Low-crowned, quadrate cheek-teeth, with rounded cusps and concave centres. Large incisors. Dental formula 1/1, 0/0, 2/1, 3/3 = 22.

Habitat – Conifer forest or mixed woodland. Large tracts of woodland preferred. See map 3.16 for modern distribution.

Behaviour – Diurnal. Does not hibernate, but may remain inactive for long periods in harsh weather. Largely vegetarian, taking tree seeds, bark, sap tissue and fungi. Occasionally nestlings and birds' eggs. Constructs spherical nest (drey) in tree, usually above 6m, from twigs and lined with moss and grass. Breeding season March-May or July-September, 1-2 litters per year, average 3 young per litter. Lifespan max. 6-7 years.

Predators – Raptors (goshawk, buzzard), pine martens.

Arvicola terrestris (water vole)

Size - head-body length 120-235mm, weight up to 320g.

Teeth - Molars prismatic, rootless. Tooth row >8mm. Dental formula 1/1, 0/0, 0/0, 3/3 = 16.

Habitat - In UK restricted to freshwater riparian habitats. Favours streams up to 3m wide, slow-flowing, with steep banks with abundant vegetation. In mainland Europe and Scandinavia, occurs away from water, favouring pasture and open grassland where it burrows extensively. In these populations, seasonal migration from wet to drier habitat may be followed. See map 3.5 for modern distribution.

Behaviour - Mainly diurnal. Largely vegetarian, feeding on sedges, grasses (particularly *Phragmites* or common reed) and roots of riparian vegetation. Riverbank burrows often have entrances both above and below water level. Swims well. Breeding - April-September, 2-5 litters per year, 4-6 young per litter.

Predators - owls, hawks, herons, foxes, weasels, mink, otters, pike.

Microtus agrestis (field vole)

Size - head-body length 78-135mm. Weight 14-50g

Teeth - molars prismatic, rootless. Tooth row <7mm.

Identifiable from other *Microtus* species by small additional 3rd loop on inside of second upper molar. Dental morphology variable. Dental formula 1/1, 0/0, 0/0, 3/3 = 16

Habitat - grassland, with preference for rough tussocky vegetation, not too heavily grazed. Road verges increasingly important, and young forestry plantation with long grass. See map 3.7 for modern distribution.

Behaviour - Mainly nocturnal in summer, more diurnal in winter. Generally herbivorous, feeding on grasses and herbs. The continuously growing teeth allow coarse, silica rich grasses to be consumed. In winter, bark is often eaten, especially when snow cover prevents grazing. Forms runs beneath ground-level vegetation and also burrows. Breeding season March-October, 2-7 litters per year, 4-7 young per litter. Females sexually mature at c. 6 weeks. Multi-annual population cycles usual in northern areas (Scotland, Scandinavia) but not in southern parts of range. All *Microtus* voles have 'an astounding reproductive potential and if conditions were absolutely ideal ... one pair could in theory produce after only two years a population of several hundred thousand or even millions' (Stewart 1992 p.69). Disperse readily into suitable habitats, especially when population levels are high in home territory. Life expectancy maximum two years, with few surviving second autumn.

Predators - many birds and mammals: owls, kestrels, hawks, foxes, mustelids. Field voles often seem to be the preferred small mammal prey species, eg. of foxes and short eared owls, frequently providing almost the complete diet of the latter in Britain (Mikkola 1983).

Microtus oeconomus (northern vole or root vole)

Earlier writers may refer to this species as *M.ratticeps*.

Size - head-body length 85-161mm. Weight 25-62g (possibly up to c. 100g)

Teeth - Molars prismatic, rootless. Distinctive long first loop of first lower molar (M_1); second upper molar (M^2) distinguished from that of *M. agrestis* by lack of third loop on inside (in common with *M. gregalis, M. arvalis* etc.). Dental formula 1/1, 0/0, 0/0, 3/3 = 16.

Habitat - Damp or swampy grassland with tall vegetation. Where field voles are also present, the Northern vole favours wetter areas than the field vole, but will inhabit drier areas when there is little or no competition from other vole species. Forms runways through reeds and sedges, with nests above ground in wet areas. In drier conditions, burrows extensively. Seasonal migration to over-winter in higher, drier habitats. See map 3.6 for modern distribution.

Behaviour - similar to field vole. Feeds on shoots and leaves of reeds and sedges, grasses and aquatic plants. Breeding season April-October in southern part of range (Netherlands etc), shorter further north. 2-5 litters per year, 2-11 young per litter. Adept swimmer and diver; climbs to reach soft vegetation - though personal observation of *Microtus* voles in captivity suggests that while they can climb upwards with relative facility, climbing downwards is usually undignified at best. Often they just let go and fall.

Predators - as field vole.

This species tends to be out-competed by other *Microtus* species (De Jonge & Dienske, 1979), which may account for its apparent disappearance from the British fauna in the early Holocene, whereas it survives on the Continent. Specimens have been recovered from Bronze Age deposits from Nornour, Scilly Isles (Pernetta J.C & Handford P.T. 1970), but the latest record from mainland Britain cited by Yalden is from the early part of the Boreal period (c. 9000 BP) at Nazeing, Essex (Yalden 1999).

Microtus gregalis (narrow-skulled vole)

Information given here is taken largely from Ognev 1964, where 14 subspecies of *M. gregalis* are described, with considerable variation in behaviour and habitat preference.

Size - head-body length 100-148mm, weight 35-60g. Largest subspecies from far north-tundra areas (Ognev *op.cit.*).

Teeth - similar to *M. oeconomus*. Molars prismatic, rootless. Morphology of first lower molar highly variable, as in *M. agrestis*. Second upper molar (M^2) distinguished from that of *M. agrestis* by lack of third loop on lingual side (inside). Distinguished from *M. oeconomus* by concave buccal (outside) edge to first loop of M_1. Dental formula 1/1, 0/0, 0/ 0, 3/3 = 16. The skull is longer and narrower, with an interorbital distance less than 3mm.

Habitat - tundra. In eastern part of range (eastern & central Asia), where climate is more continental, also inhabits steppe

and desert zone (Sutcliffe & Kowalski 1976). 'This species ... inhabits a vast range and as a result haunts extremely varied stations' (Ognev 1964, p.402), including forest-steppe, subalpine meadows, flood plains and delta areas. It has been assumed that the presence of narrow-skulled vole in British Pleistocene deposits indicates dry, cold conditions, following Stuart's comment '*Microtus gregalis* leaves the wetter habitats to *M.oeconomus* where the two species occur together' (1982, p.81). It should be remembered that *M. gregalis* is, in fact, less particular than this might suggest, and in some areas actually shows a preference for moister environments (Ognev, *op.cit.*). See map 3.6 for modern distribution.

Behaviour - Largely diurnal, particularly active at dawn and dusk. Populations studied in the USSR appear to feed on rather narrow ranges of plant species, according to local availability - Ognev cites one population living almost entirely on the stems and leaves of mountain onion, while another subsists on lilyworts. Food is stored in underground 'larders' for the winter. The voles live in colonies, with burrow systems extending to cover up to 10m² and inhabited by up to 20 individuals, including several breeding females, sub-adults and young. Lined nest chambers and larders are linked by burrows, and a radiating system of runways leads to feeding areas. Breeding season - May - September, 2 or more litters per year, 5-9 young per litter. Early litters breed in year of birth. Seasonal migration is recorded in localities where seasonal flooding necessitates a movement to higher ground in winter (Ognev, *op.cit.*).

Predators - weasels, stoats, polecats, foxes, owls and buzzards.

Lemmus lemmus (Norway lemming)

Size – head-body length 70-155mm, weight 100-130g

Teeth – molars prismatic, rootless. dental formula 1/1, 0/0, 0/ 0, 3/3 = 16.

Habitat – Tundra, mountain regions above tree line, open birch/pine woodland. Often in wet and marshy areas in summer, moving to drier open ridges in winter (Mitchell-Jones *et al*, 1999). Runway/tunnel system beneath snow but above soil level during winter, beneath moss and surface vegetation mat in summer. See map 3.3 for modern distribution.

Behaviour – Largely nocturnal. Feeds on grass, sedges, dwarf shrubs, mosses, fungi. Breeds during summer, average 6 litters per year, up to 13 young per litter but more usually 5-8. Well known for massive population explosions and migrations. Shows a 3-4 year population cycle in southern part of range, less frequent peaks in northern areas. In central Sweden the population cycle appears to have broken down, the last peak occurring in 1987. Reasons proposed for this include overgrazing by reindeer (Mitchell-Jones *et al.* 1999) and global warming (R. Engelmark, pers. comm.). The effects of the fall-out from the Chernobyl nuclear reactor explosion may also be a factor. Lemmings 'need a large, firmly-packed mass of snow [to burrow beneath] which is highly insulating against the cold. At least a yard's depth seems necessary' (Marsden 1964, p.61). They avoid very exposed areas where the snow is blown away or much reduced. Maximum lifespan c. 2 years.

Predators – owls, hawks, skuas, arctic foxes.

Dicrostonyx torquatus (collared or varying lemming)

Information from Nowak (1999) unless otherwise stated.

Size - head-body length 100-157mm, weight 30-112g.

Teeth - molars prismatic, rootless. Molars distinctive, with greater numbers of prisms on all teeth, and extremely angular folds. Dental formula 1/1, 0/0, 0/0, 3/3.

Habitat - specifically treeless arctic tundra, in dry, sandy or gravelly areas with some vegetation. During summer, digs shallow burrows underground or beneath rocks. Winter nests are formed at ground level under or within snowbanks (Nowak 1999). See map 3.3 for modern distribution.

Behaviour - Active year-round. During summer, feed on grasses, sedges, flowers and fruit. Winter diet of buds, twigs and bark, which are foraged for by tunnelling beneath the snow. The development of modified winter claws - 'the powerful middle (third and fourth) claws becoming greatly enlarged by the growth of a thick horny shield on their lower portion' (Marsden 1964 p.31) - on the front feet facilitates digging in snow or frozen earth. Insulation of thick snow essential to survival in arctic conditions, as temperatures below 60cm snow may reach 22°C warmer than surface temperatures, in addition to which the lemming's winter nest is built to add insulation - a ball-shaped affair made from plant stems, and lined with animal hair, down or feathers (Marsden *op.cit.*, p.63). With the body heat of the lemming family, the air temperature inside the nest can reach 10°C. The snow cover, nest insulation and thick fur of the animal combine to make survival possible in extreme arctic conditions, despite the lemming being 'too small to grow hair long enough for insulation and still be able to walk' (Lopez 1986, p.221). Breeding season early March-early September, at least 2 litters per year, up to 11 young per litter (average 4-5 in wild). Population density subject to peaks and troughs, (0.6/ha. to 400/ha.) but does not produce long-distance mass migrations seen in Norway lemming populations. Lifespan over 3 years in captivity, less in wild.

Predators - snowy owl, skua, arctic fox, mustelids.

Clethrionomys glareolus (bank vole)

Earlier writers refer to this species as *Evotomys glareolus*.

Size – head-body length 90-110mm. Weight 14-40g.

Teeth – molars prismatic, rooted. Roots develop by 3 months old, and continue to grow throughout the life of the vole, as the crown wears down. Prismatic angles more rounded than in *Microtus* species, and the prisms are not entirely isolated by enamel. Dental formula 1/1, 0/0, 0/0, 3/3 = 16

Habitat – favours mixed deciduous woodland with dense understorey. Also found in dense grassland and herbage, banks and hedges – wherever there is good cover. Dry areas preferred. Forms burrows and underground nests, as well as runways in ground vegetation, nests in tree trunks etc. Scandinavian populations inhabit coniferous woodland – taiga woodland has an understorey of berry bushes, dwarf shrubs etc. unlike British coniferous forest. Climbs well, unlike field voles. See map 3.8 for modern distribution.

Behaviour – Active day and night, but more nocturnal in summer. Herbivorous, feeding on fleshy fruits and soft seeds, nuts, fungi, moss, roots & flowers, leaves of woody plants. Occasional insects & worms. Breeds April-September, but season extended by favourable conditions, eg. low population, food abundance. 4-5 litters per year, 3-7 young per litter. Cyclic population in northern part of range (northern Scandinavia) with peaks every four years or so. Lifespan c. 18 months.

Island subspecies, eg. Skomer vole (*C. glareolus skomerensis*) show the ability of the species to adapt to habitats which seem less than ideal for mainland populations – the Skomer vole feeds mainly on bracken and bluebells, and there are no trees on the island. There are no other vole species present, and predators are limited to short-eared owls and large gulls.

Predators – owls, weasels, stoats, foxes. Less common in owl pellets than field vole, probably due to the voles' habitat preference.

Clethrionomys rufocanus (grey-sided vole)

Size - head-body length 110-135mm, weight 15-50g. Slightly larger than the bank vole, which is the only species of this genus present in the British Isles today.

Teeth - Molars rooted, prismatic. As in the bank vole, the roots continue to grow throughout the life of the animal, as the crown wears down. Very young specimens have no actual roots, but the bottom end of the tooth is almost closed where the roots will develop. Teeth more angular than those of *C. glareolus*. Dental formula 1/1, 0/0, 0/0, 3/3 = 16.

Habitat - Coniferous and birch forest in lowlands and on mountain slopes, also above timberline amongst dwarf shrubs and on dry peat-bogs. Rocky areas with an abundance of natural holes and fissures preferred. Present range includes Scandinavia, and through Russia to the Pacific coast and into central Asia (Mitchell-Jones et al., 1999). See map 3.8 for modern distribution.

Behaviour - active day and night. Feeds on grasses, and shoots, buds, leaves and bark of low-growing shrubs such as bilberry, crowberry and dwarf birch. Breeding season April - September. 2 -3 litters per year, up to 11 young per litter. Builds spherical grass nest with radiating burrows at ground level beneath snow in winter, otherwise nests hidden under roots, fallen wood etc or in tree-holes, sometimes in tree branches (Macdonald & Barrett 1993). Fluctuating, apparently cyclical population observed in Finland up to 1983, after which only slight, irregular variation apparent (Mitchell-Jones et al., 1999).

Predators - as *C. glareolus*.

Apodemus sylvaticus (wood mouse)

Size – head-body length 97-110 mm., weight 13-27g.

Teeth – Molars low crowned, with cusps arranged in three longitudinal rows. 4 roots in M^1, 2 in M_1. Dental formula 1/1, 0/0, 0/0, 3/3 = 16.

Note on identification – Differentiation of *A. sylvaticus* and *A. flavicollis* (yellow-necked mouse) in bone collections is possible only where complete jaws and skulls are available, allowing jaw length and thickness of upper incisor to be measured. Even where this can be done, the overlap in size range of each species makes certain identification impossible for any but the largest and smallest specimens. As the ecology of the yellow-necked mouse is very similar to that of the wood mouse, and given that the former species has a more southerly distribution (see maps 3.9 & 3.10), all *Apodemus* specimens identified in this study are assumed to be *A. sylvaticus* – in terms of environmental reconstruction the difference is not significant, and in the time period under consideration *A. sylvaticus* is the more likely species to be present.

Habitat – a very adaptable species, avoiding only very wet or very open terrain. Common in deciduous and mixed woodland, arable and ungrazed grassland, hedgerows and heather moorland. See map 3.9 for modern distribution.

Behaviour – Mainly nocturnal. Feeds on seeds, fruits, buds and shoots, nuts and fungi. Some invertebrates, particularly arthropod larvae, taken in winter. Breed March-October with some winter breeding in mild conditions. Up to 4 litters per

year, 2-9 young per litter (usually 4-7). Annual population fluctuation – no evidence of multi-annual cycles. An agile climber and leaper, the wood mouse travels through the shrub layer along branches as well as at ground level. May nest in holes in trees, but more commonly in extensive underground burrow systems. Life-span maximum 18-20 months.

Predators – Owls, kestrels, foxes, mustelids.

Micromys minutus (harvest mouse)

Size – very small. Head-body length 50-80mm, weight 5-11g.

Teeth – molars as *Apodemus sylvaticus*, but very small. Molar row <3mm. 5 roots in M^{1-3}, 3 in M_1. Dental formula 1/1, 0/0, 0/0, 3/3 = 16.

Habitat –long grass, dry reed beds, cereal crop fields. See map 3.11 for modern distribution.

Behaviour – Active night and day, with most activity at dusk. Possibly more nocturnal during summer, more diurnal in winter. Feeds on seeds, fruit, leaves of grasses and herbs, some insects. Breeding from late May to October, but favourable conditions may extend season. 3-7 litters per year, 4-8 young per litter (though records pre-1917 show litters of as many as 12 young). Ball-shaped nests of woven grasses 30-60cm above ground, attached to grass stems, built for breeding, and much activity seems to take place in the stalk zone during summer. In winter, larger nests are constructed at ground level or in a burrow. Life-span 18 months maximum.

Predators – owls, shrikes, corvids, mustelids, foxes. Small size, peculiar lifestyle and relative scarcity combine to make harvest mice a less-favoured prey item – nationally occur in only 0.8% of barn owl pellets (Glue, 1974).

The prehistory of this species in Britain is not known, nor even whether it is native or introduced.

Muscardinus avellanarius (dormouse)

Size - head-body length 70-85mm, weight 15-20g, increasing to up to 40g before hibernation.

Teeth - distinctive. Small, single-rooted premolars, large multiple-rooted molars with transverse ridges patterning the flat crowns. Dental formula 1/1 0/0, 1/1, 3/3 = 20.

Habitat - Deciduous woodland with dense understorey of shrubs and climbers. See map 3.12 for modern distribution.

Behaviour - Strictly nocturnal. Feeds on tree fruits when available - nuts, berries, ash keys etc., and on flowers and pollen during early summer. Insects frequently taken.

Hazelnuts, sweet chestnuts and acorns are eaten in large quantities to build up fat reserves prior to hibernation. Hibernation usually from October to April, induced by environmental temperature constantly below 15° C, but may not be continuous, particularly at beginning and end of winter. Hibernation nests built at or below ground level, while summer nests are generally above ground, usually in the shrub layer, but recorded at up to 10m high. Nests woven from bark of climbers etc, particularly honeysuckle. Dormice are extremely agile climbers, moving easily through trees and shrub layers along aerial pathways provided by sprawling scrub growth and tangled plants such as brambles. The protection and food supply provided by rich understorey development is essential for colonisation and survival by dormice. Breeding season May - September, one or two litters per year, c. 4 young per litter. Life span 3-4 years in wild.

Predators - secretive arboreal lifestyle leads to low predation by hawks and owls, or mammalian predators. Highest mortality during hibernation, through starvation of underweight individuals, or predation by carnivores such as foxes and mustelids. Dormouse remains are very rarely found in owl pellets.

The prehistory of the species in Britain is not certain - 'Probably a natural late post-glacial coloniser, arriving in Britain c.9000 years ago' (Corbet & Harris 1991 p.261), though no dated specimens are recorded from earlier than the late Iron Age.

Sorex araneus (common shrew)

Size - head-body length 48-80mm, weight 5-14g.

Teeth - Specialised incisors; very large beak-shaped upper first incisor, long blade-shaped lower incisor with small cusps along its length. These act as pincers to capture prey. Five unicuspid teeth, dilambdadont molars (having W-shaped cutting edge formed by buccal cusps - Hillson 1986, p.17). 3rd unicuspid smaller than 2nd. Cusp tips are pigmented, usually bright red. Pigmentation may be worn away in elderly individuals. Lower jaw length c. 12mm. Dental formula 3/1, 1/1, 3/1, 3/3 = 32.

Habitat - catholic, wherever low vegetation cover exists. Common in grassland, scrub and deciduous woodland. See map 3.13 for modern distribution.

Behaviour - active day and night, with frequent alternation between rest and foraging. Active above and below ground, with more underground activity in winter. Feeds mainly on invertebrates, particularly earthworms, slugs, snails, insect larvae, beetles, spiders and woodlice. While shrews feed voraciously, consuming 80-90% of their own body weight daily (Corbet & Harris 1991, p.56), studies by Crowcroft showed them to be selective in their predation (Crowcroft 1957). Different behaviour patterns of *Sorex araneus* and *S. minutus* are important in discerning reasons for the presence of one of the two species in the absence of the other. These

will be discussed in detail later. Breeding season April - September, 1-4 litters per year, litter size up to 10, but average 6-7 (Macdonald & Barret 1993). Life-span up to 18 months.

Predators - Owls, mustelids, foxes.

Sorex minutus (pygmy shrew)

Size - very small. Head-body length 40-60mm, weight 2.4 -6.1g.

Teeth - Similar to *S. araneus* (see above). Smaller - lower jaw length c. 9mm. 3rd unicuspid larger than 2nd. Dental formula 3/1, 1/1, 3/1, 3/3 = 32.

Habitat - As *S. araneus*. Generally less abundant, except on moorland, where live-trapping of shrews indicates *S. minutus* to outnumber the larger *S. araneus* by c. 8:1 (Yalden 1981, p150). See map 3.14 for modern distribution.

Behaviour - Equally active day and night, though 'relatively more diurnal than Common Shrew' (Macdonald & Barrett 1993, p.28). Does not burrow (unlike common shrew), taking majority of prey at ground surface. Feeds on small invertebrates, mainly beetles, woodlice, flies and spiders, but not earthworms. The small size and high energy requirement of the pigmy shrew necessitates its consumption of 125% of its body weight daily - a vast number of small prey items. Breeding season April - October, probably 2 litters per year, 4 - 7 young per litter. Life-span c. 13 months in wild.

Predators - as *S. araneus*. Less common in owl pellets than *S. araneus*, despite more frequent activity on ground surface. Possibly a combination of its smaller size and more rapid movement afford the pigmy shrew some protection.

Neomys fodiens (water shrew).

Size - Head-body length 63-96mm, weight 8-23g.

Teeth - Teeth similar to *Sorex* species, but larger - lower jaw length c. 14mm. Lower incisor long and blade-like, lacking the multiple cusplets of the *Sorex* species. 4 unicuspids. Tips of cusps generally a more orange colour than the distinctively red *Sorex* teeth, but this alone is not a reliable identifying criterion, especially in sub-fossil material. Dental formula 3/1, 1/1, 2/1, 3/3 = 30.

Habitat - Banks of rivers and streams, ponds and drainage ditches. May occur on seashore. Has been recorded up to 3km from water in broadleaf woodland, hedgerows and grassland (Corbet & Harris 1991, p.65).

Behaviour - Active day and night, but mostly nocturnal. Adept swimmer and diver. Feeds on small water animals - aquatic crustaceans and insect larvae, small fish and amphibia. Also earthworms, beetles, slugs and snails. Prey taken both underwater and on land. Excavates extensive burrow system, with entrance above or below water level. Breeding season April - September, 2 litters per year, average 6 young per litter. Life-span c. 18 months.

Predators - Mustelids, owls, herons, carnivorous fish (eg. pike). Not common in owl pellets.

Talpa europaea (mole)

Size - head-body length 110 - 150mm. Males larger than females. Weight 65 - 130g. (Macdonald & Barrett 1993)

Teeth - small simple incisors, large double-rooted upper canines, smaller lower canines (similar to incisors), small, pointed premolars, dilambdadont molars. Dental formula 3/3, 1/1, 4/4, 3/3 = 44. (Hillson 1986).

Habitat - Very adaptable, requiring only a sufficient depth of soil to construct tunnels. Originally a denizen of deciduous woodland. Avoids extremely wet areas and moorland (Corbet & Harris 1991).

Behaviour - Can be active at any time. Feed on earthworms and other soil invertebrates, hunted in the tunnel system. Moles are rarely seen on the ground surface, though weaned young may disperse over ground in search of suitable unoccupied territory. Burrow system comprises a nest chamber and surrounding tunnels at different levels, dug out by the mole. In areas prone to flooding, permanent hills may be constructed, known as 'fortresses', which allow a nest chamber and several tunnels to remain well-drained. Decapitated worms are stored underground against shortage. Breeding season - spring (according to latitude); one or possibly two litters per year, 3 -4 young per litter. Lifespan - generally 3 years, but individuals may survive up to 6. (Corbet & Harris *op.cit.*).

Predators - tawny owls, buzzards, stoats. Mainly predated when juveniles are dispersing above ground (Corbet & Harris *op.cit.*).

Erinaceus europaeus (hedgehog)

Size – Head-body length 225-275 mm, weight 400-1200g. 30% weight loss during hibernation.

Teeth – First incisors long and pointed. Molars four-cusped, with low points arranged in a square. Other teeth have low, single points, except fourth premolars (Hillson 1986). Hedgehogs have less specialised dentition than moles and shrews, reflecting their more general diet. Dental formula 3/2, 1/1, 3/2, 3/3 = 36.

Habitat – Deciduous woodland, scrub and hedgerows, moist pasture and grassland. Distribution limited by availability of invertebrate prey.

Behaviour – Nocturnal. Feeds on invertebrates, such as worms, beetles and slugs; occasional vertebrates, such as nestlings, small amphibians and baby rodents; birds' eggs; carrion; some fruit and mushrooms. Breeding season May-September, average litter size 4-6. Nest of grass and leaves for breeding and hibernation, insubstantial at other times, under cover of vegetation. Lifespan max. 7-10 years.

Predators – principal cause of death is starvation during hibernation. Spines prevent predation by most species, except in young or sickly animals. Predators include badger, fox, pine marten, polecat, golden eagle and eagle owl (Corbet & Harris, *op.cit.*)

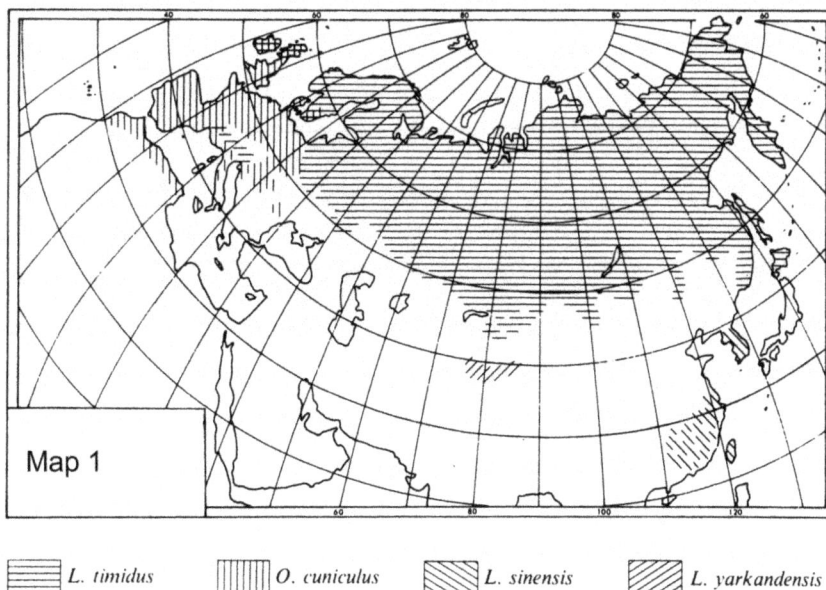

L. timidus	*O. cuniculus*	*L. sinensis*	*L. yarkandensis*

Map 3.1 – Modern distribution of *Lepus timidus*

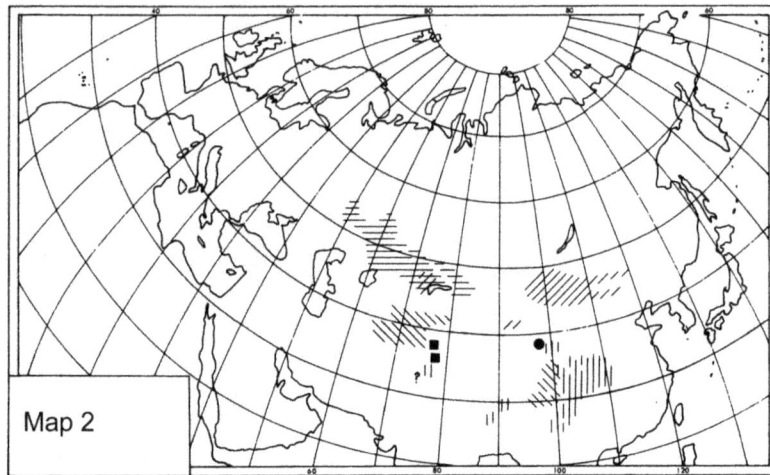

Map 2

| O. pusilla | O. thibetana | O. rutila (west), O. erythrotis (east) |
| O. pallasi | ● O. thomasi | ■ O. ladacensis |

Map 3.2 – Modern distribution of *Ochotona pusilla*

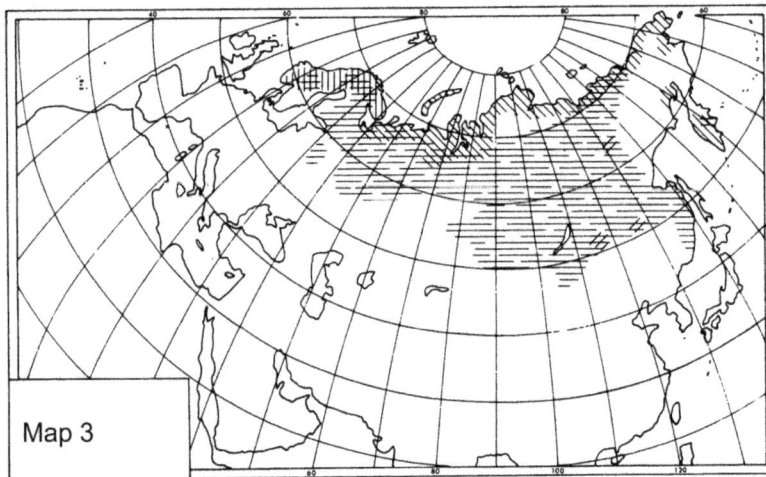

Map 3

M. schisticolor   L. lemmus   L. sibiricus   L. amurensis

Map 3.3 – Modern distribution of *Lemmus lemmus & Myopus schisticolor*

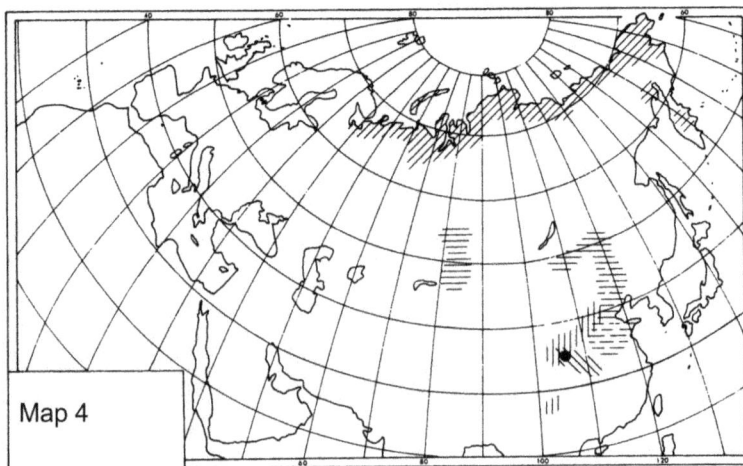

Map 4

M. myospalax   M. fontanieri   M. rothschildi   D. torquatus

● M. smithi

Map 3.4 – Modern distribution of *Dicrostonyx torquatus*

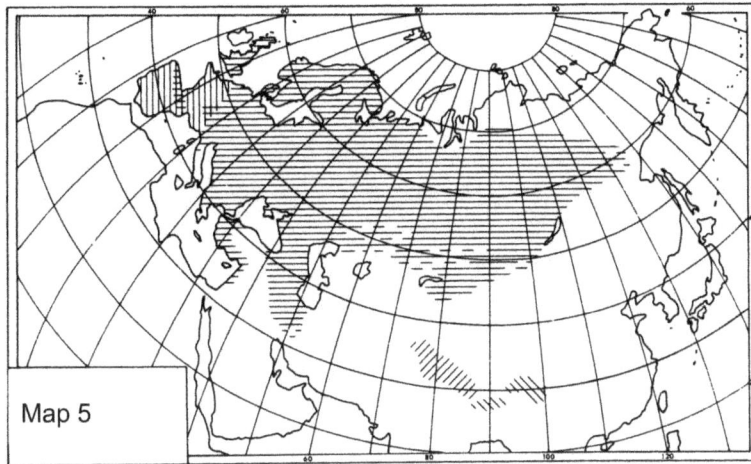

| A. terrestris | A. sapidus | P. sikimensis | P. leucurus |

Map 3.5 – Modern distribution of *Arvicola terrestris*

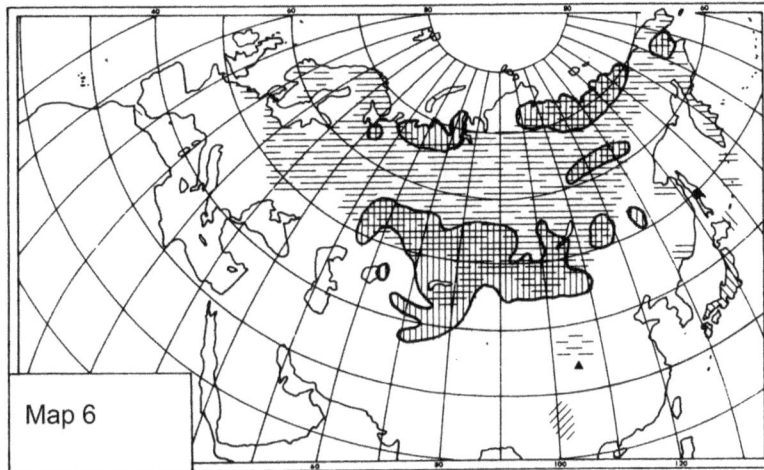

| M. oeconomus | M. gregalis | M. montebelli | M. clarkei |

● *M. sachalinensis* ▲ *M. bedfordi*

Map 3.6 – Modern distribution of *Microtus oeconomus* & *Microtus gregalis*

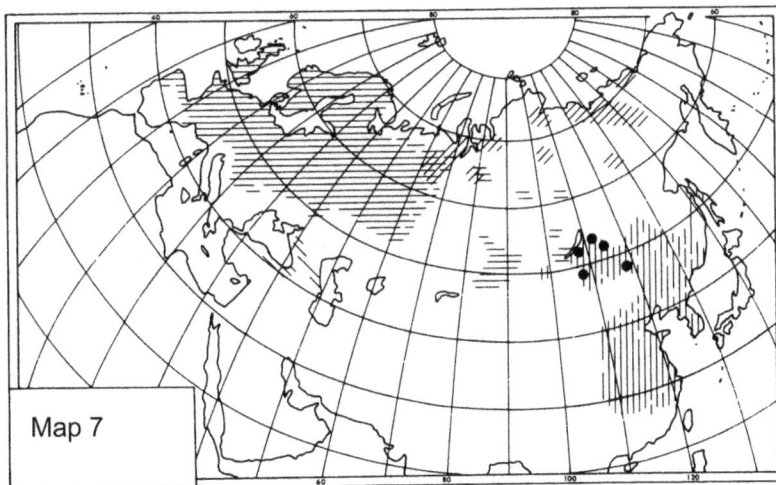

| M. agrestis | M. fortis | M. roberti, M. gud |

M. middendorffi ● *M. maximowiczii*

Map 3.7 – Modern distribution of *Microtus agrestis*

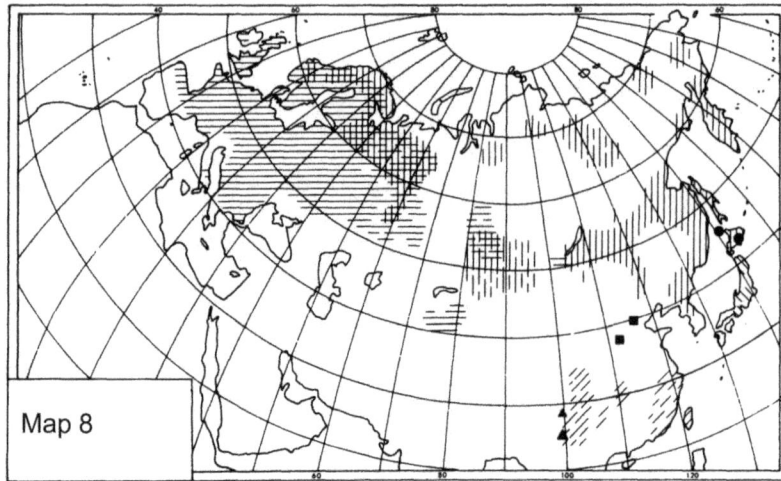

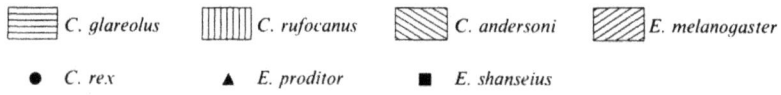

Map 3.8 – Modern distribution of *Clethrionomys glareolus* & *Clethrionomys rufocanus*

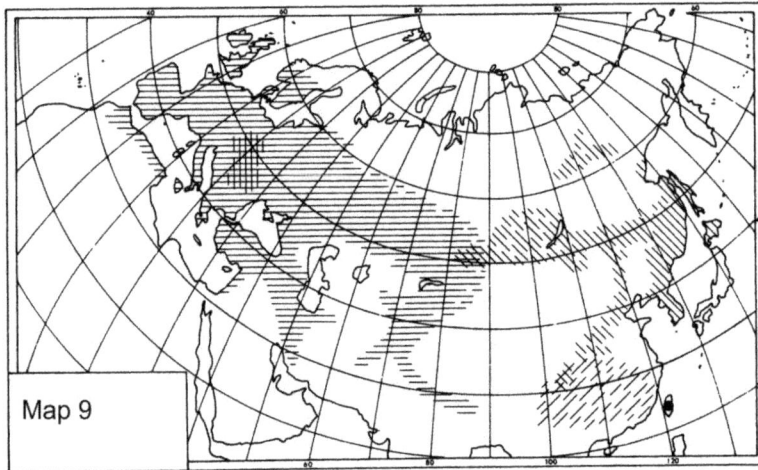

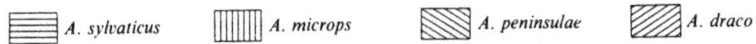

Map 3.9 – Modern distribution of *Apodemus sylvaticus*

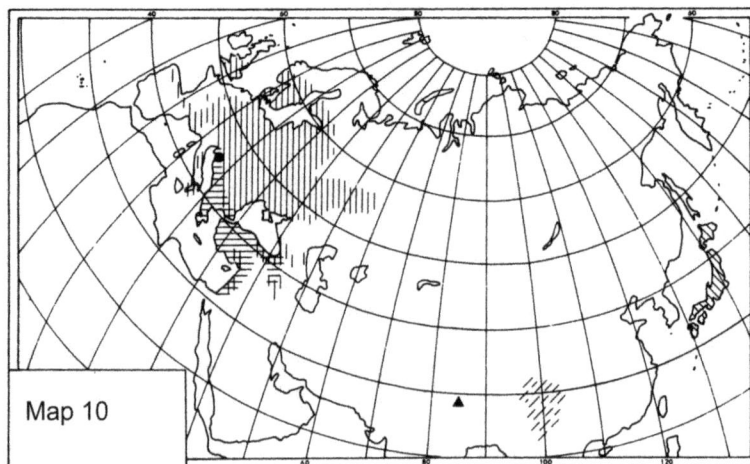

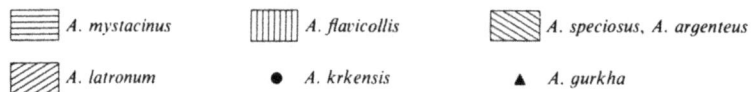

Map 3.10 - Modern distribution of *Apodemus flavicollis*

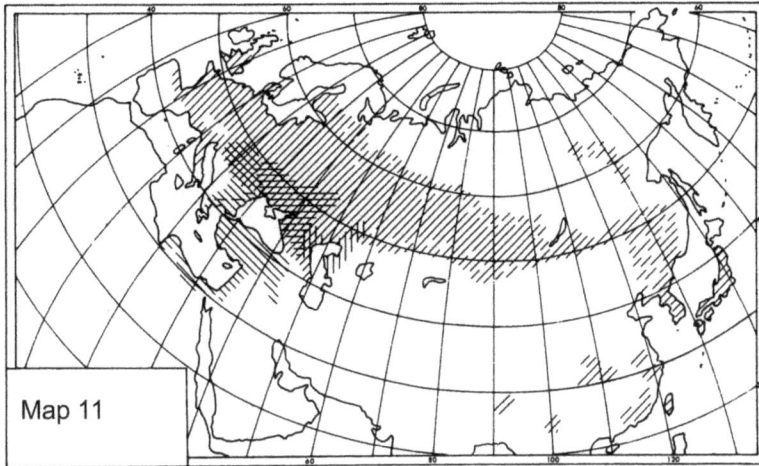

| S. microphthalmus | S. giganteus | S. leucodon | M. minutus |

Map 3.11 – Modern distribution of *Micromys minutus*

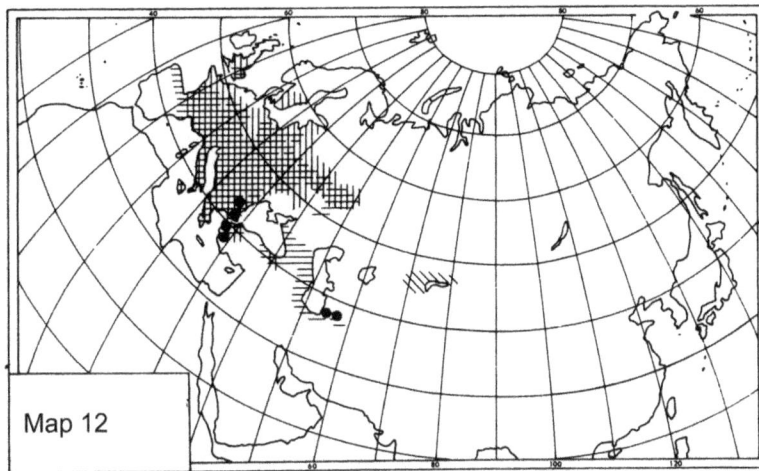

| G. glis | Mus. avellanarius | S. betpakdalensis | ● My. personatus |

Map 3.12 – Modern distribution of *Muscardinus avellanarius*

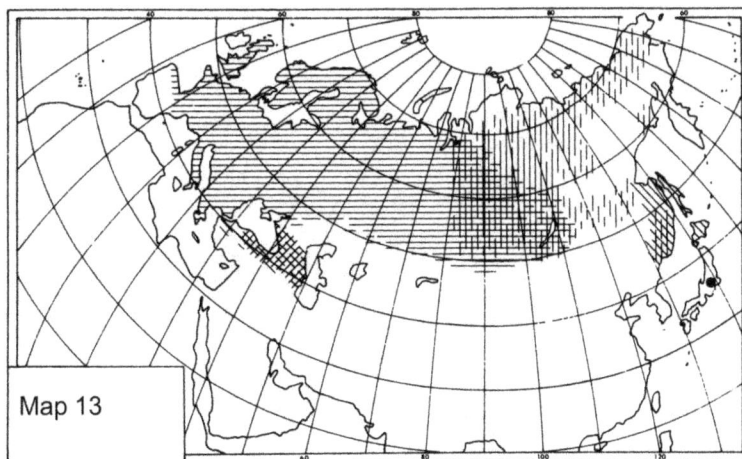

| S. araneus | S. vir | { S. caucasicus (Caucasus) / S. unguiculatus (E. Asia) } |
| S. raddei | ● S. hosonoi | |

Map 3.13 – Modern distribution of *Sorex araneus*

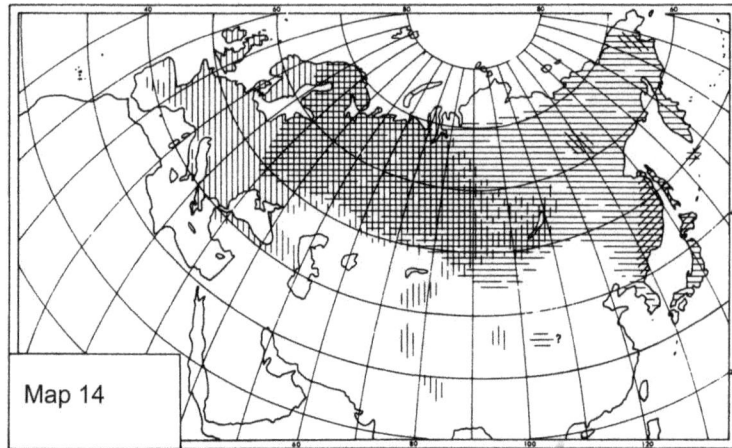

S. caecutiens   S. minutus   S. cinereus   S. gracillimus

Map 3.14 – Modern distribution of *Sorex minutus*

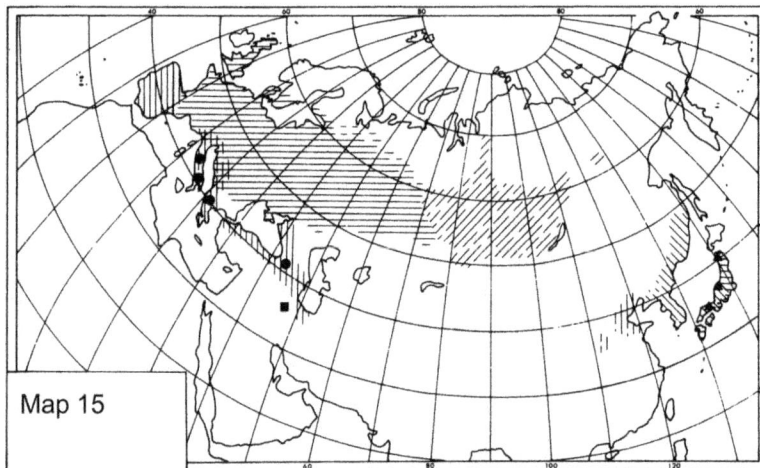

T. europaea (west), T. wogura (east)   T. caeca (west), T. moschata (east)

T. robusta   T. altaica   ● T. romana   ▲ T. mizura

■ T. streeti

Map 3.15 – Modern distribution of *Talpa europaea*

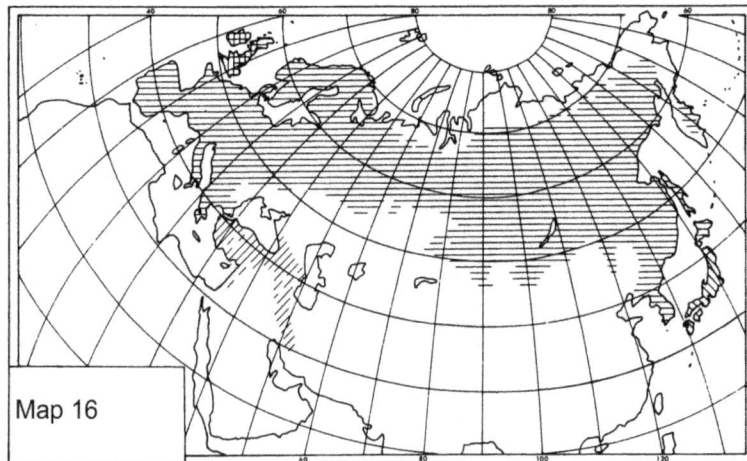

S. vulgaris   S. carolinensis   S. lis   S. anomalus

Map 3.16 – Modern distribution of *Scuirus vulgaris*

All modern distribution maps are taken from Corbet 1978, and also show the ranges of other closely related species.

Methods

The best-quality small mammal collections are likely to come from excavations where there is, from the outset, the intention to provide data for environmental reconstruction. The programmes of excavations at Torbryan Valley (directed by Alison Roberts, Ashmolean Museum, 1989 - 1992) and in the Wye Valley (directed by Dr Nick Barton, Oxford Brookes University, 1993 - 1996) both included extensive environmental investigations, and work on site was carried out by a multidisciplinary team of specialists. Where collections of material from excavations other than those in which I was directly involved have been included in this study, I have endeavoured to use only material with good stratigraphic relationships and carefully recorded documentation. In the case of Cathole Cave (Gower peninsula), I examined the material from Campbell's 1968 excavation in preference to McBurney's collection of 1958, as the Lateglacial deposits identified by McBurney as horizon B (McBurney 1959) were subdivided by Campbell into five separate contexts (Campbell 1977), providing a much more finely grained stratigraphy. Other collections were evaluated for their potential usefulness in terms of quantity of small mammal remains of a suitable age, and the integrity of stratigraphic units identified by the excavator. Where few late glacial specimens were recovered, or where there has been post-depositional stratigraphic disturbance, the collection has not been included.

Torbryan Valley caves, Wye Valley caves and Priory Farm Cave

To obtain samples of small mammal remains for analysis, bulk sediment samples were excavated from all identified contexts and returned to the laboratory for processing. A limited amount of sediment was examined on site, allowing the immediate identification of contexts containing the remains of lemmings, pikas or extinct voles and so a rough indication of *in situ* late glacial deposits.

The size of each sample was recorded, measured in litres, prior to the sediment being soaked in water to break up any clumps. In most cases, this was sufficient to allow easy sieving, but where a sample included heavy clay, a small amount of hydrogen peroxide was added to the water, as advised by Simon Parfitt (Natural History Museum). The brecciated samples from Merlin's Cave (Wye Valley) required special treatment, which will be outlined below. Once the sediment was seen to have broken down, the sample was poured through a stack of brass laboratory sieves, mesh sizes 4mm, 2mm, 1mm and 0.5mm. Water was run through the stack until no sediment was seen in the outflow. The residue was then left to dry on mesh-lined trays, in four discrete size fractions. Once dried, each fraction could be sorted either by eye (4mm) or using a binocular microscope (2mm, 1mm and 0.5mm) -

keeping the different sizes separate makes the sorting process considerably easier and more efficient. All bone was extracted, whether or not it was deemed to be identifiable, to allow taphonomic analysis. Charcoal, mollusc shells, flint microdebitage, small pot fragments and any other small pieces of cultural or environmental debris were all collected, to be passed on to their particular specialists.

The brecciated samples taken from the wall of Merlin's Cave (Wye Valley) offered an excellent opportunity to investigate an undisturbed stratigraphy. During excavation the west wall of the cave, just inside the entrance, was treated as an excavated section, and drawn as a vertical profile with the locations of bone-rich breccias indicated. These pockets of concreted fossiliferous material were then sampled, often using a hammer and chisel (see plate 9, p.61). The bones were later extracted by acid-treatment. Each block was first examined, and any bones on the surface were removed where possible, to provide samples for dating. The samples were then soaked in dilute acetic acid for four to twelve hours, rinsed under running water for the same length of time as they were in the acid-bath, sieved through a 0.5mm laboratory sieve, and dried. Any bones freed from the surface by the dissolving process were picked out before the process was repeated. This continued until all bones were recovered. Samples were taken in the more usual way from the earth of the cave floor.

The extracted bone was next examined to provide a general impression of the condition of the bone - degree of breakage, staining, surface damage etc., providing a basis for reconstructing the likely source of the bones, and the degree to which they had suffered post-depositional alteration. This will be dealt with in detail in chapter 4, but is important here because samples used to reconstruct a past environment would have to be as well-preserved as possible, and contain identifiable specimens. As small mammals rarely inhabit caves, the bones can be assumed to have been brought to the cave as food remains by one of several kinds of predator. This also may have an effect on the environmental reconstruction, as biases may be introduced by the selectivity of the predator, its hunting patterns and its feeding habits (see chapter 4).

Identifiable bones were separated, and identified by comparison with modern specimens of known species. In the case of most rodents, post-cranial remains cannot be identified to species with any confidence. However, as the teeth are the best-preserved skeletal element and therefore likely to be present even where other bones are lost, it is considered sufficient to identify species present and relative density by teeth alone. In the case of the three species of *Microtus* (grass voles) present in the Late Glacial and early Holocene, identification rests on a combination of clues. These are covered in the previous section. It is essential to consider the complete collection of *Microtus* teeth - if any second upper molars (M^2) of the *Microtus agrestis* (field vole) pattern are present, the lower first molars (M_1) and mandibles must be examined to discern whether some are referable to *M. gregalis* (narrow-skulled vole), a highly variable species which includes forms very like modern *M. agrestis* as well as distinctively separate forms. Both species may be present in the same assemblage. In the presence of *M. agrestis* M^2s, only the most typical forms of *M. gregalis* can be identified with confidence, and in many cases one can make no further identification than "*M. agrestis/gregalis*". If no M^2s of the *M. agrestis* type are recovered from a sample containing those of other *Microtus* species, it is probable that any M_1 of a similar form to *M. agrestis* is in fact *M. gregalis*. *Microtus oeconomus* (Northern vole) has a distinctive M_1, although the M^2 is identical to *M. gregalis*. Consequently, the breakdown of species present can include not only the three species identified, but also "*M. non-agrestis*" (ie. M^2s not of the *M. agrestis* pattern), "*M. agrestis/gregalis*" where mandibles or M_1s cannot be definitely identified other than that they are not *M. oeconomus*, and *M.sp.*, which covers all other *Microtus* teeth which are not identifiable to species. Fortunately this analysis is more straightforward to carry out than it is to explain.

In the case of insectivores, the innominate bones (part of the pelvis) of shrews may be separated from those of mice and voles, but generally where shrews are present in a sample, their mandibles will also be recovered. Moles (*Talpa europaea*) have frequently been identified from humeri, radii and pelves, as these are extremely distinctive in this species whereas the teeth and mandibles are more rarely recovered. This may be due to the larger size of the creature, and the fact that it provides only a minor part of the diet of owls (Mikkola 1983), which are the main accumulators of small mammal bones in caves (see below). Mole remains are more likely to be accumulated by mammalian predators or diurnal raptors such as buzzards.

The presence of a species which does not seem an appropriate part of the fauna represented by the bulk of specimens in a sample may be explained in one of several ways. Firstly, it may be intrusive - the product of post-depositional mixing. The nature of the sediment should be considered - an open structure such as scree allows the downward movement of small particles such as rodent teeth, whereas a more consolidated sediment does not. Small remains may be relocated within the soil profile by the actions of burrowing animals (bioturbation), or by climatic soil movements (cryoturbation). Human activity at any time in the history of the site may cause disturbance of stratigraphic relationships. Sometimes intrusive bone can be distinguished by a different colouration or surface condition - modern bone may appear almost translucent, and pale-coloured bones appearing in a collection of predominantly grey or dark-stained material might indicate a different depositional history. However, it should always be considered that the seemingly odd species might be genuinely part of the fauna, perhaps indicating a transitional phase of environmental development. Currant (1986) argues that during the Lateglacial period, the rapidly changing climate caused all faunas to be transitional, and that faunal mixing (in the sense of mixing in the living population) should be seen as the norm. Lack of data on the true tolerance range of small mammal species renders it impossible to identify a cut-off point beyond which a certain species could not survive. It seems probable that true tundra species such as collared lemming persisted at the edge of their tolerance range as the climate warmed, until either incoming species displaced them by direct competition in a environment to which they was

better suited, or a different species within the existing fauna, perhaps having been at the edge of its tolerance range during the colder phase, expanded and increased in a climate to which it was better adapted, and so out-competed the lemming with which it had previously shared resources. At some point, though, an invading species must make its earliest appearance in the stratigraphic record, perhaps in low concentrations, and at this stage might be mistakenly assumed to be intrusive.

It is also important to be aware of the possibility that an apparently intrusive specimen might in fact be a similar species with a different environmental niche, and all possible care should be taken to ensure accurate identification. Material from the lower (grey) scree deposit at King Arthur's Cave, Wye Valley, included several specimens of what initially appeared to be *Clethrionomys glareolus* (bank vole), a species not normally found in contexts of this age - the scree contained upper palaeolithic artefacts, indicating a Lateglacial interstadial age. The small mammal bones were chiefly of narrow-skulled and northern vole, with collared and Norway lemming. Further research into voles of the genus *Clethrionomys* and comparison with modern specimens at the Natural History Museum, London, made it possible to identify these specimens as *Clethrionomys rufocanus* (grey-sided vole), a species previously unrecorded in British contexts, but with environmental preferences agreeing with the other species present (see above).

The number and type of specimens of each species present was recorded, allowing relative frequency to be considered. In this way, where the same species might be present in two different contexts, the proportional representation of each species could be considered when reconstructing the environment. For example, if the species present were collared lemming, Norway lemming, narrow-skulled vole and northern vole, with large numbers of collared lemming and narrow-skulled vole but lower numbers of Norway lemming and northern vole, it would imply that the area surrounding the site included a greater area of drier terrain, a smaller area of damper ground (favoured by the latter two species) and that a cold climate prevailed. A collection including large numbers of field vole, with bank vole and wood mouse in moderate numbers and a small number of dormouse teeth would indicate a largely open environment (favouring the field voles) with areas of fairly dense woodland (required by dormice). If the dormouse was not present, the bank vole and wood mouse would indicate a degree of cover, but not necessarily closed woodland, as both of these species inhabit hedgerows and shrubby areas as well as woods.

Type Faunas

It becomes obvious that a single identified species will be of little use in reconstructing an entire environment. Small mammals are generally rather opportunistic, and it would be impossible to define a 'typical' environment for any but the most specialised types. Even when a species, in its modern distribution and ecology, appears to be restricted, it is necessary to consider whether this restriction is caused by factors external to the animal itself - human alteration of the landscape and vegetation, physical isolation, climatic changes. For example, the Skomer vole (*Clethrionomys glareolus skomerensis*), an island sub-species of bank vole (*C. glareolus*), while essentially very similar to the mainland species, exists in a totally treeless environment, eating bracken, sorrel and bluebells (Archer-Thomson & Bunker 1993). The mainland species is usually taken to be an indicator of woodland conditions, but in the absence of other small herbivores - the island has rabbits, but no other voles - and of any mammalian predators, the Skomer vole has adapted to fill an unoccupied niche in the island ecosystem. The specialised dietary requirements of the animal are a product of availability rather than necessity. It is important, therefore, to know as much as possible about the individual species, and also to consider the whole range of represented species as a group. By examining which species are present together, and also which are absent, it becomes possible to reconstruct a much clearer picture of the available environment than could be suggested by individual species.

Typical faunas can be constructed for each of the main subdivisions of the Lateglacial and early Holocene, from records published from excavated sites in Britain (after Stuart, 1982).

Glacial -   *Dicrostonyx torquatus* (collared lemming)
             Lemmus lemmus (Norway lemming)
             Microtus gregalis (narrow-skulled vole)
             Microtus oeconomus (northern vole)
             Lepus timidus (mountain hare)

Interstadial - *Dicrostonyx torquatus*
             Lemmus lemmus
             Lepus timidus
             Microtus gregalis
             Microtus oeconomus
             ?Microtus agrestis (field vole)

Arvicola terrestris (water vole)
?Apodemus sylvaticus (wood mouse)
Sorex araneus (common shrew)
Sorex minutus (pygmy shrew)

Stadial -   *Dicrostonyx torquatus*
             Lemmus lemmus
             Ochotona pusilla (steppe pika)
             Lepus timidus
             Microtus gregalis
             Microtus oeconomus

Post-Glacial - *Lepus timidus*
             Microtus oeconomus
             Microtus agrestis
             Arvicola terrestris
             Clethrionomys glareolus (bank vole)
             Apodemus sylvaticus
             Sorex araneus
             Sorex minutus
             Erinaceus europaeus (hedgehog)

Establishing such 'type faunas' from the faunal lists of well-known sites runs the risk of neglecting regional variation, local variation within the region, and the variation brought about by local topography. However, if these lists are regarded as guidelines only, and it is accepted that faunal differences are likely to be the norm rather than the exception, they can provide a useful starting point when studying specific small mammal bone collections. The lists above are very general, and do not reflect any particular site. Dates have not been specified, as the timing of environmental changes varies with latitude. It will be seen that the study of carefully excavated and recorded deposits can add considerably to these lists, and that relative frequencies, in no way reflected in such lists, are as important in reconstructing environments as the range of species represented.

Chapter 4
Small Mammals and Caves

1. Taphonomy - deposition

The presence of large quantities of small mammal bones in cave deposits requires explanation. With the exception of bats, whose highly specialised lifestyle is very different from the terrestrial insectivores and rodents, it is unusual to find such creatures inhabiting caves. An attractive food source might encourage them to venture into a cave - for example, the presence of dead animals or food remains leads to a large short-term population of flies and maggots, which in turn may attract scavenging shrews. It is common to find that any item of food or equipment left in a cave overnight is gnawed by rats - a caving lamp inadvertently left unprotected in Merlin's Cave during excavation there in 1996 suffered the loss of most of its cables and softer rubber parts, the remains showing very clear and distinctive tooth marks. The majority of small mammal remains recovered from cave sediments, however, are of herbivorous rodents such as voles and lemmings, and given the lifestyle of the animals and the quantities in which they are found, it is clear that some other agency is responsible for their presence. Consideration must be given to the predators of small mammals, particularly to their feeding habits and to whether their lifestyle would lead them to accumulate large collections of microfaunal remains in a cave.

a. Mammalian predators

The larger carnivorous mammals present in Britain during the time period under consideration - bears (*Ursus arctos*) and wolves (*Canis lupus*) - are both known to utilise caves, either for breeding or, in the case of bears, for hibernation. Prey remains from wolf dens show characteristic gnawing, and deposits may also contain wolf cubs' milk teeth, as collected, for example, from Price's Passage, Tornewton Cave (A. Currant pers.comm.), but small mammal remains are scarce. Such small prey items are not normally hunted, and the bones would be lost in digestion. Bears are more likely to leave their own bones in caves, due to death during hibernation.

The smaller canids, red fox (*Vulpes vulpes*) and arctic fox (*Alopex lagopus*) both prey on small mammals, primarily voles and lemmings, according to availability. Shrews and moles are avoided (Andrews 1990). Bone samples extracted from the scats of both types of fox show 'severe' corrosion of both bone and tooth enamel, and 'very great' breakage of bone; bone fragments suffer a high degree of rounding and polishing (Andrews & Evans 1983). The use of scats as territorial markers by both species of fox considered here means that large accumulations of bone are unlikely to be produced by these predators. Scats tend to be distributed around the territory of the fox, and deposited in exposed situations, often on tussocks or mounds to raise them above ground level and so allow better dispersal of the animal's scent. Andrews & Evans observed that 'the bones that do survive in the predators' scats are so weakened during the process that the chances of their surviving the further stresses of fossilisation are very low' (*op.cit*. p.306). While foxes might use a small cave or cavity within a cave as a den, then, it is unlikely that they play a major role as accumulators of small mammal remains.

Stoats (*Mustela erminea*) and weasels (*Mustela nivalis*) are commonly represented in bone assemblages from cave sites but, like the foxes, probably contributed little else but their own remains to the bone record. Analysis of the scats of small mustelids shows them to contain only splinters and flakes of bone (see plate 1) - 'generally too fragmentary for identification even to body parts' (Andrews & Evans 1983, p.302). Where more complete bone is present, it shows clear evidence of digestive corrosion, with tooth enamel etched or dissolved. A similar pattern is produced by the digestions and feeding behaviours of polecat (*Mustela putorius*) and pine marten (*Martes martes*) (Andrews 1990). It is likely that a small proportion of the bones recovered from caves are the result of mustelid predation, particularly in the later deposits at Broken Cavern, where the loose scree would have provided an attractive habitat for stoats and weasels. The presence of these creatures in the area is interesting, as they may be considered to be small mammals themselves, but they are not

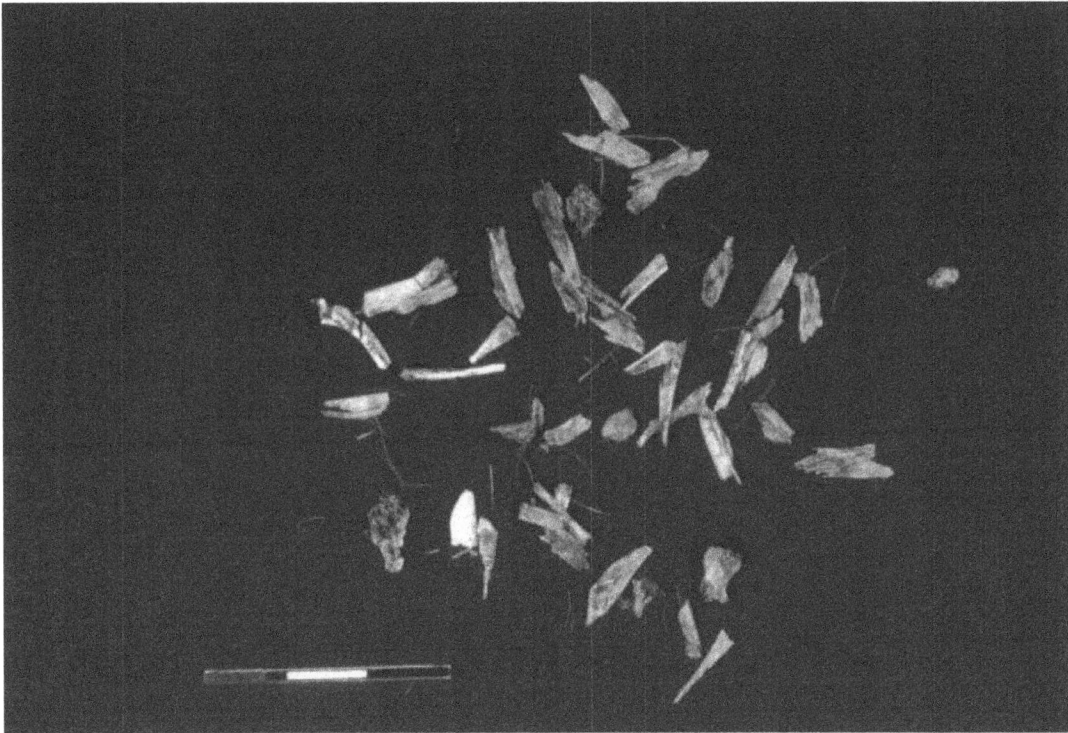

Plate 1 – Bone fragments from pine marten scats (3cm scale)

a major source of identifiable microfaunal bone. In fact, they are more likely to have arrived on site as a prey item rather than a predator.

Wild cats (*Felis silvestris*) and lynx (*Lynx lynx*) complete the range of potential mammalian predators of small mammals in Britain during the Lateglacial and early Holocene periods. The wild cat arrived with the temperate wooded conditions of the Postglacial, and is recorded from Mesolithic sites such as Thatcham (Yalden 1999), whilst the lynx was present during the Lateglacial interstadial and is recorded from Gough's Cave (Currant 1991). The cat family, like the mustelids, is highly destructive of bone, both during feeding and through digestion. Andrews' study of a feral cat (*Felis catus*) suggests that birds and rabbits form the bulk of the diet, and that bones are either not ingested or, in the case of the more fragile bird bones, are destroyed by chewing and digestion (Andrews 1990). As with the mustelids, it is unlikely that any identifiable small mammal bones from the deposits studied are contributed by felids.

b. Avian predators

i. Diurnal raptors - hawks and falcons

As all hawks and falcons dismember their prey, swallowing meat, fur and feather but avoiding the larger bones, the regurgitated pellets of these birds often contain only small bone fragments. Specialist predators of smaller birds, such as the peregrine (*Falco peregrinus*) may be discounted as accumulators of small mammal bones, as they eat only a very few rodents. Kestrels (*Falco tinnunculus*) feed mainly on voles, taking prey up to 200g (Andrews 1990). However, their efficient digestion appears to dissolve the majority of ingested

bone. Studies by Yalden & Yalden (1983) involving analysis of pellets from captive kestrels show that of 213 prey items consumed, only 80 were recovered in any form from pellets, mostly as individual molars and incisors. The kestrel is one of the bird species identified from Merlin's Cave (Harrison 1980), but it is likely this was brought into the cave as prey by a larger bird. Certainly many of the microfaunal remains from Merlin's Cave are of species too large for such a small falcon, and the completeness of many of the bones recovered is evidence against accumulation by diurnal raptors. Even larger species - buzzards, harriers, kites and eagles - produce pellets containing only fragmentary bone, and with a low representation of actual dietary range. It is considered safer, when using pellet analysis to record feeding habits and prey selection in these species, to rely on hair or feather identification. It is very likely that a certain proportion of the bone fragments and individual teeth recovered from the cave sites under investigation originated in the food remains of falcons or hawks, either feeding debris or pellets, as the cliffs surrounding most of the sites would be attractive perching or nesting sites. The Wye Valley particularly has a large modern population of raptors, with peregrine falcons nesting at Symonds Yat, many kestrels, buzzards (*Buteo buteo*) and sparrowhawks (*Accipiter nisus*), and the less common goshawks (*Accipiter gentilis*) and hobbies (*Falco subbuteo*) are often seen in the area (Birdwatching Magazine, February 2001).

ii. Owls

Despite their nocturnal habits, owls do not inhabit the depths of caves, but rock ledges inside the cave mouth provide roosting and nesting sites where owls can rest during the day, avoid harassment by other birds, and raise young in safety. The cliffs commonly surrounding caves also offer shaded niches into which owls can retreat. Rich small mammal deposits are most often found at or near the cave mouth, rather than in the depths of the cave - the sequence of breccias sampled in Merlin's Cave was located in the daylight zone, and the most productive areas for small mammal remains at both King Arthur's Cave and Three Holes Cave were along the dripline of the cliff adjacent to the cave mouth. Interestingly, the poorest assemblage of microfauna in the Wye Valley project was recovered from Madawg Rockshelter (Wye Valley), where the west-facing aspect and location combine to render the site extremely warm on a sunny day - a situation avoided by roosting and nesting birds - and exposes it to wet westerly winds. Advice on siting nest-boxes states 'north-facing and east-facing sites are best' (Chinery 1986, p.183), but local conditions also play an important part in determining the suitability of a site. Priory Farm Cave, though north-facing, yielded little microfaunal material - possibly due to its damp westerly position where 'high levels of precipitation or air saturation along the southern margins of the ice sheet [during glacial periods]... would make it difficult for raptorial species to become airborne, because their plumage readily becomes waterlogged' (Eastham 2000, p.290). Even in more temperate conditions, the site is not in an ideal position for owl habitation.

As owls feed mainly on small mammals, and generally swallow prey whole, the indigestible bone and fur which is regurgitated as a compact pellet provide an almost complete record of the owls' feeding habits (plate 2). In open conditions, the pellets are quickly disaggregated by weathering, and by the action of insect larvae feeding on them. Where there is physical protection, such as inside a cave, the pellets may disintegrate as the fur or feather matrix is consumed, but the bones will be preserved. In some circumstances.

mineralisation may produce preserved owl pellets, wherein the fur/feather matrix is replaced by a breccia-like concretion with the bones still in place. Several examples of this were recovered from the Kent's Cavern Wolf's Cave samples (plate 3). The stomach acid of owls is markedly weaker than that of diurnal raptors - c. pH 2.35 compared with c. pH 1.6 (Mikkola 1983), leading to little digestive damage to the bones. Young owls have a more acid gastric fluid, and so bones from the pellets of fledgling owls are likely to show more surface etching than those digested by more mature birds. Physical bone breakage may occur if the pellets are cast in a confined roost, where they will be trampled by the birds. This leads particularly to the loss of complete crania and of some maxillae, breakage of mandibles and an associated rise in numbers of isolated teeth, breakage and some loss of large post-cranial bones, but no breakage of small post-cranial elements such as foot bones and vertebrae (Andrews 1990).

Small mammal bone assemblages from several of the sites studied show many indications of originating from owl pellet deposits - Broken Cavern, Merlin's Cave, King Arthur's Cave, Kent's Cavern, Cat Hole, and Bridged Pot. Other sites, producing material suggestive of the same origin but with subsequent modification by other agencies, will be considered below.

iii. Other bird species

Several other types of bird are known to feed on small mammals occasionally, and to cast pellets containing bones. Most of the crow family exhibits this behaviour, most often through scavenging carrion rather than hunting. Andrews states that 'it seems unlikely ... that corvid species are

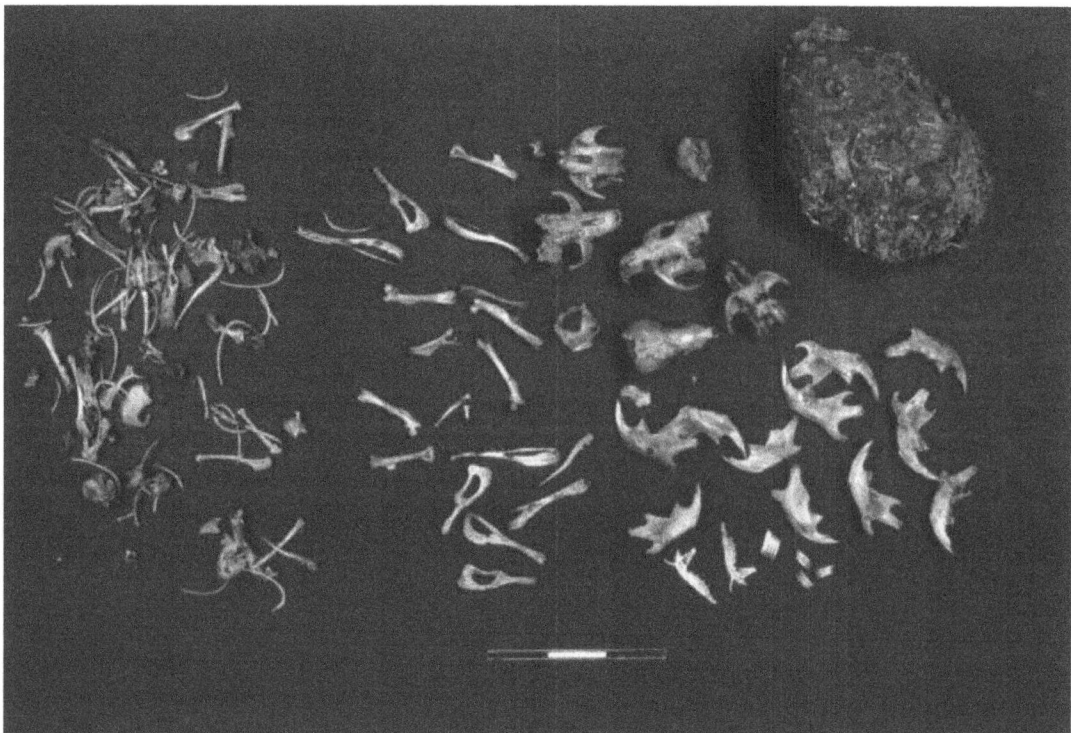

Plate 2 – Barn owl pellet, and small mammal remains recovered from barn owl pellets (3cm scale)

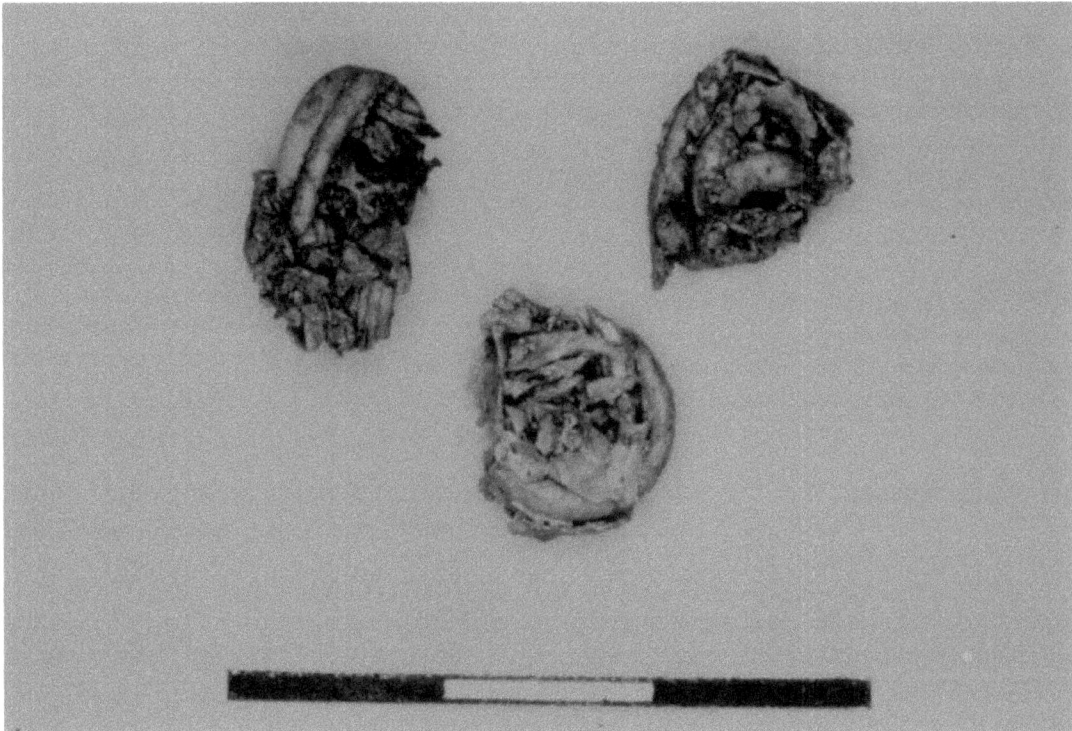

Plate 3 – Concreted owl pellet fragments, Kent's Cavern Wolf's Den, spit F

significant accumulators of mammalian bone' (*op.cit*, p.200), as his examination of 'a small number' of carrion crow pellets contained no small mammal remains. However, other sources suggest that live small mammals are frequently taken, particularly in spring and early summer when they form an especially important part of the diet, as demonstrated by the analysis of gizzard contents of crows from an agricultural area in southern England (Coombs 1978). It is probable that the pellets studied by Andrews, produced by crows in Rhulen, Wales, represented the prey remains of a different season. Herons (*Ardea cinerea*) 'may, on occasion, catch and eat any living prey which can be swallowed' (Voisin 1991, p.50), and will take available small mammals. Pellets investigated were found to contain very little bone, all of which was highly digested.

c. Transport from outside the cave

i. Water-borne sedimentation

Any animal dying within the catchment area of the water system associated with a cave might possibly contribute its bones to the cave fill, either by water flowing into the cave or by mud flow. Cave sediments act as a filter, collecting particles carried by moving water. The extent of movement depends on the size of the particles and the nature of the matrix through which they are transported. In a vaccuous deposit, small bones and teeth may be washed through the interstices and effectively graded by size as larger elements become trapped and smaller ones are carried farther. As movement by water is 'both destructive and dispersive of small mammal bone' (Andrews 1990, p.95) it is improbable that any significant accumulation of small mammal bone should occur through its agency.

ii. Pitfalls

Caves commonly have multiple entrances, opening either horizontally or vertically into the surrounding landscape. Vertical shafts, either avens or swallet holes, produce a natural trap for mammals, which having tumbled into the cave, may be unable to escape and so die of starvation. None of the caves studied here are of the kind of pothole required for this to offer an explanation for small mammal accumulation, as small mammals can survive a fall from a considerable height, and having done so would simply wander out through the main cave entrance. Vertical or near-vertical shafts can also produce an accumulation of dead-on-arrival small mammal material, usually from the pellets of owls roosting outside the cave, in trees or rocks overlooking the shaft. Bones from such a deposit will have the typical preservation of those from *in situ* pellet deposits. Where soil and rock material has also accumulated in the cave through the same aperture, a cone of deposition will form beneath it, such as is reported from Bridged Pot, which McBurney describes as 'a funnel-shaped dissolution hole ... only partially roofed, and open on the downhill side' (McBurney 1959, p. 262). He refers to 'old photographs', presumably from the time of H. Balch's excavation, showing 'that the greater part of the shelter was filled, when first discovered, by a typical cone of dejection' (*op. cit.* p.262).

2. Taphonomy - Post-depositional processes & preservation in cave sediments

The factors affecting bones in cave sites after their deposition can be divided into two main groups - geochemical processes, to do with the cave environment itself, and biological processes, wherein the bones or bone assemblages are altered by the actions of animals or plants. It must be remembered that the development of a cave stratigraphy is rarely so simple as to have restricted itself to one deposition process, and similarly, several different post-depositional processes may have left their marks on the specimens recovered from any particular context. This becomes a particular problem where there has been human use of a site, whether by Palaeolithic hunters, Bronze Age burial parties, 18th century freeminers or even 20th century archaeologists. This will be examined in more detail in chapters 6 to 9, where analyses of the individual contexts and sites investigated will be presented.

a. Geochemical processes

i. Rockfalls etc. - either complete collapse of cave roof (as in Broken Cavern) or spalling from cave walls, resulting in burial of any material lying on the surface (as in the scree deposits outside King Arthur's Cave). In the Broken Cavern example, the fall of large boulders would crush any bones on which they fell directly, but due to the uneven shape of both the boulders and the floor surface, cavities containing small bones were sealed beneath the rockfall in some places and thereby avoided subsequent alteration. These protected deposits were sufficiently distinctive as to have warranted a separate context number, and this context, 21, seems to represent the only totally uncontaminated Lateglacial Interstadial deposit found on this site. Context 14, its temporal equivalent, appears to have suffered from the 'sofa cushion' effect - small items trickling down the cracks and interstices between the rockfall scree and arriving at the same level as earlier material. Any material present on the surface above the cave roof at the time of collapse would also be redeposited in the scree. By this process it would be possible to arrive at a situation of older material being redeposited at a higher stratigraphic level than more recent debris. As a hypothetical example, if a Lower Palaeolithic knapping floor had been stratified on the plateau surface above a cave, a major roof collapse in the Younger Dryas might superimpose it on an Upper Palaeolithic occupation layer on what had been the cave floor, now at the front of a rockshelter. A similar process is seen on a smaller scale in Merlin's Cave, where brecciated deposits, having been exposed by the digging out of the cave deposits, are exposed as a sort of section on the cave wall. While the integrity of the cemented stratigraphy is preserved, material eroding from the bone-rich breccias is deposited either on the floor of the cave where it mingles with much more recent remains, or trickles down through the lower breccias to redeposit itself in a lower, earlier concretion. It is possible to see that in time this could lead to a complete inversion of the stratigraphy as the breccias erode from the top to the bottom of the section, or a complete mixing of the deposits as the material erodes randomly from the face.

ii. Consolidation

Deposits in limestone caves become consolidated by the formation of breccia. In the strictest sense, this is defined as a deposit 'consisting of angular fragments implying minimum transport of material. Breccias are generally poorly sorted and commonly contain rock fragments derived from a restricted source' (Whitten 1972, p.63). However, the word has also come to be used *sensu lato*, to refer to any consolidated matrix in a cave environment. A 'bone breccia' is

'A large unstratified mass of bones or bone fragments cemented together. The commonest type of bone breccia develops where bones accumulate in a cave, or in a sink hole in a limestone region, subsequently becoming consolidated by a deposition of calcium carbonate in the form of stalagmitic material'

(Whitten *op. cit.*, p.56)

This does not necessarily occur in a single phase. The breccia supported by angular clasts may be consolidated first, forming a cemented structure with many voids, especially between the larger rocks. These gaps might then be filled with cave earth and any small bones and bone fragments deposited by any of the processes described above (this chapter), by downward percolation. The resultant loose material between the rocks is then consolidated by the same process as the initial cementation, as water carrying calcium carbonate continues to trickle down through the deposit. The bone breccias on the west wall of Merlin's Cave present a good example of this process, with thin layers of stalagmite from the initial brecciation lining the voids in which the subsequently consolidated mass of small mammal bone were found.

b. Biological processes

i. Trampling (compaction) by humans and other large cave-dwelling mammals

In examining assemblages of small mammal bone from cave excavations, it becomes obvious that the physical condition of bone often varies according to its exact provenance. Material from occupation levels shows evidence of severe trampling, which has compacted the sediments and crushed many of the bones - for instance, in the Lateglacial occupation horizon at Three Holes Cave. Individual small mammal bones are likely to be completely destroyed by trampling, unless a particularly soft substrate allows them to be pushed into it. Robust bones such as individual teeth, and very small bones such as phalanges and caudal vertebrae will survive such treatment. The effect of trampling on pellets, rather than individual bones, depends on the state of the pellet, whether wet or dry, the freshness, and the composition of the pellet. Those containing a high proportion of feather are noticeably less compact and more fragile than those composed of fur. Dry pellets are stronger than wet or fresh, to some extent protecting the bones inside, but even a single trample will break skulls, parts of the mandibles, scapulae and pelves (Andrews 1990). Small mammal bones from occupation levels investigated in the Torbryan Caves Project and the Wye Valley Caves Project commonly showed evidence of trampling - extreme bone breakage, total lack of crania or recognisable parts of crania, and a high proportion of individual teeth, many of which had split into separate prisms or groups of prisms.

The bones were also infrequent and widely dispersed, with a significant improvement in condition at the edges of the deposit such as right against the cliff or cave wall.

ii. Bioturbation

The action of burrowing creatures, while unlikely to cause physical damage to individual bones, leads to an alteration of the assemblage. This is seen mainly in deposits outside a cave mouth. Large burrowers - from badgers down to rabbits - cause severe disturbance of stratigraphy both in excavating their burrows and later when the burrow may collapse. Such disturbance is usually clearly visible, especially where darker, more humic topsoil is introduced into subsoils and scree deposits. Disturbance by smaller soil organisms such as earthworms leads to the opening of voids in the soil matrix through which small bones may be carried downwards by water percolation, leaving larger particles higher in the profile. This can also occur where the sediment is naturally vacuous, as in a scree deposit. The growth of roots, particularly of trees and shrubs, can lead to considerable disturbance, both while the plant is living and growing, and when either an individual root or the entire plant die. Root growth may push particles, including bones, down into lower sediments, or force them upwards. The decay of dead roots leaves a void, with a similar effect to an animal burrow. Root marks are often observed on bone from true earths, which contain the humus necessary for plant growth, showing as irregular grooves and linear indentations in the bone (Andrews 1990).

iii. Chemical degradation

The organic acids present in topsoils and in deposits such as middens cause degradation of the bone, leaving it soft and brown, as observed in bones from the later deposits at Three Holes Cave. The small bones of voles and shrews are unlikely to display root marks, and their large surface area to mass ratio quickly leads to their total loss where soil conditions are acidic. This has been observed when newly-dead small mammals have been buried in flowerpots of soil to obtain cleaned comparative skeletons. Burial in acid soils leads to considerable bone loss if the specimen is not recovered as soon as all flesh has gone. Chemical effects are recognised as pitting and flaking of the bone surface, which are likely to be present over the whole bone surface (Andrews 1990).

3. Problems in the study of small mammals from cave sites

a. Multiple taphonomic effects

These are caused by a series of events acting on bones during and after deposition. The complexities of what might happen to small bones during their depositional history are profound , and the examination of at least one collection of relatively unmodified remains, provided in this study by the excavation of Merlin's Cave, gives a yardstick by which other assemblages may be evaluated. It is also important to examine as many different known taphonomic effects as possible, as comparative material cannot be replaced even by excellent photographs and descriptions such as are provided in Peter Andrews' volume, *Owls, Caves and Fossils* (1990).

b. Stratigraphic integrity

As discussed above, there are many ways in which the stratigraphy of cave sites may be distorted. Loose screes may lead to downward percolation of small bones, as is seen in the Yellow Scree deposit at King Arthur's Cave. Pockets in the scree contained the bone remains from one or two owl pellets, identifiable by matching pairs of longbones, mandibles and crania (see below for full discussion), but some small bones such as toes and caudal vertebrae were absent. Larger gaps, occurring in scree with large clasts, rockfalls, or by cave formation processes such as solution, allow the passage of larger bone. Consequently, even an assemblage from seemingly undisturbed cave sediments may show the effects of mixing, and stratigraphic blurring.

c. Human activity

As most opportunities to study ancient small mammal bones arise from their inclusion in an archaeological site, it seems churlish to complain of the effect human activity can have on the development of a useful small mammal sequence. However, it has been observed in samples from occupation levels at Three Holes Cave, Symonds Yat East Cave and Gough's Cave that the small mammal bone is not only comminuted, but also that the deposition of such material ceases. It is unlikely that the owls thought to be the major contributors of small animal remains on most sites would continue in residence when humans had taken over the cave. As a result, the fragmented microfauna associated with human occupation debris is unlikely to be coeval with the archaeological material, and may either be later, as discussed above, or may derive from a scatter of owl pellets lying on the surface when the humans took possession. In a sheltered environment, such as is offered by the cave entrance at Gough's Cave, the small mammal remains may have been lying on the surface for some considerable time before being amalgamated with the evidence of human activity. They cannot, therefore, be assumed to be totally contemporary, and this should be considered when direct dates are obtained. Dates on larger mammal bones may be inaccurate for the microfaunal assemblage, and ^{14}C accelerator dates on small mammal bone may prove unrealistically early for the cultural material with which they are associated.

d. Old collections

When research involves the study of museum collections of small mammal remains, it is impossible to determine the standard to which retrieval of specimens was carried out. The processing of bulk samples demonstrates to the researcher how much is lost when, for example, a 1mm sieve is used in preference to one with 0.5mm mesh. The more uncommon species - dormouse, bat, water shrew etc. - may be missed entirely if individual teeth are not recovered. Most collections made before 1950 comprise only the larger and more readily identified specimens (A. Currant, pers. comm.) - complete mandibles, crania and maxillae - which makes difficult their comparison with assemblages where all bone fragments above 0.5mm were recovered. It is possible only to assume that if complete mandibles are present, correspondingly complete post-cranial elements would also be preserved. The degree of bone damage exhibited by the collection can therefore be extended to offer a tentative extrapolation of the taphonomy of the complete bone assemblage.

Chapter 5
Small Mammals and Archaeology

Problems with small mammal assemblages from archaeological habitation sites

As discussed in the previous chapter, small mammal material from human occupation sites tends to be of poor quality, in terms of availability and completeness of identifiable specimens. To recap on the problems presented in such situations:

a) The more identifiable skeletal elements (mandibles and crania) tend to be broken by trampling and crushing, while only the small unidentifiable bones such as caudal vertebrae and phalanges survive intact. Surviving individual teeth tend to be damaged, with the largest and most identifiable lower first molar most likely to be broken. It is common to recover vole teeth split down the longitudinal axis and broken down into individual prisms, particularly the relatively less robust teeth of collared lemming (*Dicrostonyx torquatus*).

b) Small mammal remains tend to be unevenly distributed within cave sites, with better survival and preservation at the edges of the site, for example, against the cave wall or cliff, away from foci of human activity. Where microfaunal bones have been recovered as incidentals during the excavation of occupation sites, it is possible that the sample is unrepresentative, as potentially better preserved specimens scattered away from the habitation debris might be missed. The damage to comminuted specimens from living areas, and the total loss of much of the original assemblage, renders it impossible to offer any sort of estimation of how the small mammal remains originally arrived at the site, preventing in turn a valid environmental assessment. This is demonstrated by the condition, distribution and species range of specimens recovered from the occupation levels at Three Holes Cave in the Torbryan Valley.

c) The presence of humans in an area may lead to a hiatus in the deposition of small bones by other predators, as owls, hawks and small carnivores are generally shy of larger predators such as humans, and have a well-developed sense of self-preservation which provokes them to seek alternative living quarters when disturbed. Even infrequent short-term visits to a cave by a human hunting party could be sufficient for it to be abandoned as a nesting site.

d) The circumstances outlined in (c) above can lead to a temporal ambiguity in accumulation. As discussed in chapter 4, the small mammal bones associated with human occupation might be from owl pellets deposited the day before the arrival of the humans, or just as easily, from the residual surface litter of years before. This is most likely to occur where the deposit in question is inside the cave mouth, and so protected from weathering, and is possibly the case in the assemblage examined from Gough's Cave.

Human influences on small mammal assemblages

The effects of human behaviour on the living small mammal assemblage must be considered, as well as their impact on the 'death assemblage' present at the site through other agencies. While deliberate human actions towards species as small as voles and mice tend to be restricted to instances where the animal is either of some use, or more commonly, a problem to people, the indirect results of local human occupation may be considerable.

i) Alteration of landscape, environment, and vegetation

There is no evidence for Upper Palaeolithic hunter-gatherers having any significant impact on the environment, as the landscape would already provide suitable conditions for the hunting of large herbivores. The developing woodland experienced by Mesolithic communities, however, led not only to technological alterations in hunting equipment, but also to the practice of forest clearance. This would produce open areas, providing suitable vegetation for grazing and browsing deer, and so attract the prey species to specific locations where they could be more easily taken. Evidence for forest clearance is provided by mollusc and pollen analyses, wherein shade-loving species are seen to decrease, such as is seen in the land-snail evidence from Cherhill, north Wiltshire (Evans *et al*. 1978). The data suggests no more than small scale clearings. A larger impact would result from the deliberate burning of wooded areas to provide a regenerative flush of young growth, as is suggested by Simmons. 'Using fire as the primary tool, Mesolithic populations probably manipulated the woodland edge habitat to produce more browse for ungulates and more *Corylus* [hazel] nuts for direct consumption' (Simmons 1975, p.57). By increasing the productive ecotone between the closed woodland and the more open landscape around it, usually at the treeline, a different balance of habitats was created both for the species intended to benefit (deer) but also for the small mammals dependent on the same resources. Field voles would benefit from the growth of new grasses, while bank voles and field mice would be encouraged by the flush of new shoots and the increase in seed production which follows burning.

ii) Removal of predators

The removal of potential predators from the environment would create an imbalance in which small mammal species might experience a rapid rise in population. Several of the mammalian predators of rodents and insectivores produce valuable furs – arctic fox, marten, stoat (ermine), and polecat (fitchet) – for which they are hunted or trapped, particularly during autumn and winter. The removal of even small numbers of these predators, which tend to be thinly dispersed over the landscape, could have a marked effect on their prey species.

iii) Removal of competition

Human exploitation of large grazing animals such as deer and horse might be expected to be of benefit to the small grazers, as pressure on the potential food supply would be reduced. However, the reverse seems to be the case. This is because regular grazing and dunging by ungulates encourages a close sward, with a thicker, lower growth. Voles habitually eat the lower parts of the grass stems, favouring the white leaf bases. Consequently, taller, sparser growth typical of ungrazed grassland, does not provide as much available food per square metre. Regularly grazed grasses also set seed on shorter stems, providing an energy-rich food source at vole-

level, and so allowing the rodents to build up a good layer of fat before the winter.

iv) Removal of food supply

The concentrated exploitation of such resources as hazelnuts by human populations could potentially cause a local shortage of these supplies, which are relied upon by dormice and other rodents to provide high-calorie forage to build up fat stores and hoards for the winter. I feel that this would not have too great an impact on small mammal populations, as experience shows that whenever there is a good crop of ripening hazelnuts, the rodents usually get them first.

Human use of small mammals

i) Direct evidence

Direct archaeological evidence of human use of small mammals in the form of cut-marked, burnt or modified bones is uncommon. It is likely that, with the notable exception of the mountain or arctic hare (*Lepus timidus*), most of the animals in the size range of this study were simply too small to have been regularly exploited by Upper Palaeolithic and Mesolithic hunter-gatherers. Mountain hares, with a body weight of 2.3 to 3.6kg in specimens from Scotland and Ireland (Corbet & Harris 1991) and up to 5.8kg in the larger Scandinavian specimens (Macdonald & Barrett 1993), can provide a useful contribution to the diet, as well as a fine pelt. Awls made from the proximal tibia of mountain hare have been recovered from Late Upper Palaeolithic occupation sites at Gough's Cave (Mendip), Robin Hood's Cave (Derbyshire), Pin Hole (Derbyshire) and Church Hole (Derbyshire) (Jacobi 1991). Cut mountain hare bones from Robin Hood's Cave, Pin Hole and Three Holes Cave (Torbryan) have been AMS radiocarbon dated (Table 5.1) to provide evidence of human exploitation of this species during the Late Upper Palaeolithic.

There is also direct evidence of the exploitation of hedgehogs (*Erinaceus europaeus*) by the Mesolithic people of Denmark. The cut hedgehog mandible, cranium and tibia from the site of Akonge show clear evidence of butchery, possibly for both meat and the spiny skin (Aaris-Sørensen & Andreasen 1993). Hedgehogs are large enough, at 0.4 to 1.2kg (Macdonald & Barrett 1993), to be worth catching and eating, especially as

Table 5.1- AMS dates (¹⁴C years BP) on cut mountain hare bone (from Housley 1991; * from Roberts *et al* 1996.)

Three Holes Cave*	calcaneum	12,260 ± 140	OxA 3208
Robin Hood's Cave	right humerus	12.290 ± 120	OxA 1670
Pin Hole Cave	proximal radius	12,350 ± 120	OxA 1467
Robin Hood's Cave	left femur	12,420 ± 200	OxA 1617
Robin Hood's Cave	right humerus	12,450 ± 150	OxA 1619
Robin Hood's Cave	right scapula	12,480 ± 170	OxA 1618
Robin Hood's Cave	left scapula	12,600 ± 170	OxA 1616

their only defence is to roll up into a ball, making them easy to collect. The large dorsal muscle along the back which allows the animal to roll up, and the concentration of high-calorie brown fat below the skin of the neck and shoulders which builds up before hibernation (Freethy 1983), make an autumn hedgehog an attractive food source - 'Still eaten and enjoyed by the Romany people, the hedgehog was, until well on into the nineteenth century, a favoured food of the agricultural worker' (Freethy *op.cit.* p.41).

The Mesolithic (Ertebølle) site of Vejkonge, in Denmark, also yielded the mandible of a red squirrel (*Sciurus vulgaris*) with clear cut marks in typical locations for skinning cuts. The marks can be seen as evidence of the hunting of this species 'especially for its long, silky winter coat' (Aaris-Sørensen & Andreasen 1993, p.33) rather than as a food resource, being 'too small to be worthwhile' (Fearnley-Whittingstall 1997, p.52).

ii) Small mammals as food

Whilst there is scant evidence for the culinary exploitation of small mammals, it may be worth while to consider historical and ethnographic sources to explore the possibilities further. Apart from the use of the larger species, hares, rabbits and hedgehogs, extensive enquiry has produced no record of regular exploitation of the smaller rodents as food, even in comparatively harsh and apparently resource-poor environments. Lee's study of the !Kung Kalahari Bushmen observes that 'such animals as rodents ... which in the literature are included in the Bushman dietary ... are despised by the Bushmen of the Dobe area' (Lee 1968, p.35). This probably indicates that rodents might be eaten in times of extreme hardship, but certainly not when there is a normal availability of other potential prey species. Lemmings, in their migrating hordes, might be thought to offer an easy chance to obtain sufficient quantities of the creatures to compensate for their individual small size. However, the literature shows disagreement over their edibility. Marsden's examination of the subject offers two citations supporting, and two denying, the acceptabilty of a meal of lemming (Marsden 1964). He quotes W. Duppa Crotch, writing for the Linnaean Society in 1878 that 'lemmings are often eaten by Lapps, who compare their flesh to that of squirrels', though he himself disliked them (Marsden op.cit. p.50). These would be Norway lemmings (*Lemmus lemmus*). The species referred to in Marsden (*op.cit.*), citing 'Peter Freuchen [in the *Report of the Fifth Thule Expedition* 1921-4 (1937)] speaks of the Eskimo roasting lemmings between two flat stones' (p.51) would be one of the *Dicrostonyx* species. Freuchen found the flavour disagreeable, and averred them to be 'eaten only in cases of emergency' (p.51). Marsden ends with his most recent observation on the subject, 'I came across some British students in Nordland in 1961 who had cooked and eaten lemmings and who swore that they were delicious' (op.cit. p.51). This may be an equal reflection on both lemmings and students. In general, lemmings seem to be a low-value food source, to be exploited only when other resources collapse, though it is possible that the Sami, who it must be remembered are primarily herders rather than hunters, may have been less reluctant to eat them, or perhaps to be recorded as eating them.

iii) Small mammals as fur-bearers

The pelts of lemmings and voles are of no commercial value, owing to the high cost of processing such small skins, and the poor durability of the finished pelt. Lemmings have particularly thin skins (Marsden 1964), which makes them unsuitable as economic fur-providers. The winter coats of the larger creatures covered by this study - hares, squirrels and small mustelids - are known to be valued to the fur trade. Mole skins were regularly used in the 18th and 19th centuries, when the velvety pelts were used particularly in making hats and waistcoats (Freethy 1983). The small skins would be sewn onto the split hide of some larger species, for durability (A.P. Currant, pers.comm.). The non-directional pile of the fur was prized, and led to the development of the plush cotton fabric now sold as moleskin.

Commercial viability alone does not necessarily preclude the occasional exploitation of small mammals to provide skins and furs. Personal whim might provide the impetus to devote the large amount of time necessary to process the tiny pelts to produce an item of clothing. Mr Andrew Currant informs me of his Aunt Hilda, who had a cape made from mouse skins. Her brother prepared the skins, each about the size of a postage stamp, from mice killed by the barn cats. These were then stitched to heavy cloth (A.P. Currant, pers.comm).

iv) Ritual and mythology

The position of the lemming in Inuit mythology is not surprising, in a landscape where there are comparatively few mammals, and a culture in which intimate knowledge of the natural history of the area is necessary for survival. The varying (or collared) lemming in its winter pelage is seen as a different creature - 'many groups of Eskimos do not distinguish between the Brown Lemming (*Lemmus trimucronatus*) and the Varying Lemming in its summer coat. Not only that: they lump them both with various mice and voles' (Marsden 1964, p. 228). However, the white winter lemming is seen as a 'sky lemming', thought to have fallen from the heavens, and so having 'an altogether peculiar knowledge of the diseases of mankind and the causes of death' (Marsen *op.cit.* p.234). The Copper Eskimo shaman, Ilatsiaq, who was struck by a falling sky lemming (presumably dropped by a flying predator), was considered to have particularly valuable supernatural powers bestowed by the incident (Marsden *op.cit.*).

Amulets made from, or in the shape of, the lemming were believed to enable the possessor to row quickly, or to be skilled in the construction of igloos. A protective amulet, recorded from Canada, Greenland and Alaska is described as Marsden as follows:

'Among the most famous Eskimo amulets are the skin and skull of an ermine or a lemming, the dried skin of which is worn inside the hood. The wearer of such an amulet can, when attacked by any superior force, breathe life into it. The ermine or lemming is immediately animated and rendered invisible. Small and inconsiderable though it is in outward seeming, its powers in amulet form are violent, and disastrous to the wearer's enemies. It dashes in unobserved among the hostile party with such force as to drive right through the bodies of his foes, as a rule up through the anus and out through the mouth, exterminating a whole party in a moment'

Marsden 1964, p.233.

Many Inuit groups do not distinguish linguistically between lemmings and ermines. It is probable that in the context of folklore and mythology, the similarity between the creatures (in that they both change colour in the winter) is more important than the differences.

v) Medicinal

The uses of small mammals in folk medicine are difficult to justify. The shrew, considered to be poisonous and capable of producing serious disability in domestic animals merely by coming in contact with them, was used to procure a remedy, in the hair-of-the-dog tradition. Gilbert White, in his 'Natural History of Selbourne' describes the process, involving

'a very old grotesque hollow pollard-ash, which for ages had been looked on with no small veneration as a shrew-ash. Now a shrew-ash is an ash whose twigs or branches, when gently applied to the limbs of cattle will immediately relieve the pains which a beast suffers from the running of a shrew-mouse over the part affected: for it is supposed that a shrew-mouse is of so baneful and deleterious a nature, that whenever it creeps over a beast, be it horse, cow or sheep, the suffering animal is afflicted with cruel anguish, and threatened with the loss of the use of the limb. Against this accident, to which they were continually liable, our provident fore-fathers always kept a shrew-ash at hand, which, when once medicated, would maintain its virtue forever. A shrew-ash was made thus: Into the body of the tree a deep hole was bored with an auger, and a poor devoted shrew-mouse was thrust in alive, and

plugged in, no doubt, with several quaint incantations long since forgotten'

White 1788-9, 1987 reprint p.186.

The taphonomic analysis of remains generated by such a practice would be a nightmare, and it is doubtful that the serious-minded academic and scientific worlds would believe the results.

Equally improbable was the belief, held up to Victorian times, that various childhood illnesses, and most specifically whooping cough, could be cured by feeding the patient mice. I have found two references specifying them to be fried, in Sybil Marshall's collection of her parents' reminiscences of Victorian childhood (Marshall 1967) and in Flora Thompson's *Lark Rise to Candleford* (Thompson 1945). Alternatively, it seems they may be cooked in pies for a similar effect (Freethy 1983).

As a final observation in this short catalogue of human uses for small mammals, perhaps the most peculiar reference collected is this.

'In 18th Century England, fashionable people wore false eyebrows made out of mouse skins'

Sunday Telegraph *Disney's Planet* magazine, 28.11.99

Unfortunately, no further information was offered on the practice.

In conclusion, human populations seem to have found a remarkably wide range of uses for the various sorts of rodent and insectivore available to them. Whilst it is not suggested that all, or indeed any, of the above-mentioned were practised by the Upper Palaeolithic or Mesolithic inhabitants of south-west Britain and Wales, it is not inconceivable that the small mammal bones found in archaeological deposits may have more cultural meaning than is immediately obvious.

Chapter 6
Results and Analysis (Devon)

Note on identification and bone condition analysis, chapters 6-9.

All available specimens from each key site were examined, and where possible, identified to species. Databases were developed to record numbers of identified specimens of each species and the general condition of the bone in each sample.

Voles of the genus *Microtus* present particular problems in identification to species, as tooth morphology can be variable within a species and similar between species. The field vole *Microtus agrestis,* for example, can be confidently identified in British material by the presence of an extra loop at the proximal end on the inner side of the second upper molar (M^2). The other two microtine voles (*M. oeconomus* and *M. gregalis*) present in Britain in the Late Pleistocene and early Holocene have only two loops on the M^2 inner side. These two latter species have identical upper dentitions, so where either complete maxillae or individual M^2s are present, they are divided into '*Microtus agrestis*' and '*Microtus oeconomus/ gregalis*'. Mandibles and first lower molars (M_1) of *M. oeconomus* are distinctive (see Chapter 3), but those of *M. gregalis* can be very similar to *M. agrestis*. Because of the lack of certainty in dealing with individual teeth, where a sample contains no distinctive *M. agrestis* M^2, but includes first lower molars or mandibles of a morphology close to the modern field vole, these have been recorded as '*Microtus*

gregalis/agrestis'. '*Microtus* sp.' refers to individual teeth (other than M_1 or M^2), which are identical in the *Microtus* species present in Britain in the time period studied here. There is also variation in the third upper molar in some *Microtus* species, particularly in *Microtus nivalis* (snow vole) and in the North American *Microtus ochrogaster* (prairie vole), but not in the species present in the British Lateglacial and early Holocene.

The general condition of the small mammal bone was considered, including all bones and fragments of bone not identified to species. I defined six classes of preservation, each sample being classified according to the condition of the sample as a whole, rather than of individual specimens.

1. Torbryan Valley (Devon)

The results from Broken Cavern and Three Holes Cave will be considered together, as the deposits excavated are roughly contemporaneous, and the two caves are separated by only 50m . The small mammal remains complement each other; a similar range of species is present, though different depositional and post-depositional processes have produced a marked dissimilarity in preservation. By examining the evidence as a unit, a clear picture may be drawn of the environmental conditions in the valley, and the taphonomic differences between the two assemblages may be explained.

Table 6.1 - Categorisation of states of preservation

Category	Defining features
A	Complete crania, mandibles, longbones etc.
B	Near-complete mandibles, maxillae, longbones
C	Mandible fragments, half longbones
D	Isolated teeth, fragments of longbone, complete small bones (toes etc)
E	Fragmentary bones, including molar prisms etc.
F	Fragments, but nothing identifiable to genus.
X	Mixed - distinct division between two or more levels of preservation

a. Broken Cavern & Three Holes Cave - environmental evidence

The deposits at Broken Cavern indicate less intensively occupied horizons than those of Three Holes Cave. The bone is generally less damaged by trampling and compaction, but the looser sediments have resulted in more post-depositional movement of material (see below). Three Holes Cave produced a much smaller amount of identifiable bone, but the individual contexts exhibited far more environmentally cohesive species group

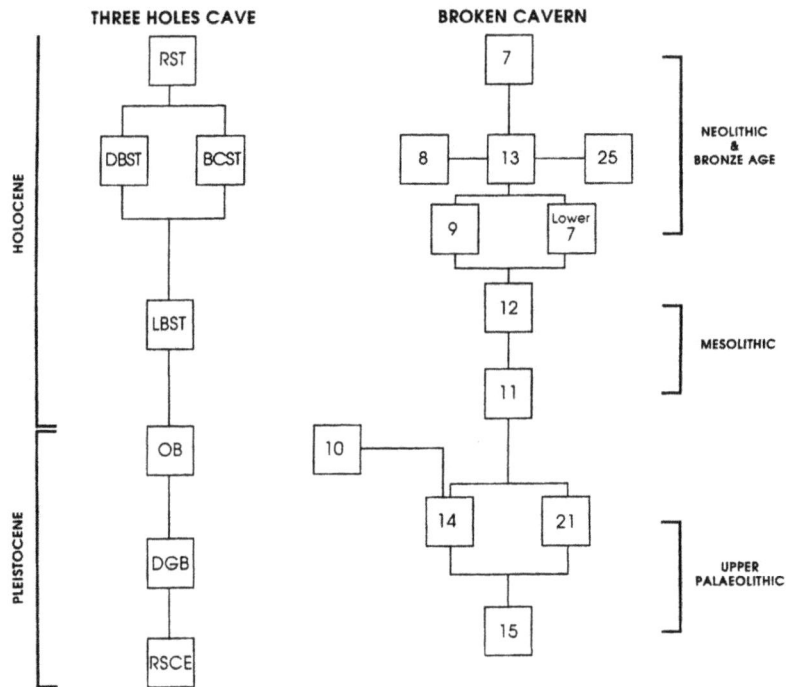

Fig. 6.1 – Matrix of stratigraphic relationships, Three Holes & Broken Cavern (Roberts et al, 1996).

Plate 4 – Broken Cavern 1990, working on Late Pleistocene level

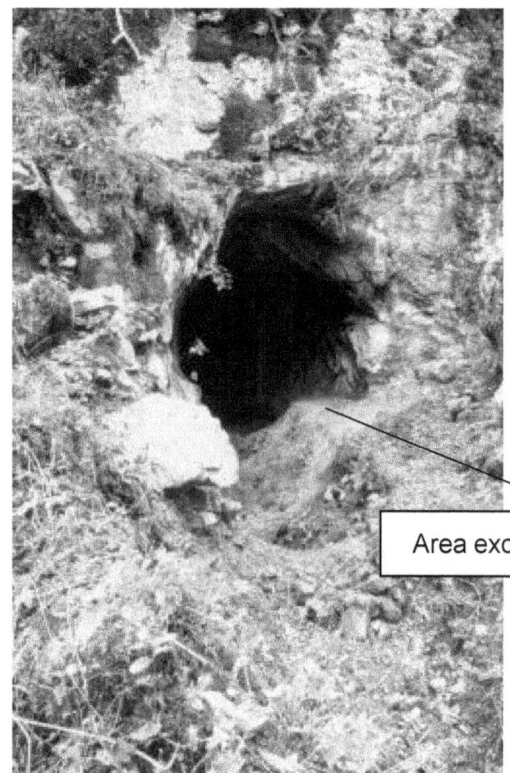

Plate 5 – Three Holes Cave entrance 1990, showing area of excavation on right of cave mouth

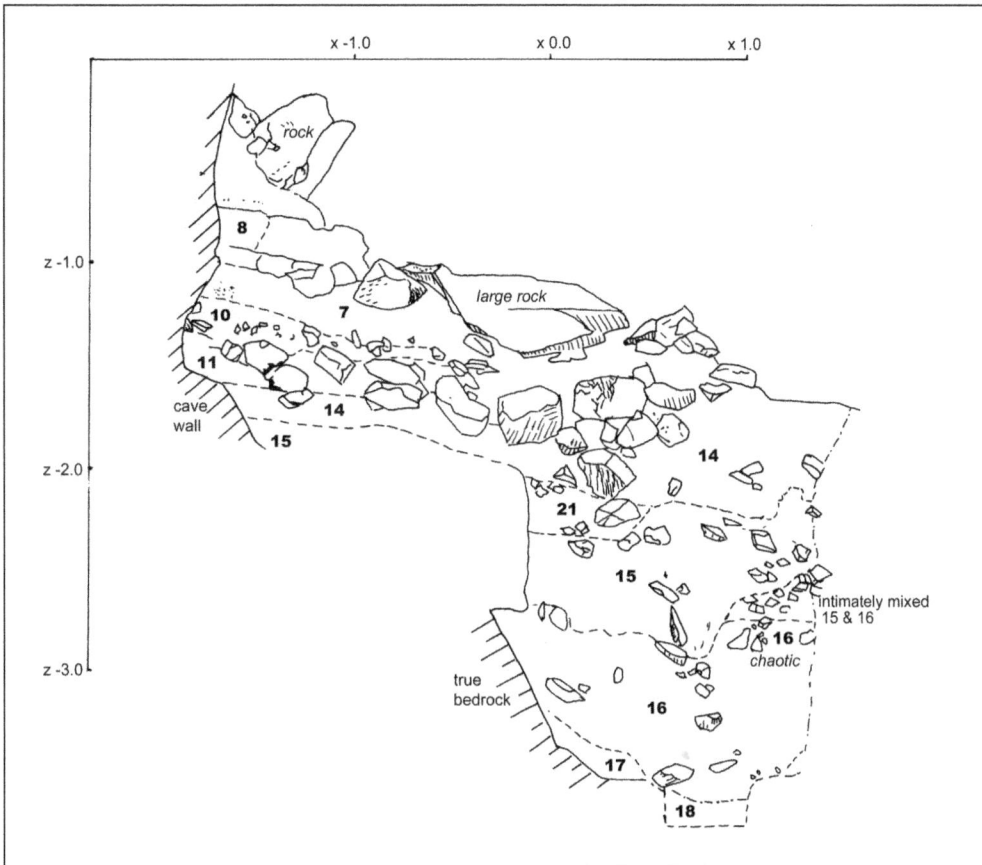

Fig. 6.2 – Section through excavated deposits, Broken Cavern

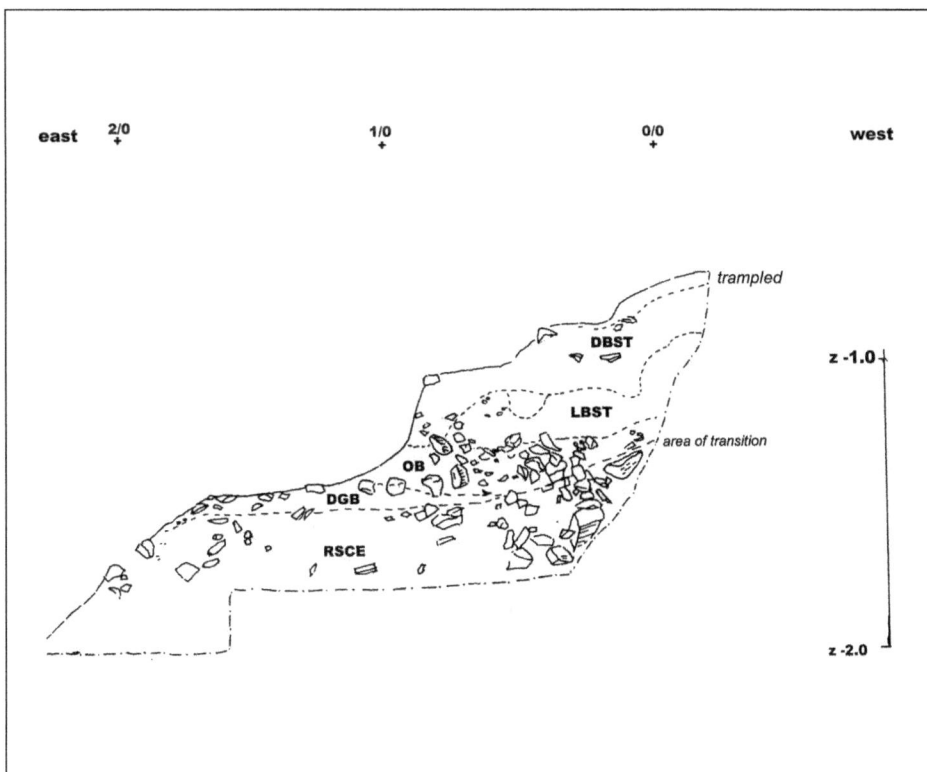

Fig 6.3– Section through excavated sediments, Three Holes Cave

Table 6.2 - Species Representation - Broken Cavern

	Late Pleistocene								Neolithic				
Context	15	14/15	21	14	10	11	12	Lwr 7	9	25	13	8	7
Lepus timidus			2	7									
Ochotona pusilla					18			33					
Lemmus lemmus				1				4					
Dicrostonyx torquatus	3	2				1		10					
Arvicola terrestris		1	2	29	5	5		12		5			3
Microtus oeconomus		1	8	57	17	29		50		1			10
M. gregalis			1	66	17	36		9					
M. oeconomus/gregalis		2	10	134	8	65		33					2
M. gregalis/agrestis		4	40	249	18	62		24					6
M. agrestis				11	2	5	3	4	1	19	11	26	36
Microtus sp.		55	250	1127	150	439	11	376	5	102		14	46
Clethrionomys glareolus				13	33	1	45	46	22	249	16	57	80
Apodemus sylvaticus		1	3	82	6	22	26	10	3	93	9	62	44
Muscardinus avellanarius							2		1	3	5	1	1
Sciurus vulgaris												1	
Sorex araneus				13	11	2	15	18	2	109	12	3	10
Sorex minutus		4	6	22	3	3	3	4		36	1		2
Neomys fodiens				1						6			1
Talpa europaea					3		3	16		15	5	5	27
Chiroptera sp.			3	2						23	8		4
Mustela erminea													
Mustela nivalis			1	10		2		11					
Total identified specimens	3	69	326	1824	291	672	108	806	34	661	67	169	272
Total samples examined	2	3	1	21	4	3	1	18	1	7	4	2	33

Table 6.3 - Species Representation – Three Holes Cave

	Late Pleistocene				Neolithic			
Context	RSCE	DGB	OB	LBST	DBST	BCST	GTST	RST
Lepus timidus		4		7				
Ochotona pusilla								
Lemmus lemmus		1						
Dicrostonyx torquatus	10	10		4				
Arvicola terrestris	4	4	2	14		1	1	
Microtus oeconomus	5	9		3				
Microtus gregalis	3	9		2				
Microtus oeconomus/gregalis	7	20		6				
Microtus gregalis/agrestis	1	21	2	10				
Microtus agrestis	2	4	1	2	1	8	4	10
Microtus sp.	114	295	32	112	20	48	32	6
Clethrionomys glareolus	1	6	4	44	63	205	54	22
Apodemus sylvaticus		3		17	51	112	5	29
Muscardinus avellanarius						3		1
Sciurus vulgaris								1
Oryctolagus cuniculus							2	
Sorex araneus		2	1	3	17	39	1	3
Sorex minutus	1	3			5	5	2	1
Neomys fodiens						2		
Talpa europaea					3	7	1	3
Chiroptera sp.		1			2	7	1	1
Total identified specimens	148	394	42	224	183	437	103	77
Total samples analysed	8	43	1	20	15	25	4	9

The earliest sediments excavated at Broken Cavern and Three Holes Cave yielding microfauna are context 15 and the Red Stony Cave Earth (RSCE) respectively. Context 15, a thick deposit of grey/green silts beneath the Lateglacial Interstadial horizon, was subjected to Thermoluminescence and OSL dating, indicating deposition at the end of the Last Glacial Maximum. A TL age of 14.1 ka BP is given by Debenham (in Roberts *et al.*, 1996). The base of the Dark Grey-Black horizon (DGB) overlying the RSCE equates with the top of context 15 (see figs. 6.1, 6.2 & 6.3). Small mammal remains are scarce in context 15, only three molars of a single species, collared lemming (*Dicrostonyx torquatus*) being recovered. The RSCE of Three Holes has a wider range of species, but some are likely to be derived from the more temperate fauna of the overlying Lateglacial Interstadial occupation horizon (see Chapter 4, section 3c). Only the two samples from the top of the context contributed specimens of any species other than collared lemming or undetermined *Microtus* vole. A single sample (511), which also included flint and is recorded as 'RSCE (probably)', from below a pocket of DGB containing a worked flint, included four water vole (*Arvicola terrestris*) molar fragments, all of the definite northern vole (*Microtus oeconomus*) remains, both of the field vole (*Microtus agrestis*) upper second molars, and the bank vole (*Clethrionomys glareolus*) molar. It seems most probable that the context designation of this sample was incorrect, as these species imply temperate conditions and are similar to the fauna of the DGB. If the specimens from this sample were removed from the totals given for the RSCE in table 6.3, the species list would be as follows.

Table 6.4 – Three Holes Cave context RSCE.

Dicrostonyx torquatus	10
Microtus gregalis	1
Microtus sp.	28
Sorex minutus	1

The single specimen of pygmy shrew (*Sorex minutus*) is from the top of the context. The environmental indications are of a cold, dry climate with open grassland vegetation in the locality, providing favourable habitation for collared lemmings and narrow-skulled voles (see chapter 3 for habitat preferences of individual species). Of the two samples of context 15, only one provided identifiable teeth, all of which were collared lemming molars. This context might therefore be taken to indicate a rather colder environment than that shown by the RSCE, though it would be preferable to have a larger sample base from which to draw conclusions. As stratigraphic indications are that context 15 is marginally earlier than the RSCE (Roberts pers.comm.), a colder climate would in any case be expected.

The Lateglacial Interstadial deposits, which include late Upper Palaeolithic occupation debris, are the DGB at Three Holes Cave, and contexts 21 and 14 at Broken Cavern. A greater diversity of species was recovered than from the underlying sediments. The small mammals recovered from the compacted DGB horizon include Arctic hare, both collared and Norway lemming, northern, narrow-skulled and field vole, all indicators of open grassland. Bank vole and wood mouse (*Apodemus sylvaticus*) are present in low numbers, as are common shrew (*Sorex araneus*) and pygmy shrew. Whilst bank vole and wood mouse are often found in woodland, they also occur in meadow and scrub environments. There is a possibility that these species are intrusive, as a certain amount of burrowing was observed during excavation of the site. However, it is not inconceivable that they are genuine Lateglacial specimens, and indicative of taller, shrubbier vegetation, if not necessarily woodland. The single bat tooth, unidentifiable to species, is possibly intrusive. The prehistory of bats is not well researched. Specimens of Natterer's bat (*Myotis nattereri*), Daubenton's bat (*Myotis daubentoni*) and lesser horseshoe bat (*Rhinolophus hipposideros*) were recovered from Neolithic levels at Dowel Cave, Derbyshire (Yalden 1986). There is a reference to 'subfossil material .... from cave deposits from Late Pleistocene in Notts/Derbyshire' identified as Serotine bat (*Eptesicus serotinus*) (Corbet & Harris 1991, p.113). The modern Serotine bat is described as 'House dwelling bat, mainly in lowlands, in areas of human settlements with parks, gardens, meadows, at the edges of big towns' (Schober & Grimmberger 1993, p.143). Its close relative, the slightly smaller Northern bat (*Eptesicus nilssonii*), has a more northerly distribution, occurring throughout Scandinavia and reaching the Arctic Circle and inhabiting areas of open scrub and mountainous regions (Schober & Grimmberger *op.cit*). Its present distribution and habitat preference imply that this species might be a potential inhabitant of Lateglacial Britain, a possibility which will be examined if sufficiently complete specimens can be recovered in future work. Six AMS radiocarbon dates for the lower part of the DGB occupation horizon range from 12,350 ±160 BP (OxA-1500) to 11,980 ± 100 BP (OxA-3891), giving a pooled mean of 12,190 years BP (Roberts *et al.*, 1996). The bones from which they were obtained were associated with a hearth and Creswellian flint artefacts. The upper hearth deposit contained a Final Palaeolithic assemblage including penknife points, a technology associated in mainland north-western Europe with the development of open birch woodland vegetation in the Allerød, later than c. 12,000 BP (Roberts *et al.*, 1996). Unfortunately, the low numbers of identifiable specimens in the individual samples of this context mean that although a block of sediment containing a section of the hearth deposits was carefully excavated under laboratory conditions by the author and A, Roberts, no biostratigraphic development could be observed in the small mammal assemblage.

Contexts 14 and 21 from Broken Cavern seem to be roughly contemporary with the upper part of the DGB, and date to the Allerød. The small mammal fauna original to this deposit is that found in context 21, which occurs in situations protected from later alteration by large rocks. These are thought to be the remains of the cave roof, which broke up and fell during the cold Younger Dryas period at the end of the Pleistocene (S. Collcutt, pers. comm). The rocks came to rest on sediments deposited on the cave floor during the Lateglacial Interstadial (context 21). Between the rocks, the cave floor remained exposed to later alteration, as smaller rocks and debris trickled between the larger rocks, filling the voids. This downward movement of material brought with it the remains of small animals from higher deposits. Burrowing animals would encourage the downward movement of earth, and also, by living in the gaps between rocks, would add material in the form of droppings, nesting material and even their own bodies after death. In this way, small mammal remains indicating widely different environments have come to coexist in a single context, and the distinction between contexts 21 and 14 has come about. The single sample from context 21 yielded 326 identifiable specimens, and a large amount of small mammal post-cranial bone in good condition. 309 of the identified specimens were of *Microtus* voles, and none of the 11 M²s and maxillae were of the modern field vole (*Microtus agrestis*), despite most of the M₁s having the typical morphology of that species - only one has the 'mitten' shape of 'typical' narrow-skulled vole (*M. gregalis*). It is suggested that they are all narrow-skulled vole, the modern species of which has extremely variable tooth morphology. Fourteen subspecies were recognised by Ognev (1964), many of which display varying forms of the lower first molar within the subspecies (see Fig.8.12). No lemming remains were present. A *Microtus* sp. mandible was dated at 12,470 ± 110 BP (OxA-4588), placing the deposit close to the suggested Interstadial thermal maximum (Atkinson *et al.*, 1987). The local vegetation at this time, as indicated by the small mammal evidence, was open grassland. There is likely to have been variation within the valley, offering the drier habitats preferred by narrow-skulled voles, perhaps on the plateau, with wetter grassland in the valley bottom where northern voles and water voles might be found. Further consideration of local habitat variation and its effects on small mammal population will be given below (chapter 10.2). Context 14 will be examined below, as the taphonomic evidence is central to the understanding of the fauna recovered from it. Suffice it to say here, that the species listed require a range of habitat conditions that could not exist in one environment.

Context 10 in Broken Cavern and the orange-brown sediment (OB) in Three Holes Cave appear to date from the Younger Dryas (Lateglacial Stadial). Only one sample was recovered from Three Holes OB, suggesting that deposition was very limited during this period. Few pure samples of context 10 were obtained, and no small mammals were recovered from the block of sediment attached to, and protected by, the back wall of the shelter (see fig. 6.2, Broken Cavern section) which is the only surviving remnant of this context *in situ*. Redeposited lenses of context 10, while containing numerous specimens of steppe pika (*Ochotona pusilla*), narrow-skulled vole and northern vole, also included many of bank vole, with some wood mouse, shrew and mole, presumably the result of depositional mixing or bioturbation. The protected deposit of context 10 included the remains of wolf (*Canis lupus*) and gnawed bones of reindeer (*Rangifer tarandus*), implying the occupation of denning wolves. A date of 10,950 ± 95 BP (OxA-3888) was obtained from a wolf metapodial. Context OB is dominated by voles, with 35 of the 42 identified specimens being of *Microtus*. The environment indicated by these and the steppe pikas of Broken Cavern, is open grassland. Context Lower 7 at Broken Cavern also contains elements of the Younger Dryas fauna, with 33 specimens of steppe pika, one of which provided a sample for AMS dating with a result of 10,180 ±90 BP (OxA-4374) and 50 of northern vole, dated at 10,370 ± 90 BP (OxA-4375). The mixed fauna also included 4 Norway lemming and 10 collared lemming teeth, 9 definite narrow-skulled vole, 33 upper second molars and maxillae of northern or narrow-skulled vole, 4 of definite field vole, and a total of 496 *Microtus* specimens. A specimen of bank vole (*Clethrionomys glareolus*) was also dated, giving a result of 5770 ± 75 (OxA-4496), proving beyond doubt that the indicators of more wooded conditions are Holocene. The high numbers of northern vole, compared with narrow-skulled vole, implies generally damper conditions in at least part of the environs of the cave. Once again, it is suggested that the valley floor provided one set of conditions, while the drier plateau offered another. The small mammal fauna does not indicate extreme cold.

The Light Brown Stony Talus (LBST) context at Three Holes Cave contained an *in situ* Later Mesolithic occupation level (Roberts, in Roberts *et al.* 1996). Contexts 11, 12, 9 and Lower 7 in Broken Cavern date from the beginning of the Holocene. Microtine voles continue to dominate the fauna in both sites, but there is an increase in wood mouse and bank vole, indicating developing vegetation cover, either from taller herbage, shrubs or open woodland. At Broken Cavern, context 11 seems to indicate the early stages of woodland development, while context 12 shows a more mature forest cover. Context 12 is represented by only a single sample but shows a marked faunal change, with a few field vole specimens but no northern or narrow-skulled vole, wood mice, bank voles and even two specimens of dormouse (*Muscardinus avellanarius*). This faunal group indicates the development of closed woodland, with a dense understorey. The requirements of dormice are considerably more specialised than those of wood mice and bank voles (see chapter 3). The roughly contemporary contexts 9 and Lower 7 (a widespread red cave earth overlying context 12) are the product of depositional mixing, containing a range of small mammal species which is environmentally uninterpretable. The taphonomic problems resulting from the site formation processes at Broken Cavern, outlined above and discussed more fully below, lead to difficulties in establishing a true biostratigraphy of the microfauna. The stratigraphy at Three Holes, despite the human occupation of the site and the subsequent trampling and compaction of the contemporary and underlying deposits, offers a more secure succession. From the four excavated squares from which LBST was recovered, a single column (square 7) can be taken to show the faunal development through the deposit.

Table 6.5 - Small mammal biostratigraphy, Context LBST, square 7.

Species	Spit	Top		Base	
		1	2	3	4
Arvicola terrestris				1	2
M. gregalis/agrestis				3	1
M. oeconomus/gregalis			1		1
M. agrestis		2		1	
Microtus sp.		3	3	17	13
Clethrionomys glareolus		5	4	1	
Apodemus sylvaticus			1	1	
Sorex araneus		1			

Table 6.6 – AMS Dates (¹⁴C years BP) from the Torbryan Caves.

Site	Context	Species	Date	Lab. No.
THR	DGB	Arctic hare	12 260 ± 140	OxA-3208
THR	DGB	Brown bear	12 180 ± 130	OxA-3209
THR	DGB	Horse	12 150 ± 110	OxA-3890
THR	DGB	Red deer	11 980 ± 100	OxA-3891
THR	LB	Red deer	6330 ± 75	OxA-4491
THR	BS	Red deer	6120 ± 75	OxA-4492
THR	BS	Aurochs	5060 ± 70	OxA-4493
THR	RB	Horse	12 220 ± 110	OxA-4494
THR	DB	Aurochs	5010 ± 70	OxA-4495
BRK	7	Sheep	4930 ± 90	OxA-3205
BRK	7	Human	4885 ± 90	OxA-3206
BRK	8	Cow	5015 ± 80	OxA-3207
BRK	14	Arctic hare	11 380 ± 120	OxA-3887
BRK	10	Wolf	10 950 ± 95	OxA-3888
BRK	Lwr 7	Steppe pika	10 180 ± 90	OxA-4374
BRK	Lwr 7	Northern vole	10 370 ± 90	OxA-4375
BRK	12 (base)	Bank vole	5770 ± 75	OxA-4496
BRK	21	*Microtus sp*	12 470 ± 110	OxA-4588
BRK	21	Natterjack toad	11 080 ± 220	OxA-6292
BRK	14	Natterjack toad	10 850 ± 90	OxA-6991
BRK	11	Natterjack toad	10 420 ± 120	OxA-6993
TB 6	Hearth	Reindeer (cut)	11 130 ± 100	OxA-3894
TB 6	Hearth	Arctic hare	12 130 ± 110	OxA-3895

The four specimens of collared lemming are from square 5, abutting the rockface. In this situation it is possible they are intrusive, having fallen into the context from above. This will be discussed below.

The Neolithic levels of the two caves are both divided into different contexts. At Three Holes Cave, the Black Charcoal-rich Stony Talus (BCST) is a thick layer of hearth material, shown by magnetic susceptibility to be redeposited rather than *in situ*. This is dated to the early Neolithic by AMS radiocarbon dates on aurochs (*Bos primigenius*) teeth (OxA-4493, 5060±70 BP; OxA-4495, 5010 ± 70 BP) (Roberts *et al*, 1996). The Dark Brown Stony Talus (DBST) surrounds the BCST, and 'appears to be its lateral equivalent outside the major area of deposition although with a lower charcoal content' (Roberts *et al*, 1996 p.173). These contexts are overlain by the Red Stony Talus (RST), containing Late Neolithic and Bronze Age archaeological material. At Broken Cavern, an occupation horizon of Early Neolithic age similar to that of the BCST and DBST is divided into contexts 8, 13 and 25, surrounded by context 7 (a red stony cave earth). The small mammal bones from these horizons show the local vegetation to be well wooded, with no evidence of clearance. Numbers of bank vole and wood mouse are considerably higher than of field vole, and there are regular occurrences of dormouse, and one from each cave of red squirrel. The dormouse is probably under-represented in archaeological deposits in relation to the living population, as the creature is not a common prey item for owls or raptors, and its arboreal lifestyle limits its predation by carnivores (see chapter 3). Neither are squirrels commonly taken by owls, being diurnal, though woodland hawks such as buzzards and goshawks are

known to predate them, as do wild cats and pine martens (Corbet & Harris 1991). The occurrence of northern vole in context 7 of Broken Cavern is interesting as a late record of the species, which is often assumed to have died out 'within about 1000 years [of the start of the Postglacial], presumably as a result of climatic change' (Yalden 1999, p.165). Northern vole has been positively identified from a midden on Nornour, Isles of Scilly, dating from the Bronze Age or possibly the Iron Age (Pernetta & Handford 1970). The continuing presence of the species in an area housing a healthy population of field voles - context 7 included a probable 42 specimens of field vole, and only 10 of northern vole - implies the existence of favourable northern vole habitat of damp or swampy grassland with tall vegetation, probably in the valley bottom. The presence of water shrew (*Neomys fodiens*), even in low densities is another indicator of this type of environment.

b. Broken Cavern & Three Holes Cave – taphonomy

The study of the small mammal remains from these two caves gives an important insight into cave deposit formation, and the effects of human occupation on the accumulation processes. The problems encountered in analysing faunal assemblages from many of the contexts in Broken Cavern require careful consideration, as is outlined above. Context 14 demonstrates the development of a mixed fauna, brought about by the loose scree allowing the percolation of fragments, including small mammal bones, from higher in the stratigraphy. This is exacerbated by the movement of living animals, burrowing through the deposits. It is fortunate that context 21 offers an opportunity to compare this with an

Table 6.7 - Condition of bone (Broken Cavern) - see table 6.1 for key.

Context	General condition
7	A to B
8	C
13	A to B
25	A to D
9	C
Lower 7	B to C, and X
12	C
11	A to B
10	E and X
14	B to D
21	B
14/15	D
15	C to E

Table 6.8 - Condition of bone (Three Holes Cave) - see table 6.1 for key.

Context	General Condition
RST	C to D
GTST	C to D
BCST	C to D/E
DBST	C to D/E
LBST	C to E (mostly D)
OB	D/E
DGB	D to F (mostly E)
RSCE	D to F (mostly E)

unadulterated sample from a protected position. The small mammal remains from context 21 are in good condition, with near-complete mandibles and longbones. All are a fairly uniform colour, with no heavy staining and no pale-coloured, fresh-looking specimens. Context 14 includes bones in a wide variety of conditions, but none of the very fragmented, trampled collections produced by Three Holes. In context 14, fresh-looking, fairly complete specimens are found in the same sample as heavily stained and grey, semi-fossilised bones. A similar range of conditions is found in the samples from context Lower 7, which includes elements derived from the Younger Dryas deposit context 10, a small remnant of which was recovered from the rear of the cave. In this case, the older, original context is physically higher than the later material, and is evidently a 'perched' deposit. Its partial collapse and subsequent amalgamation into the newly forming cave earth brought about an equally mixed and apparently similar fauna to that of context 14 by a completely different process. The deposits excavated from outside Three Holes Cave have little of the loose vacuous nature of the Broken Cavern screes, but are instead compacted by the traffic associated with human use of the cave. Much more occupation

debris is included, in the form of charcoal, burnt bone, flint chips and, in the later Neolithic contexts, pottery fragments. The small mammal remains are crushed and abraded, but not digested. Burnt small mammal bone is not uncommon, probably due to its having been accidentally in contact with hearths rather than through deliberate human action.

The range of species present at Three Holes, and the distribution of small mammal specimens across the site, implies their accumulation by owls, occupying roosts on the cliff face above the cave. The most productive samples for microfaunal remains were from the squares adjacent to the rockface, on or near the drip-line, with the quantity and condition of these declining progressively further from the cliff.

The range of species found at Broken Cavern is rather wider than at Three Holes, with the addition of steppe pika and weasel (*Mustela nivalis*), but otherwise similar. A proportion of the small mammal remains from contexts 7, 8 and Lower 7 show signs of mammalian digestion, as described in chapter 4. These are unlikely to have been the prey of the weasel, as this species is too small to swallow large pieces of rodent, despite a large part of their diet being made up of voles (Corbet & Harris 1991). Dissection of weasel scats from a moorland area of South West Scotland by the author produced only

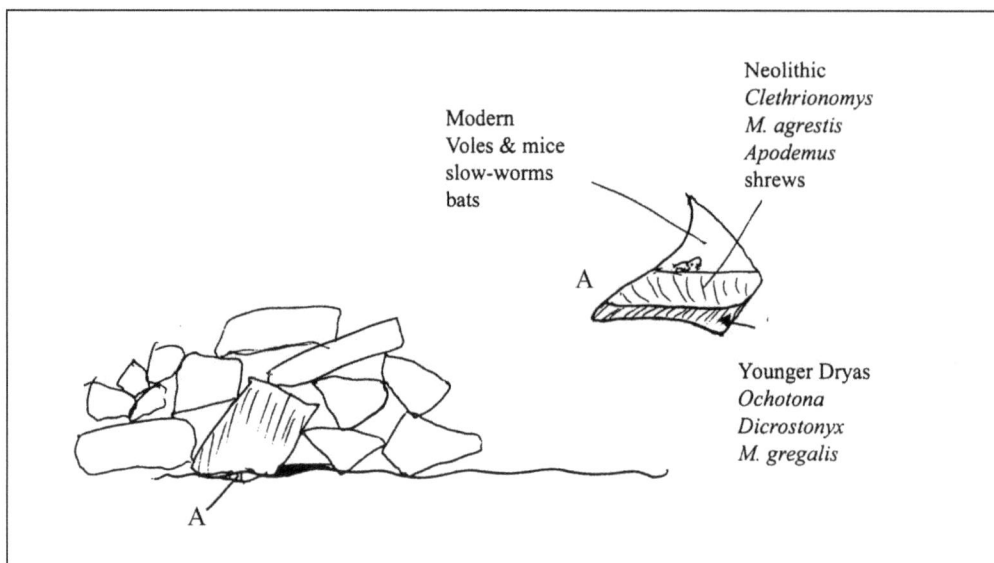

Modern
Voles & mice
slow-worms
bats

Neolithic
Clethrionomys
M. agrestis
Apodemus
shrews

A

Younger Dryas
Ochotona
Dicrostonyx
M. gregalis

Fig 6.4 - Faunal mixing due to deposition processes within loose scree (after Currant, pers.comm.)

unidentifiable bone fragments, though in this area their prey is almost exclusively field vole. The weasel remains recovered from the cave are probably from an animal which was itself a prey item - 'weasels are small enough to be regarded as, or confused with, prey by almost all other predators, including hawks, owls, foxes, cats and mink' (Corbet & Harris 1991, p.395). Mikkola (1983) lists eight species of owl known by pellet analysis to consume weasels, ranging in size from eagle owl (*Bubo bubo*) to the tiny pygmy owl (*Glaucidium passerinum*). A few of the rodent bones are marked by gnawing, which on bones of this size is restricted to post-mortem gnawing by shrews. It is impossible to determine which of the possible range of predators was responsible for individual instances of deposition.

Compared with a modern sample of owl-accumulated bone recovered from Tornewton Cave (see below), the Lateglacial and early Holocene small mammal fauna of the Torbryan caves shows a similar abundance of vole, mouse and shrew bones, with occasional bat, dormouse and fish. The predators responsible for the majority of deposition in the prehistoric levels clearly had similar dietary preferences, albeit adapted to more wooded conditions in the upper parts of the stratigraphy, and to a colder and more open environment in the lower.

Levels of concentrated human activity, the Mesolithic LB and Neolithic DB and BSCE deposits at Three Holes, yielded fewer small mammal bones than contexts of similar age but with much less intensive occupation in Broken Cavern. This is likely to be due to human disturbance of the predators, even in the case of sporadic use of the site. Owls have habitual roosting places, and once a site was deserted by the owl and a new roost chosen, the bird would not necessarily return to its original home when the humans departed, perhaps until territorial pressure or hunting patterns provoked a relocation, or a different owl took over the site. Bones would therefore be deposited between human occupations, and then trampled into the compacted land surface or swept out of the cave entrance during the next phase of occupation. The small mammal species incorporated into human habitation levels are therefore less indicative of the conditions surrounding the site at the actual time of occupation than those from caves

unoccupied by humans in the same vicinity, as can be seen by the more complete assemblages recovered from Broken Cavern. AMS radiocarbon dating of the small mammal bones themselves, in addition to those of larger species directly exploited by humans, can be seen as vital to the reconstruction of a full environmental background.

c. Torbryan 6 Cave - environmental and taphonomic indications

The only reliable *in situ* material recovered from this cave is from the possible hearth deposit on the east wall (see chapter 1). Eleven samples of this deposit were examined. No stratigraphy was apparent in the material (S. Collcutt, pers. comm.) so the recovered bones will be treated as from one context.

The small assemblage of rodent bones recovered from the Torbryan 6 hearth material indicates a cold open-grassland environment. The number of identifiable specimens is insufficient to provide more detailed environmental reconstruction. AMS radiocarbon dating of material from the hearth places it within the Lateglacial Interstadial, with a cut-marked reindeer dentary proving human activity at 11,130 ± 100 BP (OxA-3894), and an arctic hare bone dating from 12,130 ± 110 BP suggesting the hearth deposit accumulated over a lengthy period (Roberts *et al*., 1996). The condition of the bones is typical for an occupation horizon, with many of the prismatic vole and lemming teeth broken from top to bottom along the infolds. This pattern of breakage is consistent with trampling, and, as discussed above, shows the bone to have been considerably modified after its original deposition. This combines with the dearth of specimens to render it impossible to assess the primary agent of accumulation. As with the material from Three Holes Cave (see above), it is probable that the small mammal remains are slightly earlier than the human occupation, but no adequate specimen of bone from a creature smaller than arctic hare was available for dating. The collared lemming remains could be either from immediately prior to the Lateglacial Interstadial, and included in the deposit from cave floor material covered by subsequent occupation debris, or from the later part of the interstadial, as conditions once again deteriorated towards the cold Younger Dryas.

Table 6.9 - Species representation and condition of bone, Torbryan 6.

Species	Number and condition of specimens
Dicrostonyx torquatus	2 molars, 15 molar fragments (individual prisms). Most stained a dark mahogany colour.
Arvicola terrestris	1 molar fragment. Stained dark red-brown.
Microtus gregalis	5 M_1
Microtus oeconomus/gregalis	1 M^2
Microtus sp.	6 molars, 10 molar fragments (broken along prism joins)
Apodemus sylvaticus	1 molar

The small mammal bone recovered was broken and abraded, except for a few of the smallest skeletal elements such as toes. Other material present in the samples included bone fragments from larger mammals, some of which were burnt, retouched flint and microdebitage, and charcoal. The assemblage as a whole is typical of an occupation horizon, similar both in condition and in species representation to the material from Gough's Cave (see chapter 7).

d. Torbryan Valley - analysis of modern comparative owl accumulation

A collection of small mammal material taken by Andrew Currant from a ledge in Tornewton Cave was examined to compare the modern local small fauna in the valley with the archaeological assemblages. The deposit is thought to have been amassed within the last century, as the part of the cave where it was found was emptied during excavations in the late 19th and early 20th centuries (A. Currant, pers. comm.), and so should reflect modern vegetation and land use in the valley. Only complete and near-complete mandibles were counted to provide evidence of MNI (minimum number of individuals). Either left or right mandibles were counted, whichever was most numerous. Percentages are given for ease of comparison, though the numbers of individuals are too low to allow rigorous statistical analysis.

Table 6.10 - Small mammal representation in a modern owl assemblage, Tornewton Cave.

Species	No. of Individuals	%
Sorex araneus	81	29.5
Microtus agrestis	67	24
Apodemus sylvaticus	50	18
Sorex minutus	41	15
Clethrionomys glareolus	12	4.4
Micromys minutus	8	3
Neomys fodiens	8	3
Mus musculus	4	1.5
Chiroptera sp.	2	0.7
Arvicola terrestris	1	0.4
Muscardinus avellanarius	1	0.4

The wide range of species represented, and the variety of habitats preferred by those species, indicates accumulation by a catholic feeder, hunting over a large area. The condition of the bones, many of which are complete and unmarked by digestion, the location of the deposit, inside the cave mouth on a high ledge, and the modern origin of the accumulation, indicate the most probable predator to be the barn owl (*Tyto alba*). In addition to the small mammals, three fish vertebrae and low numbers of anuran bones were recovered.

The majority of the bones recovered are from prey species whose normal habitat is open grassland - field voles, common shrews and pygmy shrews. The preferred hunting territory of barn owls is over open land, as prey is easier to locate and capture than in dense cover. A greater biomass of small mammals is found in transitional areas (ecotones), for example, along woodland edges, hedgerows and field boundaries. Suitable habitat is found in such areas for the most numerous species in the Tornewton sample. Bank voles, occurring in lower numbers, prefer more cover - woodland and scrub - where available. In the Torbryan valley, populations of this vole would be concentrated in the wooded areas, where there are dense bramble patches and undergrowth. The actual population of bank voles is therefore likely to be considerably higher than indicated by this assemblage, which can be seen to represent the fauna of an environment rather different from the immediate surroundings of the cave. Tornewton is today set in fairly dense woodland with a thick, tangled understorey of briar, bramble and honeysuckle. It is unusual for shrews to be found to form the majority of such an assemblage, which would more normally be dominated by voles. However, it has been recorded that the percentage of shrews in barn owl diets increases during the winter (Taylor 1994), so while it is clear that this is not solely a winter roost - the presence of dormouse (a hibernator) affirming this - it is possibly an 'off-season' roost rather than a nesting site. The wide range of species also indicates the owls' occupation of a large and varied territory: it has been observed that barn owl winter hunting patterns cover a greater area than those of nesting birds. In Britain, water voles (*Arvicola terrestris*) are restricted to riparian habitats, which are also the most likely areas to catch water shrews (*Neomys fodiens*) (see chapter 3), implying that the owl was also hunting along a local watercourse. While the number of specifically water-loving specimens in the assemblage is low, the water's edge ecotone is also habitat to many of the less specialist creatures which appear in larger numbers, and a rich hunting ground for the predators of small mammals.

This assemblage is typical of the diet of owls feeding over the range of environments such as are found in the Torbryan area, with mature deciduous woodland on the hillside, rich pasture in the valley bottom and coarser, drier grassland on the higher plateau. It includes a suite of species in similar proportions to the archaeological assemblages - the medium-sized and easily caught prey species such as voles, mice and shrews are common, with a small number of the rarer or more elusive prey items such as dormouse, harvest mouse and bat. Similar patterns of species range and density have been observed repeatedly in this study of small mammals from cave sites, indicating that the vast majority of microfaunal assemblages encountered during the excavation of archaeological deposits in caves are either primary or redeposited owl accumulations.

2. Kent's Cavern: Wolf's Cave (Devon)

Material from Kent's Cavern High Level Chamber was also examined, but as deposition in this location was halted at around 53,000 BP (C. Proctor pers.comm.), the results will not be considered here.

The small mammal remains from the Wolf's Cave sample column (see fig. 6.5 for location in cave) were considered with reference to the age interpretation given by Proctor in his doctoral thesis (1995). The accumulation is thought to

Table 6.11 - Species representation – Kent's Cavern Wolf's Cave.

	Earliest								Latest
Sample	I	H	G	F	E	D	C	B	A
Lepus timidus						1	4		
Ochotona pusilla							1	4	1
Lemmus lemmus							1		
Arvicola terrestris	1	1	1	16			1	1	
Microtus oeconomus		2		1				1	
Microtus gregalis				4	1			2	
Microtus oeconomus/gregalis				1			2	1	
Microtus gregalis/agrestis				14	5		1		
Microtus agrestis				5					1
Microtus sp.	3	20	10	238	41	12	18	20	4
Clethrionomys glareolus				9					
Apodemus sylvaticus				4	3	1	1		1
Sorex araneus		1					1		
Talpa europaea				1					
Total identified specimens	4	24	11	293	50	14	30	29	7

Table 6.12 - Condition of bone – Kent's Cavern Wolf's Cave. See table 6.1 for key.

Sample	Condition of Bone
A (Top)	C
B	C
C	B/C - broken, but no evidence of digestion
D	B/C - as sample C
E	B - Large amount of small mammal bone, one piece of 'fossil' owl pellet
F	B - large amount of small mammal bone, some in 'fossil' owl pellets, some in anatomical association.
G	D
H	D - majority of bone is of larger mammals
I	D - majority of bone is of larger mammals
J	E - majority of bone is of larger mammals
K	F - very few, small fragments
L	E - very few, small fragments
M (Bottom)	F - very few, tiny fragments

date from 55,000 BP or earlier, terminating in the early Holocene, when granular stalagmite capped the deposit. The inclusion of steppe pika (*Ochotona pusilla*) in the three uppermost samples (A, B & C) indicates deposition during the Younger Dryas, as this species occurs in Britain almost exclusively during this last cold phase of the Devensian, with very few instances of attribution to earlier horizons. Four samples from lower in the column (J - M) are not included here, as they represent the earliest accumulations, which lie outside the parameters of this work. They contained no small mammal bones identifiable to species and only five molar fragments of indeterminate *Microtus* in the four samples.

The three lowest samples examined here (I, H and G) are comparatively poor in specimens. The species identified are indicative of open grassland, but there is inadequate evidence to suggest any further detail. Spit F yielded a much greater number of species. The *Microtus*-type teeth in this sample cover an unusually wide size range and show different states of preservation. The single specimen of *Microtus oeconomus* is particularly big at 3.25mm from proximal to distal end. Such large specimens generally occur only in early or middle Pleistocene cold faunas, where they tend to be the only vole species represented (Currant, pers.comm.). This is clearly not the case in this sample, with temperate species such as mole (*Talpa europaea*) and field mouse (*Apodemus sylvaticus*) present, albeit in low numbers. Either the *Microtus* or the temperate indicators must be intrusive or derived. Few complete mandibles were recovered, limiting identification of individual specimens to species. It is possible that the sample includes an advanced type of *Pitymys* (pine vole), a genus not found in British contexts after IOS 11 (Currant, pers. comm.), and thus much earlier than the scope of this study. The stratigraphy appears to have been sealed at the end of the Pleistocene, so it is not thought that the thermophilous species are intrusive from the Holocene, but rather that the sample represents the warmest part of the Lateglacial Interstadial, with earlier material derived perhaps from the slump of a perched deposit or deposits. The majority of the identified specimens resemble the assemblage from Broken Cavern context 21, but with slightly more emphasis on scrub or woodland conditions in the locality. This might be expected from the more coastal situation of Kent's Cavern where climatic conditions are likely to have been milder, as discussed in chapter 2.

In spit E, directly above F, a dark horizon was noted in the section corresponding with the layer of intense microfaunal remains, suggesting a concentrated layer of owl pellets (Berridge, pers. comm.). This is confirmed by the cemented bone agglomerations recovered from E and F, recognisable as concreted owl pellets (see plate 3). There are also several instances of articulated bones cemented in their original anatomical positions in spit F. This shows that the deposited owl pellets decayed *in situ*, relatively undisturbed. The sample location is around 30 metres inside the cave from the North Entrance, close to the 'Cave of Rodentia'. It is most likely that the owl nests or roosts from which the pellets were deposited in the cave were not actually inside the cave, but on the hillslope outside, from which allochthonous materials, including owl pellets, 'may enter the system through fissures and solution holes ... to form deposition cones' (Campbell & Sampson 1971, p.2). The four highest spits indicate an increasingly cool, open environment, with the Lateglacial Stadial (Younger Dryas) maximum in spit B - where there are no mice or shrews - and deposition ceasing shortly thereafter. The lack of collared lemmings, and the single specimen of Norway lemming, may suggest that the effect of the Lateglacial Stadial was much less marked in lowland South Devon than is indicated by results from the more northerly Mendip and Wye Valley sites (see chapter 6 and below), though the pollen evidence from the upland areas of the region suggests high snowfall during this period (see chapter 2).

While the small mammal assemblage from Wolf's Cave is not entirely consistent with the evidence of faunas from other sites of Late Pleistocene and early Holocene age, an AMS date on a single specimen, the ilium of a Natterjack toad from spit F, gave an age of $9,690 \pm 140$ [14]C BP (Gleed-Owen 1998) and can be taken to prove that at least a proportion of the microfauna of the deposit is of this period.

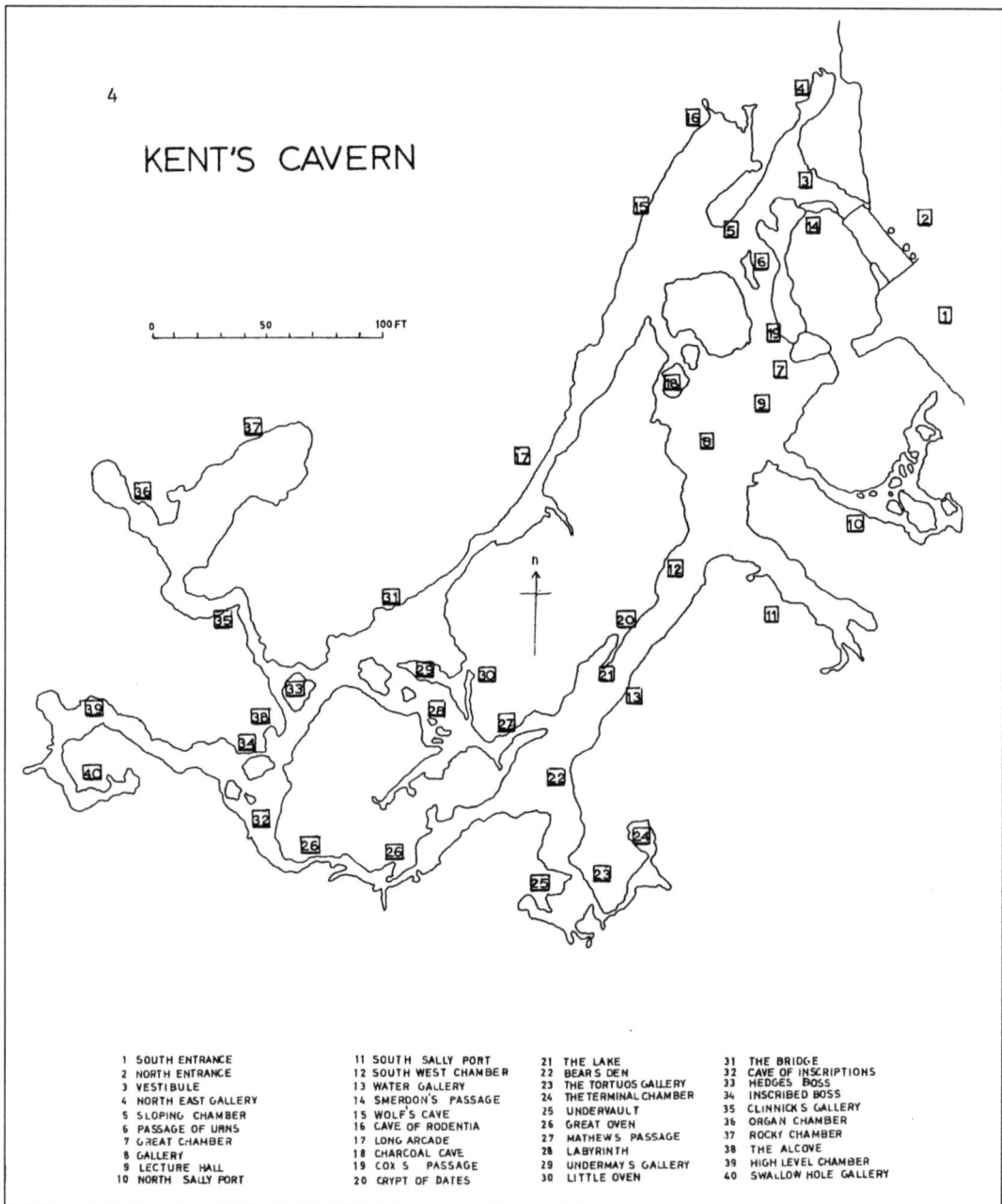

KENT'S CAVERN

1	SOUTH ENTRANCE	11	SOUTH SALLY PORT	21	THE LAKE	31	THE BRIDGE
2	NORTH ENTRANCE	12	SOUTH WEST CHAMBER	22	BEARS DEN	32	CAVE OF INSCRIPTIONS
3	VESTIBULE	13	WATER GALLERY	23	THE TORTUOS GALLERY	33	HEDGES BOSS
4	NORTH EAST GALLERY	14	SMERDON'S PASSAGE	24	THE TERMINAL CHAMBER	34	INSCRIBED BOSS
5	SLOPING CHAMBER	15	WOLF'S CAVE	25	UNDERVAULT	35	CLINNICK'S GALLERY
6	PASSAGE OF URNS	16	CAVE OF RODENTIA	26	GREAT OVEN	36	ORGAN CHAMBER
7	GREAT CHAMBER	17	LONG ARCADE	27	MATHEWS PASSAGE	37	ROCKY CHAMBER
8	GALLERY	18	CHARCOAL CAVE	28	LABYRINTH	38	THE ALCOVE
9	LECTURE HALL	19	COX'S PASSAGE	29	UNDERMAY'S GALLERY	39	HIGH LEVEL CHAMBER
10	NORTH SALLY PORT	20	CRYPT OF DATES	30	LITTLE OVEN	40	SWALLOW HOLE GALLERY

Fig 6.5 – Plan of Kent's Cavern (Campbell & Sampson 1971), showing location of Wolf's Cave (15) and High Level Chamber (39).

Chapter 7
Results and Analysis (Mendip)

1. Gough's Cave

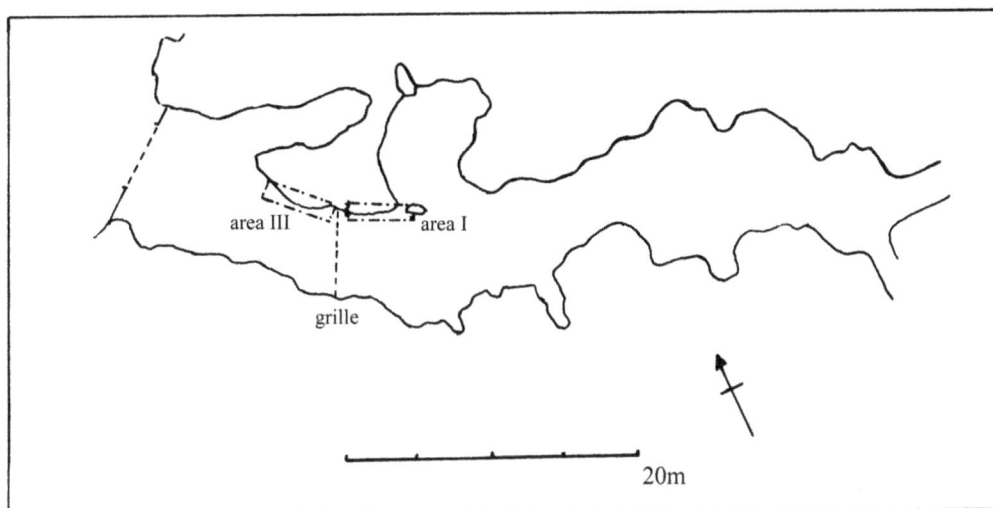

Fig. 7.1 – Plan of Gough's Cave, showing approximate area of 1989-90 excavation
(after Currant, Jacobi & Stringer 1989).

The 1989-90 excavations at Gough's Cave were conducted by Currant, Jacobi and Stringer, following exploratory work in 1986-7. Three areas were opened, areas I and III by the north wall of the cave (see fig. 7.1), and area II, which proved sterile, by the south wall. Gough's Cave is a popular tourist attraction, and to allow safe access the floor is concreted. The trenches were therefore restricted to the narrow gap between the concrete and the cave wall, and extended beyond the undercut wall shown in the plan. This allowed a 2m wide trench to be dug in each area. The squares were lettered from the front of the cave, so in Area III the nearest to the entrance is A, running back to F nearest the grille gate. They were numbered from the centre of the cave towards the wall, with the outside line of squares being A1 to F1, and the inner line, mostly beneath the overhang, A2-F2. An indentation of the wall permitted a third square, F3, at the eastern end of Area III. Area I was divided similarly, with squares L - M from south to north, and 100 to 103 from west to east. The sediment excavated was water derived red silt with some fine gravel, with no stratigraphic division.

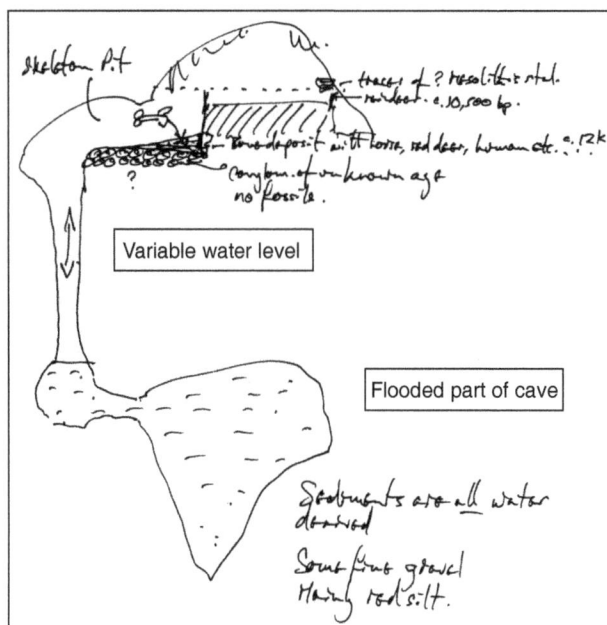

Fig. 7.2 – Sketch section of excavated deposits at Gough's Cave (Currant, pers. comm.).

49

a. Environmental reconstruction

The small mammal fauna recovered in the 1989 and 1990 excavations in Gough's Cave indicates a cold, open grassland environment in the Cheddar Gorge area. Collared lemming is the commonest species recovered from area III, with narrow-skulled vole the most abundant *Microtus* species. As discussed in chapter 3, these two species, when present with Norway lemming and northern vole, tend to dominate in the drier habitats, while the latter two concentrate in damper, lower-lying biomes. As collared lemmings are considerably more numerous in this deposit than the Norway lemming, of which only a single specimen was recovered, the implication for reconstruction of the local environment at the time is that a much greater area of dry grassland than damp sedgey terrain was available locally. The local topography supports this hypothesis, with the steep-sided gorge cutting through the Mendip uplands peaking at around 260 metres above modern sea level, and dropping down to Cheddar Moor at 6 metres. The agent of small mammal bone accumulation in the cave evidently concentrated its hunting on the upland surroundings of the gorge, rather than following the valley down to the low plain. The limited nature of the evidence offered by the selective prey-range of a predator with a very different set of priorities from those of human hunters shows only a fraction of the resources available to the human inhabitants of the cave, who would have exploited both high ground and valley. It is essential, here, to consider the nature of the deposits and the taphonomy of the bones included in them, at the same time as the implications of the species range.

b. Taphonomy

The small mammal remains examined showed a distinct deterioration in condition from the squares towards the front of the cave (area III) to those further to the rear (area I). Area III provided a much larger collection of bone, in a considerably better state of preservation, than was recovered from Area I. The largest number of small mammal bone was seen in square B1, area III, but as 28 samples were taken from this square, this can be seen as a factor of the quantity of sediment examined rather than actual density of bone. A more accurate calculation of the frequency of identifiable bone is given by averaging the number of specimens recovered per sample.

Table 7.1- Species representation (Gough's Cave area III)

Square	A1	B1	B2	C1	C2	D1	D2	E1	E2
Lepus timidus	1	2							
Lemmus lemmus		1							
Dicrostonyx torquatus	18	73	1	40	11	11	10	3	2
Arvicola terrestris		1	1?	2				18	6
Microtus oeconomus	1	2					1		
Microtus gregalis		8		6			8	4	8
Microtus oeconomus/gregalis	2	9				2	3	8	6
Microtus gregalis/agrestis		3						3	
Microtus agrestis									
Microtus sp.	8	29		13	2	4	15	25	7
Clethrionomys cf. rufocanus								1?	
Sorex araneus		1							
Chiroptera sp.									1
Total identified specimens	30	129	2	61	13	17	37	62	30
Total samples analysed	10	28	1	8	1	1	3	3	2

Table 7.2 - Species representation (Gough's Cave area I)

Square	L100	L101	L102	M101	M102
Dicrostonyx torquatus		2	1		
Arvicola terrestris	1				1
Microtus oeconomus		1			
Microtus gregalis	1	1			1
Microtus sp.			2		
Total identified specimens	2	4	3		2
Total samples analysed	3	14	6	5	5

Table 7.3 - Condition of bone (Gough's Cave)

Condition	Number of samples - Area I	Number of samples - Area III
A	0	0
B	0	11
C	1	13
D	5	32
E	1	1
F	13	1

Table 7.4 - Relative bone frequency, Area III

Square	A1	B1	B2	C1	C2	D1	D2	E1	E2
Total identified specimens	30	129	2	61	13	17	37	62	30
Total samples analysed	10	28	1	8	1	1	3	3	2
Average specimens per sample	3	4.6	2	7.6	13	17	12.3	20.6	15

Here it can be seen that the greatest concentrations of bone were found in E1 and E2. Samples from E1/2 also contained cemented lumps of small mammal bone, which appear to be owl pellet fragments.

The red silty sediment containing the small mammal remains, together with those of larger animals such as wild horse and red deer, also included human bone, occupation debris and flint artefacts. AMS radiocarbon dating of bone samples from earlier collections from the cave produced a range of dates between 12,940 ±140 BP (OxA-3413) and 11,900 ± 140 BP (OxA-813) for mammals consistent with the temperate Lateglacial Interstadial, with a further two dates on reindeer bone from the Lateglacial Stadial (Currant 1991). The human utilisation of the cave covers an extended period, and, as discussed above (chapter 5), this may well prevent the continual input of small mammal remains by discouraging roosting of avian predators. It is likely that the rodent bones, associated as they are with human occupation debris, represent the period immediately prior to the coming of the Upper Palaeolithic hunters, rather than a continual record of the Lateglacial Interstadial. The deposit examined seems to have been the result of material being swept under the overhang of the cave wall, where it was protected from continual trampling and, indeed, later excavation and the development of the site as a show cave. In two ways, then, the small mammal fauna is somewhat biased - first, by the chosen hunting range of the owl or owls responsible for the initial deposition, and subsequently, by the interruption of accumulation and reworking of the material in secondary deposition. The result is that an environmental reconstruction based on the small mammals alone is likely to indicate colder, more open conditions than were necessarily experienced by the human occupants throughout their use of the cave, and that the evidence of Leroi-Gourhan's pollen analysis (1985) for a limited amount of woodland development in the gorge itself during the Lateglacial Interstadial, while not supported by the small mammal record, should also be considered (see chapter 10).

2. Bridged Pot (Ebbor Vale, Mendip)

The site was excavated in 1958 by McBurney, as part of a programme of research into Upper Palaeolithic cave deposits. The small mammal remains were studied at the University of Cambridge Museum of Archaeology and Anthropology. Previous excavation by Balch in the nineteenth century removed the upper part and inner slope of the cone of dejection, leaving the outer talus slope 'largely intact' (McBurney 1959, p.262). A trench was cut through this, east to west, from the inside to the outside of the cave. The stratigraphy and sediment descriptions are shown in section (Fig. 7.3).

a. Environmental reconstruction

The samples examined from McBurney's 1958 excavation of Bridged Pot are from a single context, B - the Lateglacial Stadial thermoclastic scree deposit. The majority of the collection is of complete mandibles and maxillae, indicating a selective policy of specimen extraction and retention. The samples were probably dry-sieved through a relatively coarse mesh (ie. 2mm or larger), as was common practice of the time. It is therefore difficult to compare the findings with those

Table 7.5 – Species representation (Bridged Pot - bulk sample of Context B)

Species	Number
Lepus timidus	1
Ochotona pusilla	75
Lemmus lemmus	104
Dicrostonyx torquatus	121
Arvicola terrestris	69
Microtus oeconomus	283
Microtus gregalis	1121
Microtus oeconomus/gregalis	138
Mustela nivalis	2
Total identified specimens	1914

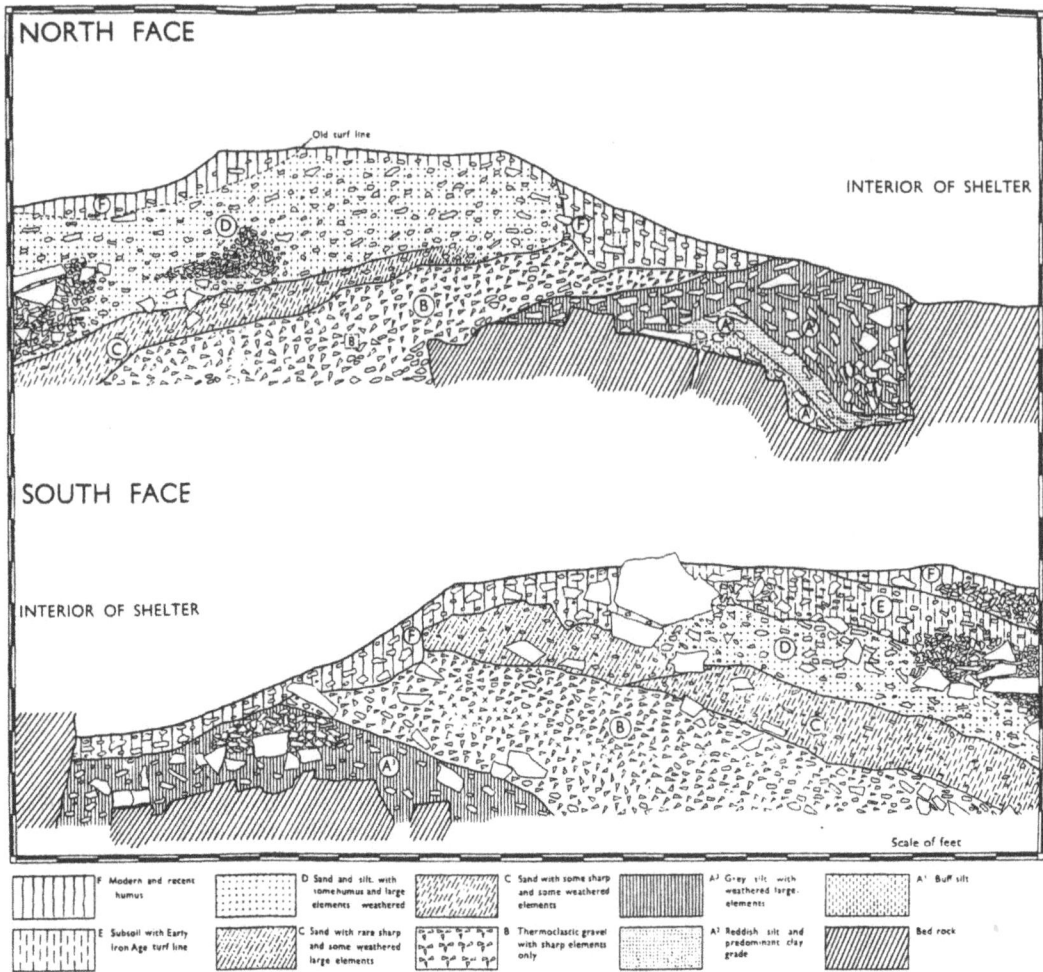

Fig. 7.3 – Bridged Pot stratigraphic section, with sediment descriptions (McBurney 1959).

of the more recent excavation examined in this work, where the retention of much smaller fragments has been the norm. However, the material does provide an excellent collection of small mammal remains which, from the faunal range, appears to demonstrate the local environment during the Younger Dryas.

The relative frequencies of identified specimens can best be shown by expressing them as percentages. These are calculated for the complete collection, with the specimens from the bulk sample of context B, taken at the same time but sieved after the excavation, added to those from samples taken during excavation.

The three specimens of rabbit (*Oryctolagus cuniculus*), recovered from a single sample, have been omitted from the calculation. They are clearly intrusive, the species having been

Table 7.6 – Species representation (Bridged Pot - samples taken during excavation)

Species	Number
Lepus timidus	5
Ochotona pusilla	22
Lemmus lemmus	12
Dicrostonyx torquatus	52
Arvicola terrestris	23
Microtus oeconomus	42
Microtus gregalis	122
Microtus oeconomus/gregalis	8
Microtus gregalis/agrestis	13
Microtus sp.	4
Apodemus sylvaticus	2
Talpa europaea	1
Oryctolagus cuniculus	3
Total identified specimens	309
Number of samples examined	55

Table 7.7 – Relative frequency of small mammal species, Bridged Pot context B

Species	Total	%
Lepus timidus	7	0.34
Ochotona pusilla	97	4.68
Lemmus lemmus	116	5.60
Dicrostonyx torquatus	173	8.35
Arvicola terrestris	92	4.44
Microtus oeconomus	325	15.69
Microtus gregalis	1256	60.65
Mustela nivalis	2	0.09
Apodemus sylvaticus	2	0.09
Talpa europaea	1	0.05
Total	2071	99.98

introduced to this country post-1066 AD (Corbet & Harris 1991). The wood mouse (*Apodemus sylvaticus*) and mole (*Talpa europaea*) are likely to be of later prehistoric date; the upper levels of context B from which these species came included fragments of prehistoric pottery. McBurney (1959) describes 'a few wall fragments of a dark relatively hard pottery similar to common Iron Age fabrics in the region' (p.264) from the upper part of context D, but the sherds from the samples examined for this study were of a red/brown fabric with coarse grits, and more similar to Bronze Age or Neolithic material. Both wood mouse and mole would be more fitting to the known faunas of these periods than to the rest of the faunal suite of context B. As no definite field vole (*Microtus agrestis*) maxilla or M^2 was recovered, those mandibles with M_1 of a similar form to field vole were considered to be one of the more extreme variations of narrow-skulled vole (*Microtus gregalis*).

The dominance of narrow-skulled vole over northern vole, and collared lemming over Norway lemming once again points to a local environment of dry grassland. This is supported by the presence of steppe pika, which also indicates extensive scree deposits in the area. The lower numbers of northern vole, water vole and Norway lemming are indicative of damper habitats, probably existing in the bottom of the Ebbor Gorge below the cave. The avian accumulator of the small mammal bones (see below) appears to have favoured the easier hunting offered by the plateau above the cave, in the same way as is seen at Gough's Cave.

b. Taphonomy

McBurney comments on the likely origins of the small mammal bones of context B as 'most easily explained as the residue of the pellets of some bird of prey - perhaps the snowy owl (to accord with the ecological implications of the rodents)' (1959, p.263). The current research finds no reason to disagree with this. The completeness of the remains is consistent with the argument, and the assemblage is similar in condition and faunal range to the undisturbed material recovered from Merlin's Cave, Wye Valley (see below). The density of the deposit suggests a long period of undisturbed owl occupation. A single radiocarbon date of 9090 ± 350 BP (BM-2101R) (Bowman *et al*, 1990), obtained from fragments of large mammal limb bone shaft, unfortunately gives no impression of the actual duration of accumulation, and the stratigraphic position of the samples used is not recorded.

Chapter 8
Results and Analysis (Wye Valley)

A fieldwork programme directed by Dr R.N.E. Barton (Oxford Brookes University) ran between 1993 and 1997, examining some of the many caves and rockshelters in the southern part of the Wye Valley near Monmouth, Gwent. The research aims to examine both the human uses of the caves and surrounding area, and the past environments of the valley. Four of the caves excavated provided valuable samples of well-stratified deposits containing small mammal bones, which are examined here.

1a. King Arthur's Cave - environmental reconstruction

The sequence of deposits uncovered to the west of the cave entrance (fig 8.1) provided a succession through the Lateglacial Interstadial, the Lateglacial Stadial and the beginning of the Postglacial. Context 5, underlying the

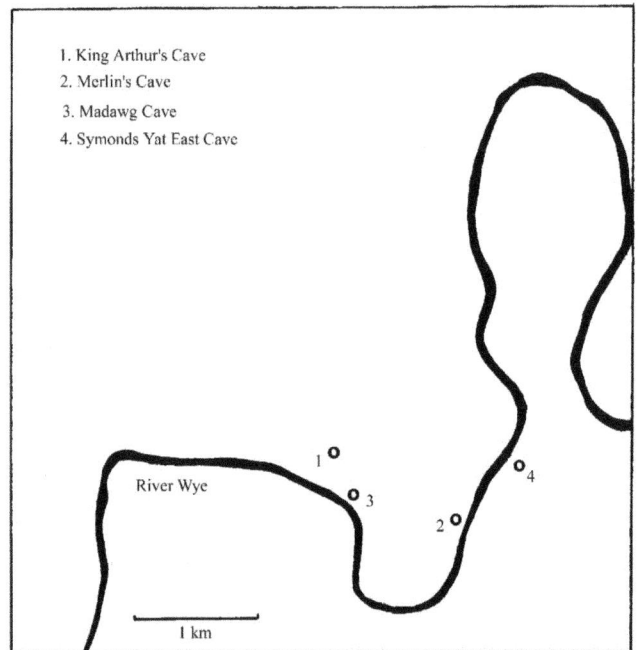

1. King Arthur's Cave
2. Merlin's Cave
3. Madawg Cave
4. Symonds Yat East Cave

River Wye

1 km

Map 8.1 – Location of sites in the Wye Valley

Plate 6 – King Arthur's Cave entrance

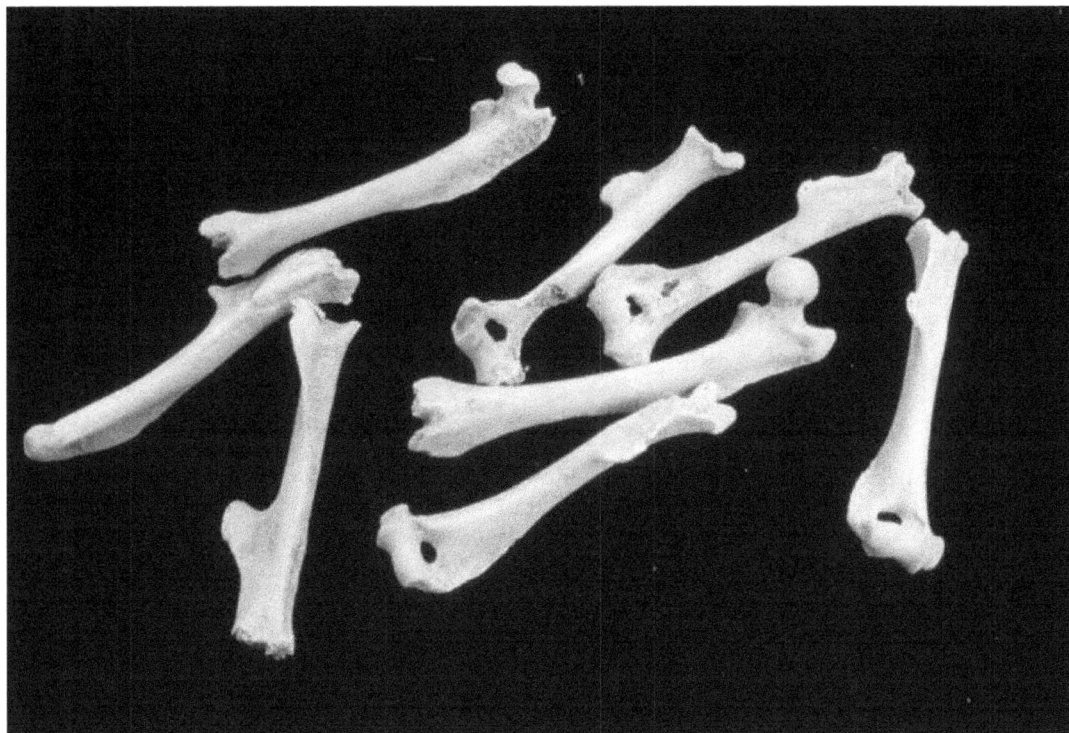

Table 8.1- Species Representation, King Arthur's Cave

	Earliest					Latest
Context	**5**	**4**	**4/3**	**3**	**3/2**	**2**
Lepus timidus	1	2		14		
Ochotona pusilla		2		2		
Lemmus lemmus	3	17	3	89	15	
Dicrostonyx torquatus	56	8		52		2
Arvicola terrestris		3	1			2
Microtus oeconomus		1		8		
Microtus gregalis	4	23	1	21		
Microtus oeconomus/gregalis	3	7	1	15		2
Microtus agrestis		3		2	1	22
Microtus sp.	29	94	9	79	1	110
Clethrionomys rufocanus		7				
Clethrionomys glareolus		6		21	1	300
Apodemus sylvaticus	2	2	1	34		95
Scuirus vulgaris				1		
Sorex araneus		1		6		19
Sorex minutus		2		2		
Talpa europaea						5
Mustela nivalis		1				
Total identified specimens	98	179	16	346	18	557
Total samples analysed	18	53	6	78	1	50

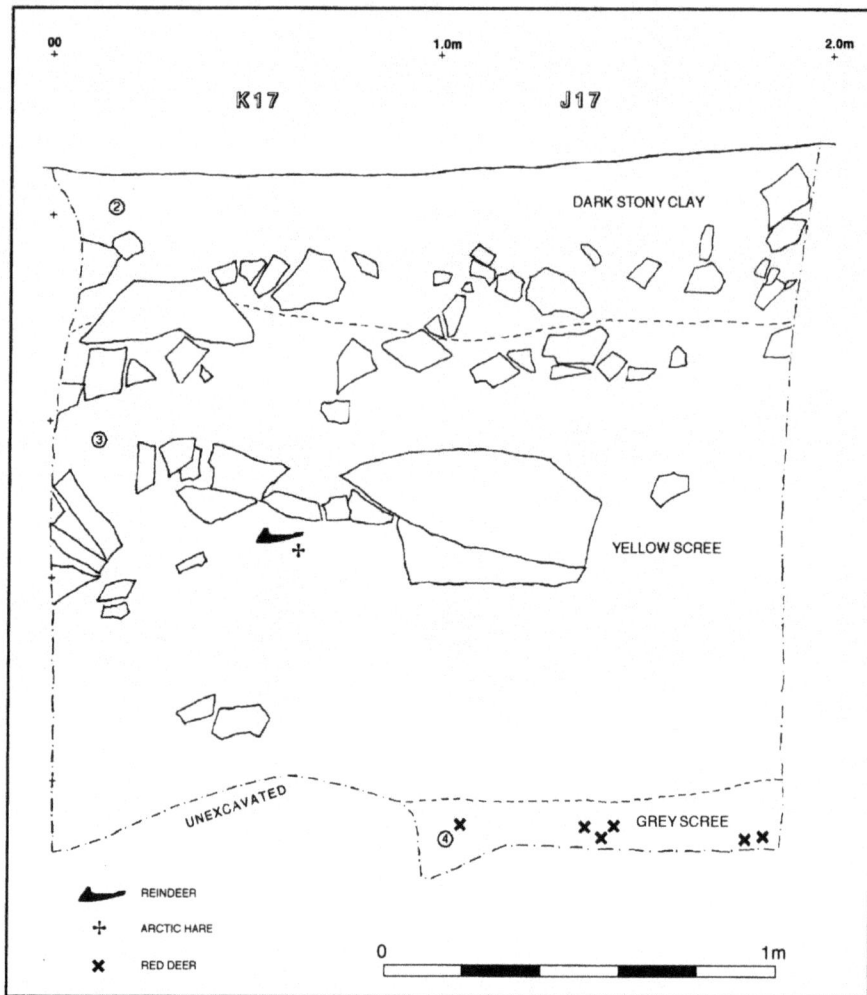

Fig. 8.1 – Section through deposits on west side of main entrance, King Arthur's Cave
(Barton *et al.* 1997)

Lateglacial Interstadial context 4, is a reddish clayey silt with frequent stones. Apart from two specimens of wood mouse, the small mammal fauna is wholly consistent with a cold climate supporting a grassland environment. The dominance of collared lemming suggests dry conditions. This is clearly the upper part of the 'Unit 3 silt loams' described from previous excavations (ApSimon *et al*, 1992, p.195), which included Unit 3c, the 'Mammoth Layer', so-called 'because it was the latest stratum in which remains of mammoth, wooly rhinoceros and hyena were found' (*ibid*). Three isolated mammoth teeth recovered from the cave mouth and platform by Taylor were radiocarbon dated to 34,850 ± 1500 (OxA-1564), 38,500 ± 2300 (OxA-1565) and >39,500 BP (OxA-1566) (Hedges *et al*, 1989). The small mammal fauna fits well with the environment suggested by these large herbivores and their predators, or indeed with the colder conditions around the glacial maximum between 25,000 and 13,000 BP. It is possible that there is no hiatus in the stratigraphy, and that the deposit dates from immediately before the Lateglacial Interstadial. The presence of narrow-skulled vole remains argues against the extreme cold of the glacial maximum, and could well indicate the gradually warming conditions following it.

Context 4, the dark scree deposit, contains an interesting fauna with elements indicating both cold and temperate conditions.

Microtus species are dominant, with 92% of the *Microtus* specimens identifiable to species being of narrow-skulled vole (*M. gregalis*). It is interesting to note that, while the dominant vole is the species taken to indicate drier conditions, the two lemming species identified would seem to indicate a rather damper environment, with Norway lemming identified from 17 specimens and collared lemming only from 8. This context is the first from which teeth of the grey-sided vole (*Clethrionomys rufocanus*) were identified, a species previously unrecorded in Britain. This creature is common in Norway, and in central and northern Sweden, where it occupies a variety of habitats including coniferous and birch forest and fells above the timberline, but 'prefers stony (rocky) places with many natural holes' (Mitchell-Jones *et al*, 1999, p.214). It is also possible that at least 12 of the 17 specimens attributed to Norway lemming (*Lemmus lemmus*) might, in fact, be of wood lemming (*Myopus schisticolor*). On initial examination it was noted that these specimens were particularly small, but the dentition of the two species is remarkably similar except in size. As only isolated teeth were recovered, comparison with modern examples of wood lemming were not conclusive, despite the specimens from King Arthur's Cave being identical to known wood lemming specimens at the Natural History Museum. The small number of identified specimens makes it impossible to apply a statistical analysis of the size range involved to demonstrate the probability of their belonging to

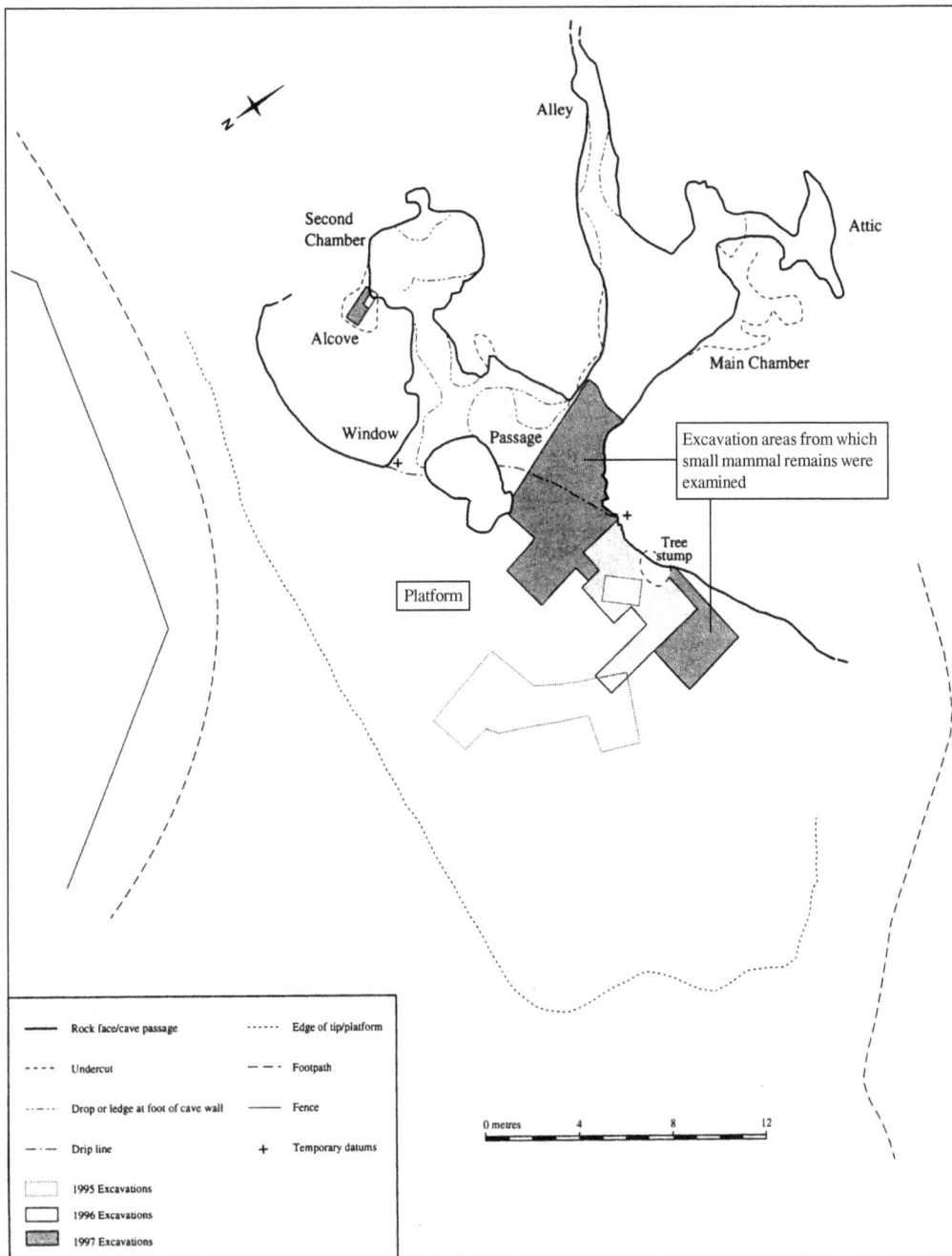

Fig 8.2 – Plan of King Arthur's Cave (after Barton *et al*,1997)

one or other species. The examination of specimens of Norway lemming recovered from contexts of known Lateglacial Interstadial age at other sites might provide more conclusive evidence of the presence of wood lemming in Britain during this period, and it is hoped that the opportunity for such research is available in the future. The preferred habitat of modern populations of wood lemming is spruce forest with a thick moss carpet (Mitchell-Jones *et al*, 1999), and the current distribution extends through the boreal forest zone from Norway to eastern Siberia and northern Mongolia (Corbet 1978) as shown in map 3, chapter 3. While it is not suggested that an exact parallel of this habitat was available in the Wye Valley during the Lateglacial Interstadial, it is possible that the species, currently 'dependent on a rather narrow set of ecological conditions that may be easily disrupted by human activity' (Nowak 1999, p.1483), might have exploited a wider range of environments in the past.

The complete small mammal fauna of context 4 suggests a mosaic of grassland and open woodland in the vicinity of the cave, distributed according to the local topography. The context provides a similar species list to that obtained from context 21 of Broken Cavern, Torbryan Valley, with the addition of lemmings. The stratigraphic position of context 4, King Arthur's Cave, suggests that it developed throughout the Interstadial. As can be seen from table 8.2, where a single column is examined, a degree of internal biostratigraphy can be seen within contexts 3 and 4. In context 4, collared lemming (*Dicrostonyx torquatus*) is only present in the top spit, at which point the climate would have been deteriorating towards the cold Lateglacial Stadial represented by context 3. The presence of steppe pika (*Ochotona pusilla*) in this spit also implies a change towards stadial conditions. There is no indication of woodland development in the vicinity during the Lateglacial Interstadial in the remains from this site.

Table 8.2 - Results from environmental column K18

Context	4b		4						3/4	3								
Spit	18	17	16	15	14	13	12	11	10	9	8	7	6	5	4	3	2	1
Ochotona pusilla							2											
Dicrostonyx torquatus							2						2					
Lemmus lemmus			1	3	8	9	4	5										
Arvicola terrestris					2			1										
Microtus oeconomus					1													
Microtus gregalis	1	1	1	3	3				1			1						
M. oeconomus/gregalis								1	1							1		
M. agrestis						1												1
Microtus sp.	3		10	6	12	9	5	10	3			1		1		2		
Clethrionomys rufocanus	3			2														
Clethrionomys glareolus																		1
Apodemus sylvaticus																		
Sorex araneus				1														
Sorex minutus					1	1												

The small mammal fauna of context 3 clearly demonstrates a return to cold conditions. The boundary between the two Lateglacial contexts is diffuse, but the number of samples available and the dearth of specimens retrieved from them do not allow a conclusive reconstruction of the fauna during the period of change. No species disappears completely between contexts 3 and 4, but their relative densities show a distinct alteration. In context 4, *Microtus* voles form 71.7% of the total identified specimens and the two species of lemming only 14%. In context 3, the balance is more even, with 40.8% lemmings and 36.1% *Microtus* voles. Surprisingly few specimens of steppe pika were recovered, despite their relative frequency in the deposits from Merlin's Cave (see below).

This is thought to be due to the method of accumulation rather than to the rarity of the species in the area. The presence of wood mouse, bank vole and red squirrel are almost certainly due to post depositional mixing, and will be discussed below.

The sample described as context 3/2 is not thought to represent a transitional stage between the Lateglacial Stadial context 3 and the Postglacial context 2, but a diffuse boundary between the two. The high number of Norway lemming teeth at this level might suggest that damper conditions prevailed at the boundary of the Pleistocene and Holocene, but the number of specimens recovered is too low to draw a definite conclusion.

Table 8.3 - Results from environmental column I17, King Arthur's Cave

Context	5	4		3/4		3			2							
Spit	16	15	14	13	12	11	10	9	8	7	6	5	4	3	2	1
Dicrostonyx torquatus	1	3						2								
Ochotona pusilla								1								
Arvicola terrestris										2						
Microtus gregalis			1													
M. oeconomus/gregalis										1						
M. cf. agrestis										3	1		6	2	1	
M. agrestis										2		2				1
Microtus sp.	1		5			2	1	1	3	39	10	1	2	18	11	3
Clethrionomys glareolus									7	88	55	9	24	46	41	19
Apodemus sylvaticus				1						44	18	1	3	23	4	3
Sorex araneus										4			2	7	3	2
Talpa europaea														1	1	

The temperate conditions following the end of the Lateglacial Stadial are seen in context 2, with increasing humic content from the base to the top of the deposit (Barton *et al*, 1997). The development of the woodland environment is marked by a fall in the numbers of *Microtus* voles (indicators of open grassland) and the disappearance of the species with a more northerly modern distribution, collared lemming, Norway lemming and narrow-skulled vole. A second column of samples (square I17), with a greater depth of Holocene deposit, shows this change.

The small mammal faunas of all but the lowest spit of context 2 are dominated by bank vole (*Clethrionomys glareolus*) and wood mouse (*Apodemus sylvaticus*), with much lower proportions of field voles. This shows a significant increase in vegetation cover, and with bank vole numbers so much higher than those of wood mouse, deciduous woodland rather than scrub is indicated. The presence of mole (*Talpa europaea*) shows that by this stage there was sufficient development of soil for these burrowing animals to construct adequate tunnel systems. Postglacial records of the mole in Britain are 'unreliable because of intrusion' (Corbet & Harris 1991, p.46), but as the species is thought to be 'a natural post-glacial colonist' (*ibid*), it must be assumed that it was present by the time of the severance of the landbridge with continental Europe at around 8,000 BP (Jones & Keen 1993). Context 2 is overlain in places by Victorian spoil, the result of Symonds' 1871 excavations (Barton *et al*, 1997).

1b. King Arthur's Cave – taphonomy

In assessing the condition of the small mammal bone from King Arthur's Cave, samples which produced only very small amounts of bone have not been included. As can be seen from Table 5.10, the condition of microfaunal remains was very variable. In Context 5, only one sample included a large amount of rodent remains, and in this assemblage the state of preservation is mixed. Some specimens are stained black, whilst others are white and fresh-looking. Context 4 includes some relatively well-preserved material, but most shows evidence of physical breakage. This is consistent with the condition of material of similar Lateglacial Interstadial age from other sites which also have evidence for Upper Palaeolithic occupation. The condition of the assemblage from King Arthur's Cave is considerably better than that of collections from Gough's Cave, Torbryan 6 and Three Holes

Cave Context DGB. This is probably a result of the vacuous nature of the scree deposit, which would prevent compaction.

The general taphonomy of the small mammal remains from King Arthur's cave shows a distinction between contexts deposited during periods of human occupation and those with no evidence of human use. There are particular problems of disturbance in the excavated area to the west of the cave entrance, from which the environmental samples were taken, as a large beech tree had grown close to the limit of excavation, causing root disturbance (see plan, fig.8.2). This meant that no samples of context 2 were available from the squares affected (K16, K17, L16, L17).

The specimens from context 5 are commonly dark-stained, and in all but one sample only isolated teeth or tooth fragments were recovered. The sample containing 2 wood mouse teeth (1402, square J17) shows differential staining, with all specimens of collared lemming almost black, but the wood mouse and one vole tooth very pale. Typically, the teeth and many of the post-cranial fragments show signs of mammalian digestion, with the corners of dental prisms smoothed off and the epiphyses of longbones dissolved. Small fragments of coprolite were also recovered from samples of context 5, suggesting that at least part of the deposition process resulted from carnivore denning. Access to this context was restricted by the depth of the excavation, limiting the number of samples obtained.

The upper part of context 4, the dark scree deposit, was identified as a buried palaeosol with associated Final Palaeolithic archaeology (Barton *et al.* 1997). The preservation of small bones is rather varied, with samples from squares close to the cliff (16 & 17) containing more complete specimens than those from farther down the talus slope. Two conclusions are drawn from this. The first is that the material was deposited close to the cliff, probably as owl pellets cast from roosting birds perched on ledges, and that the pellets either broke up where they landed, producing well-preserved prey remains below the cliff, or were blown, washed or rolled down the slope either entire or during their decomposition, producing more fragmented residues. The second hypothesis is that areas further from the cliff face were more thoroughly trampled than those close to it, and so suffered greater comminution and compaction. The natural line of access to the cave mouth passes in a curve around the cliff corner, avoiding the steeper slope close to it. A combination of these two factors accounts for the preservation

Table 8.4 - Condition of bones, King Arthur's Cave – see table 6.1 for key.

context	Number of samples in condition class						
	A	B	C	D	E	F	X
2			1	27	13	4	1
3	2	13	12	29	9	6	1
4/3			1	1	2	2	1
4		7	5	25	7	3	
5		1		7	5	1	1

differences and reconstructs the combination of site formation processes operating in the context.

Context 3, the yellow scree overlying context 4, is a loose deposit, 'entirely clast supported in a matrix of smaller limestone rubble and gravel' (Barton *et al.* 1997, p.66). There is no soil development in the rapidly accumulated thermoclastic scree. The small mammal remains give a clear indication of their accumulator. Within the deep deposit, several rich pockets of microfaunal remains were located, containing well preserved, undigested bones of *Microtus* voles and lemmings (see plate 7). Most skeletal elements were present, and the mandibles, femora and humeri could be paired to demonstrate their belonging to particular animals. Several individuals, not necessarily of the same species, were represented in each small deposit. For example, one sample (756) was found to contain the remains of five Norway lemmings and two narrow-skulled voles, with many of the mandibles and maxillae or partial crania complete. Given the size of the prey involved and the open conditions indicated by the species represented, the most likely predator is the snowy owl, *Nyctea scandiaca*, a large owl with a modern circumpolar holarctic distribution in the tundra zone (Mikkola 1983). These owls feed almost exclusively on voles and lemmings, and the pockets of prey remains recovered are consistent with the contents of the one to three pellets which would be cast within a forty-eight hour period. These have then been rapidly covered by scree deposition, to decay *in situ* and so lose little of their bone content. The preferred nesting or roosting site of the modern snowy owl is a raised hummock on the open tundra, affording a good all-round view (Mikkola *op cit.*). At King Arthur's Cave this would be provided by a position on the top of the cliff, above which the ground slopes fairly gently uphill. Before the growth of the thick woodland now abundant around the cave, it would have been possible to see for at least a mile in most directions.

The small mammal bone from the Holocene context 2, the Dark Stony Layer, is generally in poor condition. No complete mandibles were recovered, and many of the isolated teeth are broken and abraded. The post-cranial remains are fragmentary, and evidence of digestion was observed in many samples. Burnt fragments of larger mammal bones are frequent, and the presence of pottery fragments of Bronze Age and Iron Age types, and occasional late prehistoric worked flints, shows the resumption of human traffic, if not actual occupation, at the site. The effects of trampling, and the consequent movement of bone fragments, are once again evident, with the greatest number of identifiable specimens recovered from the excavated squares adjacent to the cliff. From the patterns of digestion seen in the rodent bones, the accumulation of such remains is likely to have been through predation by mammalian carnivores. It is conjectured that the faeces of domestic dogs might have been a major contributor here, given the human activity around the site. Unfortunately, no modern material is available for direct comparison. The dogs of my acquaintance are too well-fed or too idle to bother with such small prey species; when confronted with voles and shrews even within the house a springer spaniel was observed to harass the creatures by poking them with her nose but showed no inclination to kill

or eat them. Terriers will kill small mammals, but rarely eat them. However, dogs are recorded as enthusiastic predators of voles during times of exceptionally high vole density, for example, the 1890-92 vole-plague of southern Scotland. An Eskdalemuir farmer recorded that 'his dogs, who devoured large numbers [of voles], became so emaciated that they were quite unfit for work' (Elton 1942, p.148). One can only assume that sheepdogs do not thrive on a diet of voles. Comparison with Andrews' analysis of the scats of canids shows considerable similarity between the majority of the small mammal remains from context 2 and those extracted from the scats of red fox and coyote. In the case of red fox, 70% of all molars recovered were digested, incisors show extensive loss of enamel, and surface damage to post-cranial bone and the rounding of broken longbone shafts are typical of canid digestion (Andrews, 1990). The identification of these indicators is complicated by the further modification of the assemblage by the decay of the putative scats, and the subsequent movement and possible trampling and comminution of the exposed bone specimens. However, sufficient evidence remains that the small mammals were the prey of mammalian rather than avian predators. and that given the nature of the deposit, the most likely predominant carnivore to have been responsible is the dog. As is common in cave deposits, it is unlikely that the small mammal remains were generated by a single predator species, and any of the carnivores present in the area at that time, such as red fox, wolf or wild cat, might have contributed a proportion of the specimens.

2a. Merlin's Cave - environmental reconstruction

Merlin's Cave (plate 8) was known to have contained rich deposits of small mammal remains, examined and collected by Dorothy Bate in 1901 and by Martin Hinton in 1924-5. The specimens from these excavations are held by the Natural History Museum, London. Unfortunately, no stratigraphic information pertaining to the microfauna was recorded. Examination of the collection provided a good taxonomic record, but this was restricted to presence or absence of species in the cave. The Wye Valley Project investigated the cave in 1996, supervised by the author under the direction of Dr Barton, to determine the extent of surviving fossiliferous material and collect stratified samples which would provide a small mammal biostratigraphy for the period of deposition.

The samples from Merlin's Cave are divided into three categories. On the west wall of the cave, towards the entrance, many pockets of bone-bearing breccia (plate 9) were observed. This was the richest area of *in situ* deposit, and was extensively sampled. The cave wall was treated as a section, and a detailed drawing prepared on which the pockets of breccia were shown (see figure 8.5). Photographs were also taken, with the sample points marked. The samples were then removed with hammer and chisel. Below this 'section', a one metre square trench was excavated, in nine 5cm spits, adjacent to the west cave wall. The material from the cave floor was a uniform red earth, with frequent limestone clasts, breccia fragments and bones. No stratigraphy was observed. Where more than one 6 litre bag of sediment was extracted,

Plate 8 – Merlin's Cave entrance, 1996

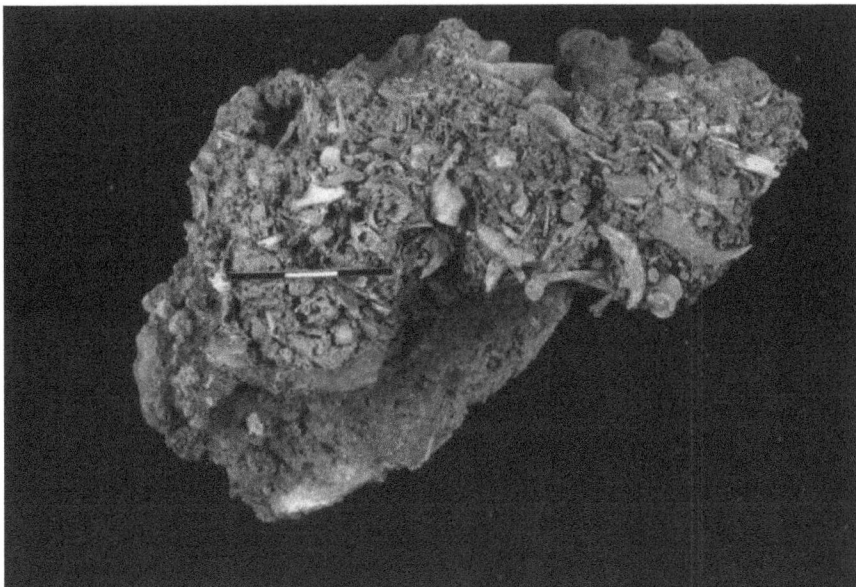

Plate 9 – Sample D, Merlin's Cave 1996, showing small mammal bone in consolidated sediment

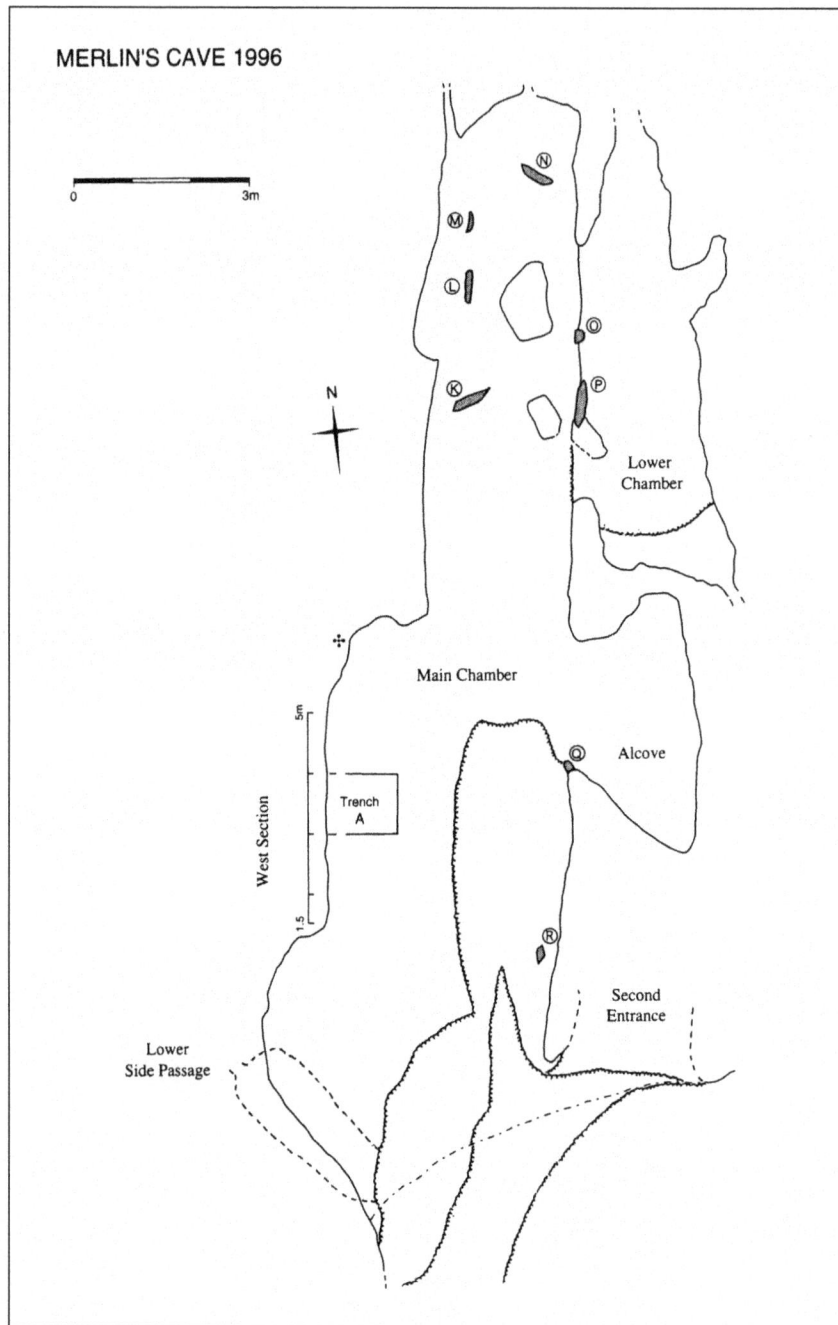

Fig. 8.3 – Plan of Merlin's Cave (Barton 1996)

only one bag was retained for fine-sieving, the remainder being dry sieved at 3mm on site. The samples became smaller towards the bottom of the trench, as more rocks were encountered, and the cave wall shelved out. Further isolated pockets of brecciated deposit were located on the east wall of the cave, marked on the site plan with levels, and removed as blocks.

c.i – Cave Floor

H - Hinton Collection (Natural History Museum, London). This material is also from the floor of the cave, and was apparently sieved at the cave. Complete mandibles and crania were retained, and other bones discarded in the residue. A deposit of cave floor material was recovered at the base of the cliff below the cave - some of the residue may have been

dumped there, while the rest was redeposited on the cave floor. No stratigraphy was apparent in the small trench excavated in the floor deposits, the whole being a fine red cave earth with frequent stones and bones. The mixed nature of the fauna is consistent with the history of disturbance in the cave.

The material from the cave floor appears to be backfilled spoil from earlier excavations, and contains a mixture of environmental indicators throughout. Temperate woodland species such as dormouse and wood mouse are present at the same level as pika and lemming. A similar range of species is represented in the Hinton Collection (Natural History Museum) from Hewer's 1924 excavation. From the site report (Hewer 1925) it is clear that the excavation concentrated on the cave floor, and no material was taken from the walls. 'The

Table 8.5 - Species representation - cave floor trench

	Bottom									Top	
Spit	10	9	8	7	6	5	4	3	2	1	H
Lepus timidus			1	2	1	2	1			1	2
Ochotona pusilla	2	9	12	17	19	19	14	2	2	9	118
Lemmus lemmus	3	18	35	19	37	14	16	18	2	11	54
Dicrostonyx torquatus	9	23	50	47	48	33	33	21	10	17	425
Arvicola terrestris	2	6	9	11	15	13	4	7	2	4	35
Microtus oeconomus	1	15	16	20	34	17	10	10	5	27	700+
Microtus gregalis	18	64	92	113	163	57	32	40	15	74	1233
Microtus oeconomus/gregalis	4	13	9	32	37	9	5	8	4	18	113
Microtus gregalis/agrestis	2	3	1	10	20	10	22	3		31	
Microtus agrestis		1	1	1	1		1				8
Clethrionomys glareolus	1	6	6	8	6	9	5	7	8		31
Apodemus sylvaticus	5	16	20	6	25	16	10	6	7	5	35
Rattus sp.											2
Muscardinus avellanarius						1				2	2
Sorex araneus	2	4	7	12	3	16	9		1		+
Sorex minutus		4	4	5	4	8	3	2			+
Neomys fodiens			1				1				+
Talpa europaea				1	3	2					
Chiroptera sp.	2		2		1	2					
Mustela nivalis		1	1	2							1
Mustela erminea								1			
Total identified specimens	49	184	266	306	417	228	166	125	56	199	
Size of sample (litres)	2.0	2.0	5.0	6.0	6.0	5.5	5.0	2.5	1.0	1.0	

material removed shewed (*sic*) manifest signs of earlier disturbance, there was no stratification of any kind' (Hewer *op.cit*, p.148). Crania and mandibles were extracted as the sediment was 'carefully sorted' (*ibid*) on site. As neither Hinton's collection nor that resulting from our own excavation are ecologically discrete, or provide biostratigraphic information, no environmental reconstruction will be based upon their evidence.

c.ii - West Wall

The west wall 'section' offers a coherent, homogenous assemblage of small vertebrate remains. Radiocarbon accelerator dates on small mammal bone from different levels of the section show the deposits to have accumulated rapidly during the latter part of the Lateglacial Stadial (Younger Dryas). The lowest dating sample, arctic hare from area G (Z = 98.83 to 99.01), is dated at 10,270 ± 65 BP (OxA-8071), a sample of water vole from the middle of the deposit (H lower front, Z = 99.00 to 99.17) at 10,160 ± 65 BP (OxA-8146), and steppe pika and Norway lemming from area F (Z = 99.68 to 99.79) at 9915 ± 60 (OxA-8073) and 9685 ± 60 (OxA-8072) respectively.

A specimen of northern vole also from area G was dated at 9450 ± 80 (OxA-8167), but as this was a loose specimen from the surface of the breccia it is probable that it fell into the sample from a higher deposit while samples were being chiselled from the wall. A distinct slope downwards towards the cave entrance was observed, so the samples are grouped into 'low', 'middle' and 'top' respective of this stratigraphy. Samples G and I are from the low section; E, H lower front, H lower back, A, C and H upper are the middle section, and J, D and F are from the top section (see fig.8.4).

As the samples varied greatly in size and in the quantity of bone extracted from them, they can be compared more easily by presenting the species representation as percentages, as well as in actual numbers. It must be remembered that in some cases the numbers are low, so the percentage figures should be used only as an indication of relative density.

This shows that there is no clear alteration of species representation related to stratigraphic position within the deposit, indicating that during the time period represented here there was a relatively stable small mammal fauna in the area. Voles are dominant throughout, with narrow-skulled vole at consistently higher numbers than northern vole. Collared

Table 8.6 - Species representation - West wall 'section' (See figure 8.4)

	Lowest G	I	E	H l/f	H l/b	A	C	H up	J	D	Highest F
Lepus timidus			2			1		1			6
Ochotona pusilla	1	2		1	2	4	3	1		6	23
Lemmus lemmus	2		5	2	6	10	1	4	3	6	26
Dicrostonyx torquatus	4		6	4	7	9	3		3	10	44
Arvicola terrestris	1		1			2		2	2	2	8
Microtus oeconomus	2	2	8	9	6	17	3	2	2	4	35
Microtus gregalis	10	3	19	16	10	19	5	6	5	19	82
Microtus oeconomus/gregalis		1	13	5	7	20	9	6	4	14	66
Microtus gregalis/agrestis	1					1			2		
Microtus agrestis											
Microtus sp.	22	15	24	37	44	109	6	24		44	162
Clethrionomys glareolus											
Apodemus sylvaticus							1				
Sorex araneus			1		1	2		1			1
Mustela nivalis				1		2					
Total identified specimens	43	23	79	75	83	196	31	47	21	105	454

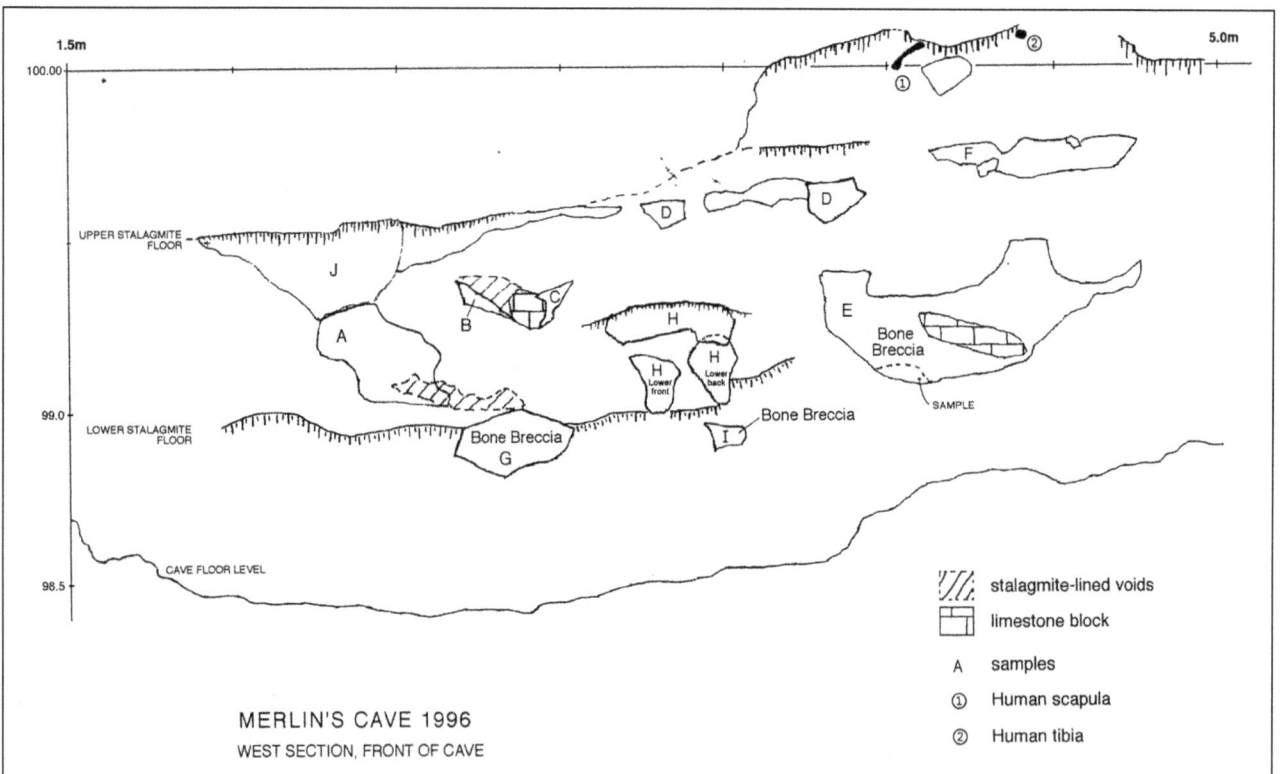

MERLIN'S CAVE 1996
WEST SECTION, FRONT OF CAVE

lemming is more frequent than Norway lemming in all but one sample. As discussed above in relation to the Bridged Pot fauna, this implies a cold, dry grassland environment, which also matches the requirements of the steppe pika, a species relatively common at this site. The single specimen of wood mouse, an isolated molar from sample C, was recovered prior to acid treatment of the breccia, and is possibly intrusive. It would be necessary to have recovered specimens from the cemented material to prove the presence of the species during the Younger Dryas conclusively. The specimens of common shrew, however, are from within the breccia and therefore confirm the species' existence at this time. The low density of the species may reflect its relative scarcity in the small mammal fauna, but equally may be a product of the

Table 8.7- Species representation as percentages - Merlin's Cave west wall

| | Low | | Middle | | | | | | | | Top |
	G	I	E	H l/f	H l/b	A	C	H up	J	D	F
Lepus timidus			2.5			0.5		2.1			1.3
Ochotona pusilla	2.3	8.7		1.3	2.4	2.0	9.7	2.1		5.7	5.1
Lemmus lemmus	4.7		6.3	2.7	7.2	5.1	3.2	8.5	14.3	5.7	5.7
Dicrostonyx torquatus	9.3		7.6	5.3	8.4	4.6	9.7		14.3	9.5	9.7
Arvicola terrestris	2.3		1.3			1.0		4.3	9.5	1.9	1.8
Microtus oeconomus	4.7	8.7	10.1	12.0	7.2	8.7	9.7	4.3	9.5	3.8	7.7
Microtus gregalis	25.6	13.0	24.1	21.3	12.0	10.2	16.1	12.8	33.3	18.1	18.1
Microtus oeconomus/gregalis		4.3	16.5	6.7	8.4	10.2	29.0	12.8	19.0	13.3	14.5
Microtus sp.	51.2	65.2	30.4	49.3	53.0	55.6	19.4	51.1		41.9	35.7
Apodemus sylvaticus							3.2				
Sorex araneus			1.3		1.2	1.0		2.1			0.2
Mustela nivalis				1.3		1.0					

feeding habits of the agent of accumulation (see below). The relatively high numbers of water vole, together with the Norway lemmings and northern voles, suggests the availability of damper ecological niches in the vicinity of the cave. The proximity of the cave to the River Wye would offer a variety of different biomes according to the drainage patterns and elevation of the ground. To illustrate the effect of the topography, a scale elevation through the valley can be used to reconstruct the possible ecological diversity (see Chapter 10.2). This is based on the study of vegetation patterns of the Umeålven valley in northern Sweden, at around 65° North. In colder climates, such as are found in northern Scandinavia today and would have been experienced in the Lateglacial Stadial in Britain, a greater vegetational difference is observed to occur with increasing elevation than is the case in temperate regions. The effect of the river itself should also be considered, as 'under lakes and rivers, permafrost is forced to great depths, or is absent completely, because water has such tremendous heat-retaining capacity' (Pielou, 1994, p.81). Riverside vegetation therefore benefits from the microclimate produced by the insulation of the water. In such sheltered locations, it is possible that there was a limited survival of tree birch, and particularly the more damp-tolerant downy birch (*Betula pubescens*). The rapid regrowth of woodland at the end of the Younger Dryas suggests that sufficient trees survived in dispersed refugia to provide nuclei for expansion as conditions became more favourable. Even if stands of birch did persist along the Wye, one would not expect to find rodents indicative of woodland conditions, as the same fauna is found in the open type of woodland surviving under such conditions as would indicate grassland.

c.iii - Other locations on cave wall

Area Q: The sample was taken from a dark brown cemented deposit on the east wall (see fig.8.4)

This fauna is indicative of a woodland environment, and its stratigraphic position shows it to be post-glacial. The presence of dormouse (*Muscardinus avellanarius*) shows that the woodland development was advanced, with mature broadleaved trees such as hazel and oak, and a dense understorey of such species as bramble and honeysuckle (see chapter 4). The antiquity of this species in Britain is uncertain. It is described as 'Probably a natural late post-glacial coloniser, arriving in Britain c. 9000 years ago, but the earliest subfossil finds date from just before the Roman period, at Ossom's Cave, Staffordshire' (Corbet & Harris 1991, p.261).

Table 8.8- Species representation - Area Q, Merlin's Cave

Species	Specimens recovered
Microtus oeconomus	1 mandible
Microtus agrestis	1 cranium, 2 mandibles
Microtus sp.	4 molars
Clethrionomys glareolus	2 mandibles, 2maxillae, 2 molars
Apodemus sylvaticus	1 cranium, 2 mandibles, 1 maxilla, 9 molars
Micromys minutus	2 molars
Muscardinus avellanarius	1 cranium
Sorex araneus	2 crania, 2 maxillae, 1mandible, 2 teeth
Neomys fodiens	1 mandible

Similarly, the harvest mouse (*Micromys minutus*), an uncommon species in fossil assemblages, 'may be a late post-glacial invader or an accidental introduction as a result of agricultural activities' (*ibid.*, p.236). The location of the sample site, at site level 99.89m just below the broken remnant of the uppermost stalagmite flow, gives an indication of its antiquity. The equivalent horizontal stalagmite layer on the west wall is at around 100m, and includes fragments of human bone and the impression of a human skull. This is assumed to be associated with the human remains collected during Hewer's excavation, which are considered to belong with the late prehistoric artefacts recovered at the same time (Barton, pers.comm.). The bone bearing breccia immediately below the speleothem must, therefore, predate the human remains, and postdate the long sequence of breccia from which the west wall samples were obtained. The specimens of dormouse and harvest mouse are themselves too significant and too small respectively to request a direct date, but it is hoped that an application for dates on both human bone from the speleothem layer and a wolf rib recently recovered from the breccia sample from area Q will be successful, providing a date of deposition and a *terminus post quem* for the sample. The presence of harvest mouse is not considered to be proof of arable crop production in the area, as the species is also found in any tall, dense vegetation such as reedbeds, hedgerows and bramble patches (Corbet & Harris, 1991). The specimen of northern vole is interesting, both as a late record of the species (see chapter 6 section1, Three Holes Cave & Broken Cavern environmental evidence, for discussion of the antiquity of the species), and as an environmental indicator. In the presence of field vole (*Microtus agrestis*), the northern vole exploits moister grassland and is excluded from the drier areas by the field vole (De Jonge & Dienske, 1979), with little overlap in territories. Sufficient damp grassland must have been available in the vicinity of the cave to allow the persistence of the northern vole against invading species more suited to the climate and environment of the Holocene.

Area R: The sample was taken from a pale buff cemented fine-grained sediment, at site level 99.18m, towards the front of the cave on the east wall.

The small mammal bones recovered from the deposit are consistent in species and relative frequency with the fauna of the west wall section.

Area K: The sample was taken from an uncemented grey-brown sediment, on the west wall towards the rear of the cave, between site levels 100.80 and 100.76m. Charcoal was also recovered during sieving.

This sample contains a post-glacial woodland fauna, similar to that of area Q (see above).

Further samples were examined from other locations around the cave, but are not discussed here as few small mammal remains were recovered from them. Their locations are indicated on the plan (fig. 8.3).

2b. Merlin's Cave - taphonomy

The small mammal bone from Merlin's Cave is in excellent condition, with a high proportion of complete mandibles and crania (see plate 9). The longbones show no signs of digestion or abrasion, though physical breaks, such as sharp mid-shaft fractures, are not uncommon, particularly in the loose material recovered from the cave floor. The condition of the bone and the species represented both indicate this to be an owl pellet assemblage. In this instance, unlike that of King Arthur's Cave

Table 8.9 - Species representation - Area R, Merlin's Cave

Species	Specimens recovered
Ochotona pusilla	1 molar
Lemmus lemmus	2 molars
Dicrostonyx torquatus	1 mandible, 3 molars
Arvicola terrestris	1 molar
Microtus oeconomus/gregalis	1 maxilla, 1 M^2
Microtus oeconomus	1 M_1
Microtus gregalis	3 mandibles
Microtus sp.	1 mandible fragment, 16 molars

Table 8.10 - Species representation - Area K, Merlin's cave

Species	Specimens recovered
Microtus sp	2 crania (no teeth), 1 mandible (no teeth), 3 molars
Microtus cf. agrestis	1 M_1
Clethrionomys glareolus	2 molars
Apodemus sylvaticus	1 cranium, 2 maxilla fragments, 2 mandibles, 4 molars
Muscardinus avellanarius	1 molar
Sorex araneus	1 cranium
Chiroptera sp.	1 maxilla fragment, 1 molar

and the Torbryan caves, the material is considerably less altered by post depositional movement, crushing and decay, due to the sheltered conditions inside the cave. Dorothy Bate's account of her investigation of the cave gives evidence of the undisturbed nature of the deposits. 'The walls of the cave have not been disturbed, for here numerous minute bones are found in a good state of preservation. These were lying even in exposed situations where they might easily have been destroyed. This is perhaps the most curious feature of the cave, for at its inner end on every ledge and in every crevice were found small bones, most of them belonging to one or other of the smaller species of voles and mice. These remains have disappeared from the ledges near the entrance, doubtless on account of exposure to wind and wet, and to the presence of jackdaws, which nest in large numbers on all the cliffs' (Bate 1901, p.101). Very few loose bones were found to be lying on ledges during our investigation of the cave in 1996. This seems to indicate that they were collected up by Bate or Hinton, and that there has been little or no owl activity in the cave since Hewer's excavation in 1924. A modern jackdaw (*Corvus monedula*) nest site was found on a small ledge at the cave entrance, site level 101.69m or *c*. 3.20m above the cave floor, on the west wall. The fill was collected and found to contain modern materials such as cellophane sweet wrappers, shiny pieces of foil and plastic, and strands of red, yellow and turquoise wool. A few bones of unidentified small bird species were recovered, together with several small mammal specimens.

Table 8.11 - Small mammal remains from jackdaw nest-site, Merlin's Cave

Microtus agrestis	2 crania, 1 mandible, 4 molars
Clethrionomys glareolus	5 molars
Apodemus sylvaticus	2 maxilla fragments
Sorex araneus	3 mandibles

Blue eggshell fragments with black blotches were also recovered, these being positively identified by comparison with complete specimens of jackdaw eggs at the Natural History Museum, London. Jackdaws are omnivorous, the majority of their diet provided by plant seeds and insect larvae. Nestling birds are taken, but vertebrate food is more usually exploited in the form of carrion, and such foods form a very small part of the diet (Coombs, 1978). A proportion of the small mammal remains found in the rest of the cave is likely to have been brought in by jackdaws, but not the great majority. Evidence of specific owl inhabitation is restricted to the frequent inclusion of eggshell fragments in the bone-bearing deposits. These are generally small, less than 1cm square, and their slight curvature shows them to be from larger eggs than those of the jackdaw. No fragment exhibits a more marked curvature, indicating the intact egg to have been rounded rather than pointed. This is typical of all species of owl. In colour, the egg fragments are the creamy white typical of owls' eggs (Harrison, 1975), but as this is not necessarily the original colour, which may have faded or disappeared during burial, it cannot be taken as an indication of species.

The identification of the particular species of owl involved in the formation of the Merlin's Cave deposits can only be conjectural. The Lateglacial Stadial accumulation on the west wall, of primary interest here, if analysed on species content and modern environmental parallels, would suggest predation by snowy owls (*Nyctea scandiaca*). However, these owls are not known to nest in caves, preferring a situation offering an all-round view (Mikkola 1983). Of the other species of owl with a modern distribution including northern Scandinavia, three are specifically woodland birds and nest in trees (hawk owl, ural owl and pygmy owl); the short-eared owl is, like the snowy owl, a ground nester; the great grey owl habitually uses a twig nest in a tree or stump, with only 0.5% of nests studied in Finland being on cliffs or rock faces. However, 80% of eagle owl (*Bubo bubo*) nests studied in Sweden were on cliff ledges, with most sheltered by an overhanging cliff (Mikkola, *op.cit*). It seems reasonable to expect that a relatively inaccessible cave such as Merlin's might provide a desirable nest place for this species. Modern populations of the owl are found both in mature conifer forest and in mountainous areas. A specimen of eagle owl was identified from Chelm's Combe Rock Shelter in the Mendips, from which 'the material collected .... appears to date from the end of the Devensian, in the short cold Loch Lomond Readvance stage following the Windermere Interstadial' (Harrison 1987, p.89), that is, the Lateglacial Stadial or Younger Dryas, confirming its presence in South West Britain at the time of the deposition in Merlin's cave. Comparison of the Merlin's Cave assemblage with the much smaller collection from the roughly contemporaneous context 3 at King Arthur's Cave shows a far higher proportion of steppe pika in the former, particularly if the large number of specimens in Hinton's collection is included. Although the dates on small mammal species from King Arthur's are slightly earlier than those from Merlin's, the earliest being 10,380 ± 90 (OxA-6843) against Merlin's earliest of 10,270 ± 80 (OxA-8071), the Younger Dryas deposit at King Arthur's also provided a later date of 9930 ± 90 (OxA-6839) on reindeer bone, showing deposition to continue well into the time range covered by the breccias at Merlin's. As a temporal difference does not appear to account for the higher count of pika remains in Merlin's, either a slightly different ecology around the cave or a different predator must be responsible. Given the proximity of the two caves, around 1km apart as the owl flies, the range covered by a hunting owl from either cave would be unlikely to exclude habitats available from the other. The eagle owl, considered to be the most likely occupant of Merlin's Cave (see above), has an average weight of 3,025g (female) and 2,225g (male) in Finland, compared with average weights of 2,120g and 1,730g for Finnish snowy owls (Mikkola 1983). It is likely, therefore, that the diet of the eagle owl at Merlin's Cave would include a greater number of larger mammals, such as pikas and water voles, than that of the snowy owl at King Arthur's Cave.

The Holocene small mammal remains from areas K and Q are equally well preserved, and are also likely to have been deposited by owls. The woodland environment surrounding the cave by this time would support a different range of predator species than the more open Late Pleistocene conditions. The putative eagle owl might continue to exploit the cave as a nesting or roosting site, but these birds prefer to hunt over open ground even when living in forest (Mikkola

1983), so dormouse would be an unusual prey item. Barn owl (*Tyto alba*) and tawny owl (*Strix aluco*) are recorded from early Holocene faunas in South West Britain (Harrison 1987), and either might have used Merlin's Cave. The barn owl is more likely, as tawny owls are more inclined to nest in trees than on cliff ledges.

2c. Merlin's Cave - morphological change in vole teeth

As a large stratified sample of mandibles and isolated molars of both northern vole and narrow-skulled vole was available from the west wall breccias of Merlin's Cave, it was possible to examine the teeth for possible changes in form and size through the period of deposition.

No diagnostic M^2 of field vole (*Microtus agresis*) was recovered from the brecciated samples, despite the many maxillae and individual M^2s present. This indicates that all of the mandibles and M_1s are either northern vole (*Microtus oeconomus*) or narrow-skulled vole (*Microtus gregalis*). It is possible, therefore, to divide the specimens between the two possible species by extracting those with the typical M_1 form of the northern vole. All others can then be taken to be narrow-skulled vole, despite the slight mophological differences. The specimens of narrow-skulled vole exhibited a continuum of forms, from those very similar to *Microtus agrestis*, through intermediate types with a less pronounced concavity of the buccal (cheek) side of the first loop, to specimens very close in form to *Microtus oeconomus* but lacking the totally convex buccal edge (see fig.8.5). The same morphological variation is seen in Late Quaternary *Microtus gregalis* from Mamutowa, Koziarnia and Raj caves in Poland (Nadachowski, 1982 p.84-85).

The different types did not form distinct groups, but rather a progression between the extremes, and while some were clearly of one 'type' or another, the majority fell morphologically between two stools. This is true for specimens from all levels of the Lateglacial deposit, and there seems to be no increasing dominance of one end of the shape spectrum over the other. As no morphological development

could be discerned, the size of the individual specimens of both northern vole and narrow-skulled vole was considered. Each M_1 was measured to ascertain if any change in overall size of voles occurred during the period of deposition. Measurements were taken from front to back of the grinding surfaces of the teeth (see fig. 8.6), as this allowed those specimens still set in mandibles to be measured in the same way as individual teeth, thereby collecting data from the complete collection. A *Mitutoyo* digimatic caliper was used, giving measurements to 0.01mm by LCD. No sub-adult teeth were measured.

To give meaningful results, the west wall samples were divided into three sloping sections, following the line of the upper speleothem flowstone and a lower stalagmite floor (see fig 8.4). This meant that sufficient specimens were included in each sample for statistical analysis. To produce easily understandable graphs, the tooth sizes were grouped in 0.05mm intervals (length classes), from 2.41mm to 3.20mm, and the number of teeth in each category plotted against the length class for each of the three 'strata' of deposition; top, mid and low (figs 8.7 & 8.8). The size distribution of northern vole specimens shows a fairly even spread of sizes between 2.50mm and 2.90mm, with the largest in the 3.01 to 3.05mm class. The graph shows no clear difference in size distribution relating to stratigraphic position in the top and mid samples, drawing a conclusion that the size of northern voles remained stable. The low sample, however, shows this species to have been generally smaller during the earlier part of the deposition. Mathematical averages also show this to be the case.

Unfortunately, the number of specimens available for measurement is rather low in all levels of the deposit, but particularly so in the lowest stratum. A much greater number of narrow-skulled vole teeth was recovered, and the graph produced from their measurements shows a clear increase in average size from the low samples to the top. The largest specimen from the low samples measured 2.95mm, while largest from the top stratum was 3.11mm.

The steadily increasing average size of individual narrow-skulled voles between the onset of deposition (c. 10,300 BP) and the date of the highest analysed sample (c. 9,700 BP)

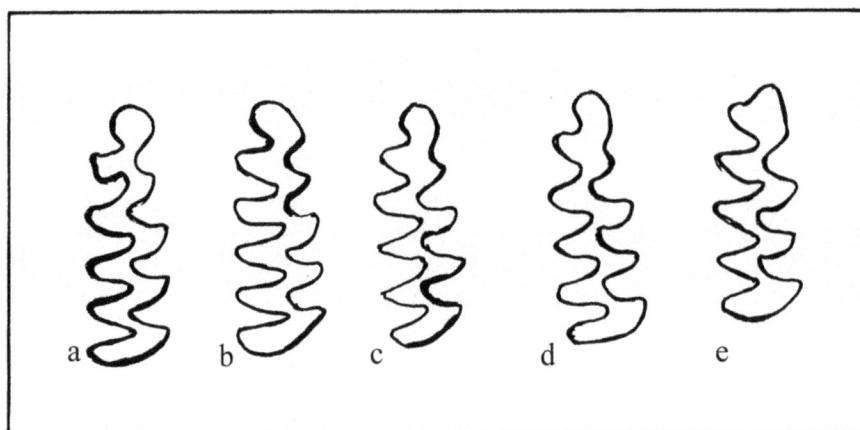

Fig 8.5 – Morphological variation in Late Quaternary *Microtus gregalis* M₁ from Koziarnia (a-c) & Mamutowa (d-e) caves. (after Nadachowski, 1982)

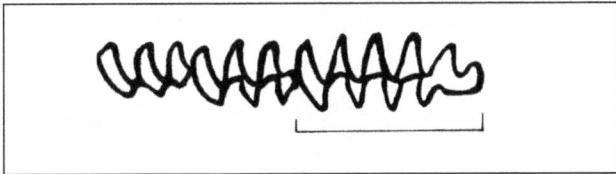

Fig. 8.6 – Measurement point for length of M₁ (*Microtus sp.*)

Table 8.12 - Mean length of lower first molar, *Microtus oeconomus.*

Stratum	Mean length (mm)	n
Top	2.72	43
Mid	2.72	31
Low	2.68	14

Table 8.13 - Mean length of lower first molar, *Microtus gregalis*

Stratum	Mean length (mm)	n
Top	2.83	132
Mid	2.81	62
Low	2.68	33

implies conditions particularly suitable for the species, with an abundance of good quality grazing. It appears that the northern voles were perhaps less well-suited to the prevailing conditions at the time of deposition of the upper two strata (c. 10,200 - 9,700 BP) than those of the earlier phase (c. 10,300 - 10,200 BP), as their average size increases from

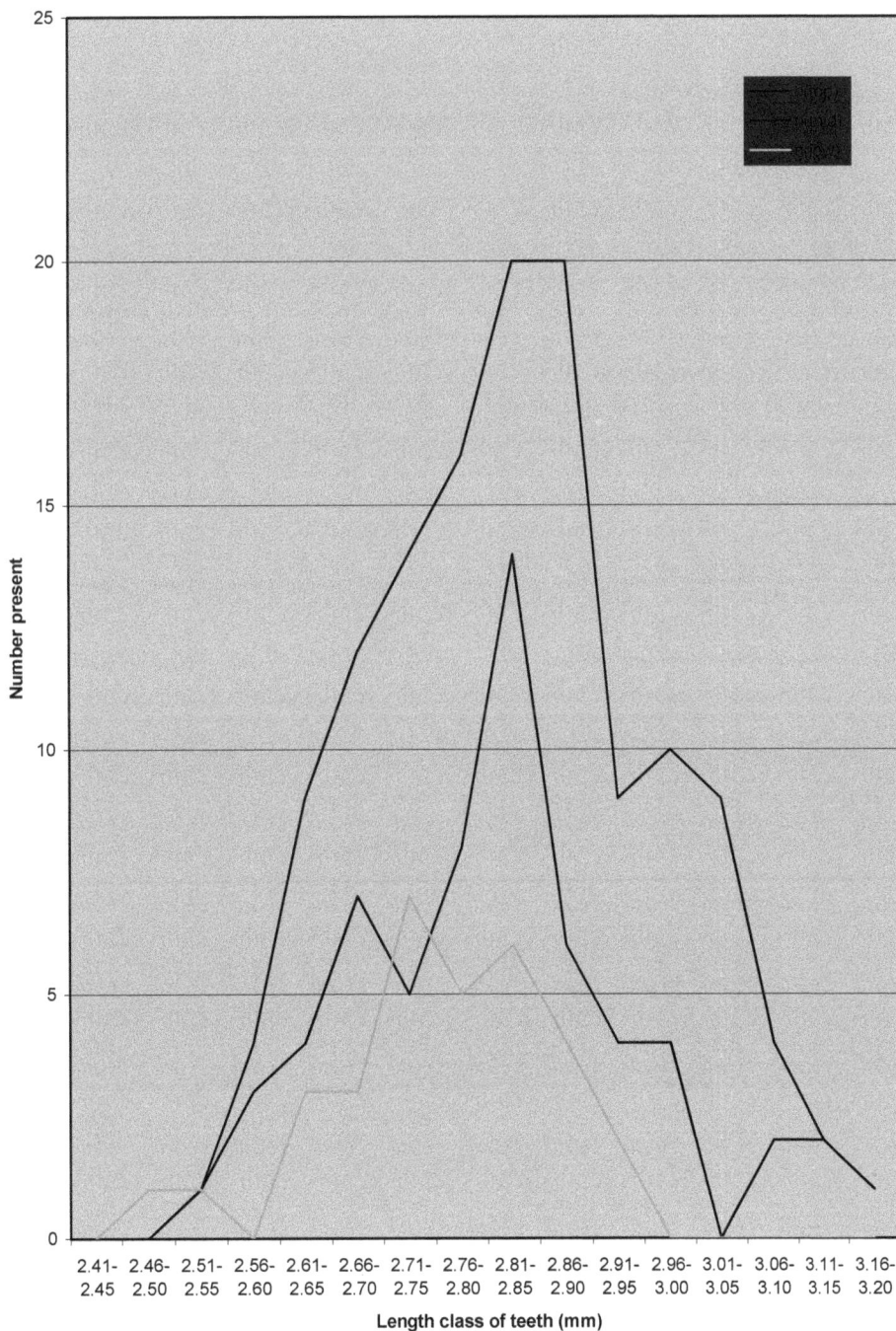

Fig 8.7 - Size distribution : Microtus gregalis (Merlin´s Cave)

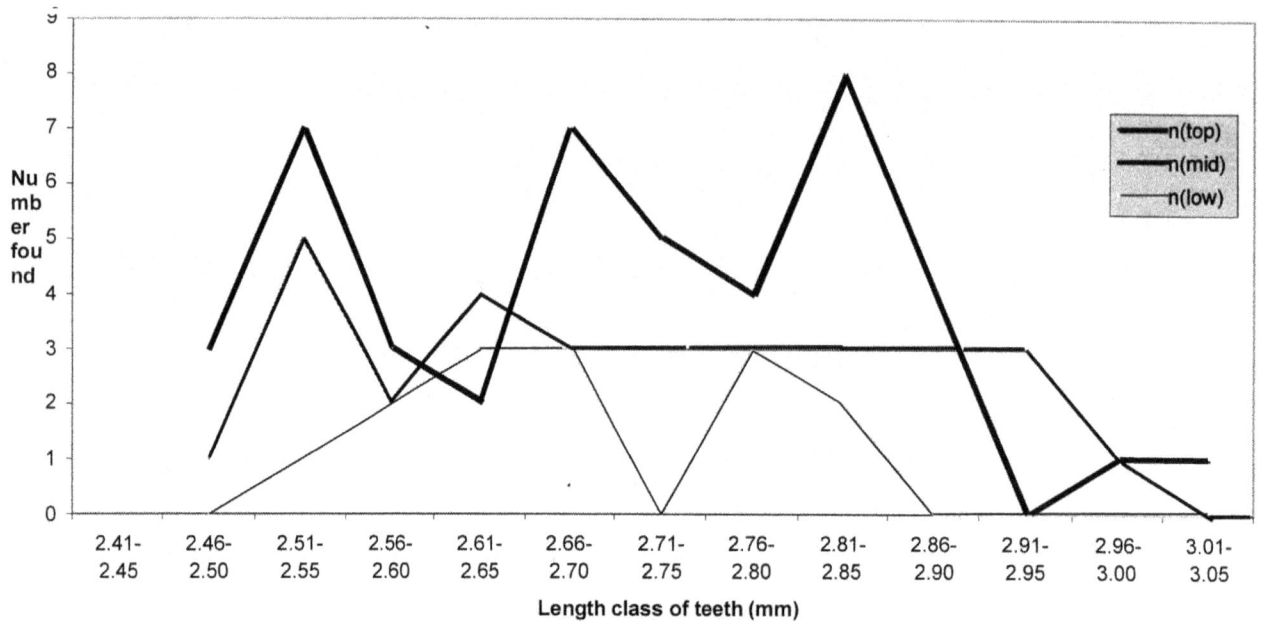

Fig. 8.8 - Size distribution : Microtus oeconomus (Merlin's Cave)

low to mid, and then stabilises. Measurements given for modern populations of the two species show northern voles to have the potential to grow larger than narrow-skulled voles, but also to have a wider adult size range (see chapter 3 for details). Larger individuals are found in the colder parts of the range of each species, showing greater body mass to be an advantage in extreme environments for the species. The subsequent extinction of the narrow-skulled vole in Britain at the beginning of the Holocene shows it to be less adapted to more temperate climates, while the northern vole survives well into the Holocene in Britain, and persists to the present day in the Netherlands (Mitchell-Jones et al, 1999). It is likely that the latter species was at its ecological limit here during the Younger Dryas, whereas the narrow-skulled vole was comfortably within its normal environmental boundaries.

3a. Madawg Cave - environmental reconstruction

The species recovered from this site are consistently indicative of a temperate wooded Holocene environment. The archaeology confirms all of the deposits investigated to be of Holocene date. The Grey Tufaceous Earth included Early Bronze Age pottery and human remains, possibly part of a disturbed burial (Barton, 1994). The underlying Brown Stony Cave Earth (BSCE) yielded Late Mesolithic aretefacts, including narrow geometric microliths and a concentration of perforated cowrie shell beads (Barton et al, 1997). The BSCE was observed to be darker towards the southern end of the trench, where a depression c. 0.30m deep was found to contain a concentration of charcoal in a very dark, ashy soil (DB2). This does not appear to be the result of in situ burning,

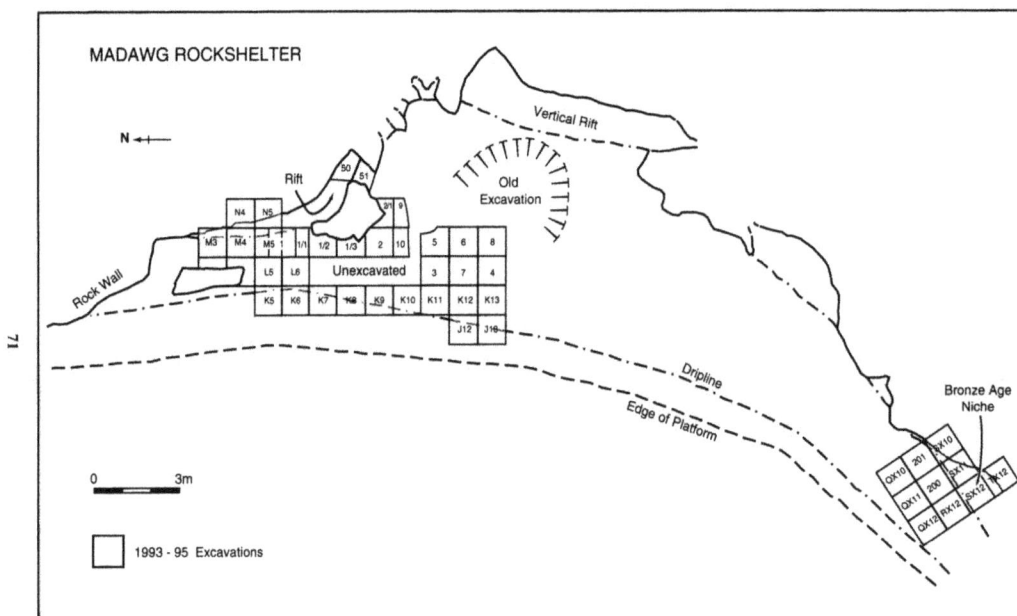

Fig. 8.9 – Plan of Madawg Cave (Barton et al.1997)

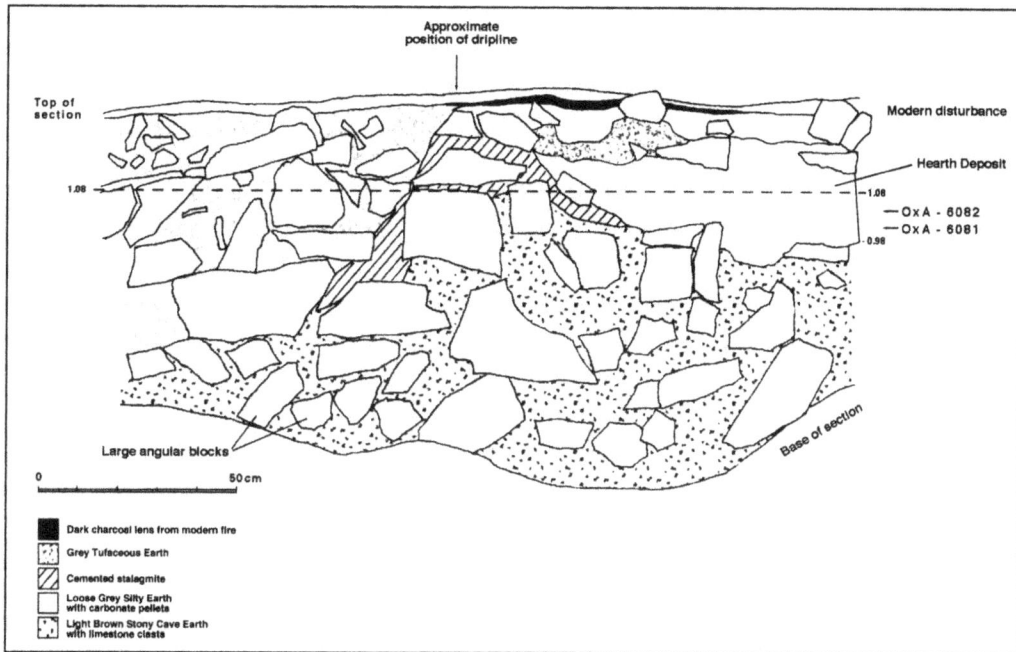

Fig. 8.10 – Section through deposits in squares J12 – K12 (Barton *et al.* 1997)

Plate 10 – Madawg Cave 1993

but probably of the redeposition of material from a nearby hearth, either through natural or human processes. Analysis of the charcoal extracted from this feature identified ash (*Fraxinus*), oak (*Quercus*), elder (*Sambucus*), pine (*Pinus*), yew (*Taxus*) and hazel (*Corylus*) from the upper layers, and pine, yew, hawthorn (*Crataegus*) and blackthorn (*Prunus spinosa*) from the lower levels. AMS radiocarbon dates on charred sloe stone and hazelnut shell from the lower levels of the depression gave results of 8710 ± 70 BP (OxA-6081) and 6655 ±65 BP (OxA-6082) respectively, indicating more than one episode of deposition. The later date is from a higher

spit, c. 7cm above the level of the earlier specimen, and 'the only unequivocally Late Mesolithic artefact recorded *in situ* in this feature (a narrow scalene triangle) was found within the same spit as the earlier of the two dated samples' (Barton *et al*, 1997, p. 73). The tree species represented in the charcoal accumulation show there to have been a fully developed mixed woodland, with both canopy and understorey species present at the time of deposition of the upper layers, and at least a dense shrubby scrub with pine trees when the lower layers were accumulating. The low number of field vole specimens in contexts BSCE and DB2 indicate that little open grassland

Table 8.14 - Species representation, Madawg Cave

| | Lowest | | | Highest |
	GB	DB2	BSCE	GTE
Arvicola terrestris				1
Microtus agrestis	3	5	2	20
Clethrionomys glareolus	31	91	116	66
Apodemus sylvaticus	8	42	25	30
Scuirus vulgaris		2	1	
Sorex araneus		7		6
Sorex minutus		1		
Neomys fodiens				1
Talpa europaea		1		1
Chiroptera sp.		1		
Number of identified specimens	41	150	144	125
Number of samples	15	24	35	19

Table 8.15 - Proportional representation of field vole & bank vole specimens

Context	GB	DB2	BSCE	GTE
Microtus agrestis	7.3%	3.3%	1.0%	16.0%
Clethrionomys glareolus	75.6%	60.7%	80.6%	52.8%

was available in the area. The red squirrel specimens from DB2 show the woodland indicated by the charcoal to have been sufficiently extensive to support a population of squirrel. Bank vole is dominant throughout the stratigraphy, showing a wooded environment to be predominant in the locality of the cave continuously through the accumulation of the excavated deposits. Field vole percentages, compared with those of bank vole, show the gradual increase in the density of the woodland and ground cover from the earliest deposit (GB) through the subsequent DB2 and BSCE. A slight rise in the percentage of field vole specimens in the Early Bronze Age GTE shows a small increase in open ground at this time, either through natural causes such as lightning strikes or wind-blow, or through human action to provide deliberate clearance.

Two specimens of collared lemming (*Dicrostonyx torquatus*) were recovered, a single molar from a sample of 'stony brown clay silt' taken from the rear of the shelter, and a partial mandible from a sample of light brown sediment taken from the environs of Hewer's 1920s excavation. These are difficult to relate to any of the stratigraphy defined by the Wye Valley Caves Project 1993-95 excavations, or to Hewer's findings,

which reported the excavated pit near the centre of the rockshelter to be sterile, except for 'a few shrew bones in the first foot' (Hewer 1925, p.155), and recorded no definite Pleistocene material from the investigation of fissures to the left of the rift (see figure 8.9). It is probable that they are stray specimens from Pleistocene material, eroded, redeposited and then lost from the cave through flooding or some other natural agency.

3b. Madawg Cave – taphonomy

The material from Madawg Cave was in generally poor condition, and small mammal bone was sparse. 159 samples were sieved and analysed; many of these contained no identifiable bone, or no bone at all. In the Mesolithic contexts DB2 and BSCE, much of the small bone shows clear signs of having been digested, and conforms to the examples given by Andrews (1990) of material recovered from the pellets of diurnal raptors or mammalian faeces and feeding remains. The vole molars are flaky and brittle, with eroded enamel along the prism angles and at the ends of the occlusal surfaces,

Table 8.16 – Condition of bone, Madawg Cave.

Context	Number of samples in each condition class				
	E	D/E	D	C	B
GTE	6	2	4		
BSCE	7	2			
DB2		3	6		2
GB	4	3	4		

and the roots when present (on more mature specimens of *Clethrionomys*) are broken. Very few complete molars were recovered. The cusped teeth of mice often have no roots, with only the enamel crown surviving. Incisors are longitudinally split and snapped across, and the surface enamel is pitted. Longbones are frequently reduced to fragments, and articular ends, where present, are usually eroded. Material from the overlying Grey Tufaceous Earth (GTE) is very similar, excepting that bone is even less frequent, and the condition is slightly worse. As with the material from King Arthur's Cave context 2, the bones appear to have arrived at the cave in the scats of either wild or domestic carnivores, which have then broken down and suffered from the trampling and movement associated with human use of the cave. The unsuitability of the cliffs surrounding the shallow cave as a roosting or nesting site for owls or diurnal raptors, discussed in chapter 4.1, is considered to be the main reason for the paucity and the poor condition of small mammal bone on the site.

4. Symonds Yat East Cave – environmental reconstruction & taphonomy

As the species representation, environmental reconstruction and taphonomy proved to be mutually dependent at this cave, they are not examined here as separate subjects.

Two trenches were opened in Symonds Yat East Cave in 1994 (see fig.8.11). Area 1, close to the passage entrance, provided a section through deposits shown in figure 8.12. Below the dark grey-black topsoil (1) was a white tufaceous stalagmite layer (2), which contained the jaw of a bear (*Ursus* sp.), and thought to be early Holocene (Barton, pers.comm.). The underlying reddish-brown clays were divided into gritty clay or 4a (labelled '3' on the drawn section), and 4b, a silty clay marked '4' on the section. Initially, these two contexts were not differentiated, and the contact between theme is diffuse. Many large rocks were removed from the trench.

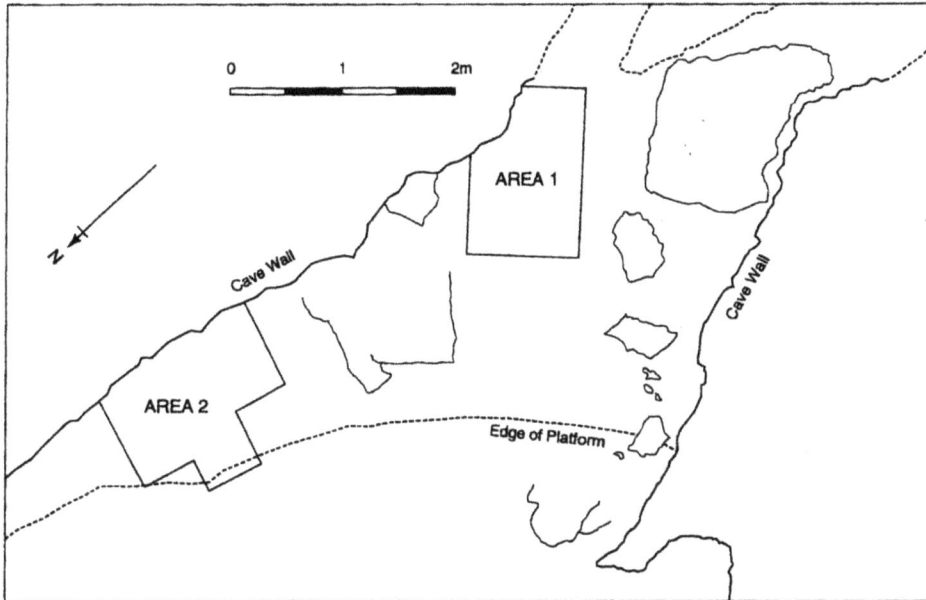

Fig.8.11 – Plan of Symonds Yat East Cave (Barton 1994).

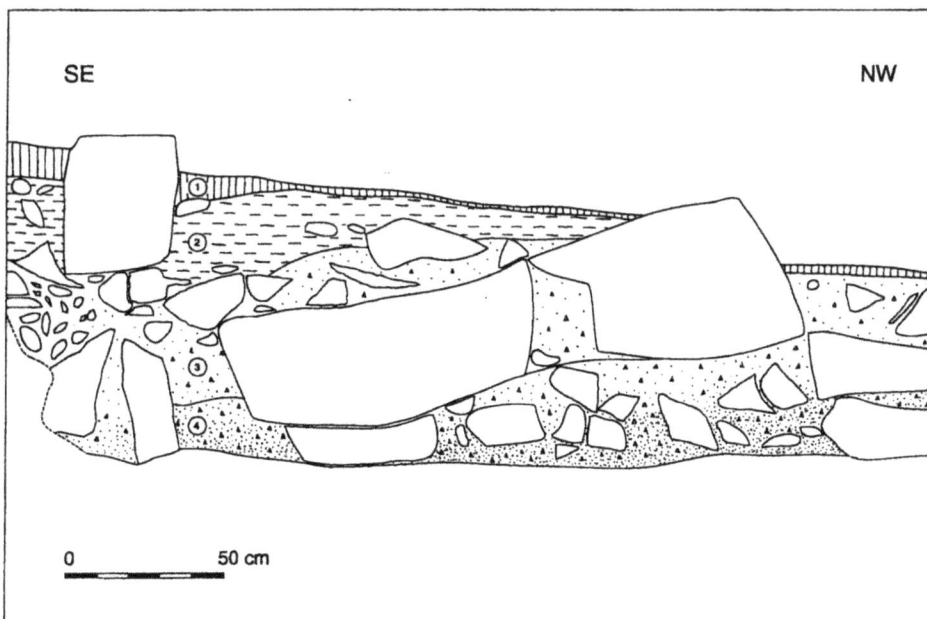

Fig. 8.12 – Section through deposits, Area 1 (Barton 1994). See text for descriptions.

In area 2 the stratigraphy was confused by the proximity of Rogers' 1980 trench, which was found to cut through squares AA and Z (see fig. 8.13). A black plastic sheet lining Rogers' trench was exposed, covered with a layer of leaf litter and rotting wood. Below the plastic was a thin, black layer over a 'reddish layer of hard rocky surface' (site notebook, 7/7/94) which was difficult to excavate. The stratigraphy of the squares outside Rogers' excavation is topped by brown compacted topsoil (1). Context 1b, a grey-black humic layer with loose rocks, lies directly on context 5 in the square furthest from the cliff (DD), but in square X, between Rogers' trench and the cliff, a more complex stratigraphy was revealed. Here, the sequence shows context 1b, the grey tufaceous context 2, a reddish clay silt (context 3) and a reddish sandy silt (context 4) in a similar succession to that of area 1. The top of the basal layer 5, described as a 'gritty light brown silt' (Barton, pers.comm.), yielded many tiny flint chips, some refitting, and a burin and its refitting spall of Final Palaeolithic type (Barton 1994). This appears to be an undisturbed late Lateglacial Interstadial deposit. Its junction with the overlying reddish sandy silt is confused by frequent rock inclusions. See figure 8.14 for a matrix showing relationships between the deposits.

The basal layer 5 in area 1 was found to be sterile. There is evidence of the translocation of specimens downwards through the sediments, creating a mixed fauna in contexts 4a and 4b. The Late Pleistocene species, collared lemming, Norway lemming and narrow-skulled vole, occur in the same layer as bat, mole, bank vole and wood mouse, creating a fauna which no single environment could support. The small

mammals from context 2 show temperate conditions with woodland vegetation. The relatively high proportion of field vole specimens, which form 20% of the identified remains, while bank vole contributes 48%, shows there to have been areas of more open grassland in the cave environs. These may have been grassy glades within the wood, or rocky patches which could not support tree growth but had a thin soil covering where grasses might flourish.

In area 2, the context 5 small mammal fauna is completely temperate, consistent with its suggested deposition in the Lateglacial Interstadial, implied by the flint assemblage. Some of its components, however, are unlikely to be Lateglacial. Dormice require more developed woodland than is indicated by the analysis of any other deposit of this age, and the pedogenesis needed to provide an adequate depth of soil for moles is unlikely to have occurred by this stage. It seems probable that the loose rocky matrix, and the position of the trench close to the break of slope, produced a similar effect as is seen at Broken Cavern (chapter 6, 1a). Small carnivores are likely to have used the interstices between the rocks as dens, and so introduced the bones of small mammals both as feeding remains and in scats. Dormice are more likely to be predated by small mustelids than by avian hunters, due to their secretive behaviour and reliance on thick woodland cover. They are most often taken from their nests during hibernation (Corbet & Harris, 1991).

Contexts 3 and 4 in area 2, the reddish clay and reddish sandy silts, both with frequent rock inclusions, have cold faunas, suggesting deposition during the Younger Dryas. The small

Table 8.17 – Species representation, Symonds Yat East Area 1.

	4a	4b	4	2
Lepus timidus				2
Ochotona pusilla		1		
Lemmus lemmus	3	4	1	1
Dicrostonyx torquatus	16	16	29	
Arvicola terrestris	2	4	4	
Microtus oeconomus		2	2	
Microtus gregalis	2	2	6	
Microtus oeconomus/gregalis	5	5	1	
Microtus gregalis/agrestis	1	10		
Microtus agrestis	3	2		2
Microtus sp.	73	93	97	13
Clethrionomys glareolus	14	2		36
Apodemus sylvaticus		1		4
Sorex araneus	1	1		1
Sorex minutus			1	
Talpa europaea	1			
Chiroptera sp.	1	2	2	16
Total identified specimens	121	145	143	75
Total samples analysed	4	5	3	3

Table 8.18 – Species representation, Symonds Yat East area 2.

	5	4	3	2	1b
Lemmus lemmus			6	2	
Dicrostonyx torquatus		4	1	2	
Arvicola terrestris	4	14		1	3
Microtus oeconomus					
Microtus gregalis				1	
Microtus oeconomus/gregalis		2		1	
Microtus gregalis/agrestis	1				
Microtus agrestis	6			13	1
Microtus sp	66	28	9	69	4
Clethrionomys glareolus	259		4	107	20
Apodemus sylvaticus	82		2	81	9
Muscardinus avellanarius	3			7	
Sorex araneus	10		1	10	3
Sorex minutus	2			3	
Neomys fodiens				1	
Talpa europaea	1			1	
Chiroptera sp	1		1	16	1
Total specimens identified	435	48	24	315	41
Total samples analysed	5	2	1	3	2

mammal remains from the samples sieved in the lab are generally in poor condition, suggesting a similar origin to those from layer 5. However, the material from spoil sieved on site includes several complete or near-complete mandibles and longbones of *Microtus* species and collared lemming, suggesting the input was in part from owl pellets. These specimens are not included in table 8.18, as the conditions under which the samples were processed were less stringent than employed in the laboratory, and there is a risk that an imbalance would be produced by the loss of smaller specimens. Contexts 3 and 4 are considered to be the equivalent of the older parts of the mixed fauna recovered from contexts 4a and 4b in area 1. When converted to percentages for comparison, the faunas of area 1 (4a and 4b) and area 2 (4) show a distinct similarity, while that of area 2 (5) is quite different.

Context 2 yielded a mixture of a few cold climate and many temperate condition small mammal specimens. Small mammal bone is much more frequent, with an average of 105 identifiable specimens per sample in layer 2, and of only 24 per similar sized sample in layers 3 and 4. Area 1 contexts 4a and 4b have an average of 30.25 and 29 identified specimens per sample respectively, again showing their similarity to area 2 contexts 3 and 4.

Context 1b includes no cold climate indicators, and with 48% of specimens identified as bank vole, shows woodland development.

Water vole (*Arvicola terrestris*) is relatively frequent in both areas, but as the species is tolerant of a wide range of climates (see chapter 3 for modern distribution), this indicates only the proximity of the River Wye and its riparian environment. The cave is located 80 metres above the east bank of the Wye, but at this point the escarpment slopes extremely steeply, and the cave lies only c. 90m east of the river. The difficulties of negotiating the slope render it an arduous trek for humans, but for an avian predator, the distance is very short.

The post-depositional mixing indicated by the small mammal species is also seen in the bone condition. Generally, as in the Broken Cavern assemblage, the teeth of obligate cold climate species such as collared lemming are dark-stained and in poorer condition than those of woodland species. The lack of evidence of digestion shows this to be another owl assemblage, modified by subsequent trampling by prehistoric occupants of the cave, and by the movement of particles within the soil matrix. The remains of burrowing creatures such as slow-worm (*Anguis fragillis*), toad (*Bufo bufo*) and frog (*Rana* sp.) are frequent throughout the

Table 8.19 – Proportional representation of key species in area 1 (4a & 4b) and area 2 (4 & 5), Symonds Yat East Cave.

Context (area)	4a (1)	4b (1)	4 (2)	5 (2)
Dicrostonyx torquatus	13.22%	11.03%	8.33%	0%
Microtus sp (total)	69.42%	78.63%	62.5%	16.78%
Clethrionomys glareolus	11.57%	1.38%	0%	59.54%

Table 8.20 – Condition of bone, Symonds Yat East area 1. See table 6.1 for key.

Context	Condition of bone
2	B. Fresh. Some physical breakage. No digestion.
4	B/C. Many small bones. Some staining, no digestion.
4b (gritty	B/C/X. As 4a.
4a (silty)	B/X. Visible distinction between stained teeth in poor condition, and fresher, paler specimens. Physical breakage. No digestion.

Table 8.21 – Condition of bone, Symonds Yat East area 2. See table 6.1 for key.

Context	Condition of bone
1b	D/E. Fragmentary. Physical breakage, some stained or burnt.
2	X. Large amount of bone. Some burning & digestion.
3	D. Most of teeth fragmentary. Some staining, burning & digestion.
4	D. Teeth brittle, fragmentary. Some staining.
5	B. Physical breakage. Some digestion.

sediments (Gleed-Owen 1998), and their movement through the deposits would have encouraged the translocation of inclusions in the soil.

The analysis of the small mammal bones from Symonds Yat East Cave is complicated by the nature of the deposits. In area 1, the large rocks in the trench produced similar conditions as are seen at Broken Cavern, and the small mammal fauna are similarly mixed. In area 2, there is the possibility of a clearer picture, with more distinct division between temperate and cold faunas. However, the fauna of the basal layer 5 is not perceived as a genuinely Lateglacial Interstadial assemblage, due to the presence of dormouse, not only in the squares close to the break of slope, but also from square YY adjacent to the cliff (see fig. 8.13), where a mandible fragment and an isolated molar were found. This presents two possibilities. Layer 5 may be at least in part

disturbed, calling into question the integrity of the overlying layer 4 with its putative Younger Dryas material. Alternatively, if layer 5 is a discrete Allerød deposit, it would suggest that, at that time, the environment in the locality was more densely wooded than previously thought, and that dormouse was present in Britain much earlier than existing records suggest. The species is described as 'probably a late post-glacial coloniser, arriving in Britain c. 9,000 years ago, but the earliest subfossil finds date from just before the Roman period, at Ossom's Cave, Staffordshire' (Corbet & Harris 1991, p.261). The question will only be resolved by direct AMS dating of specimens from layer 5, including one of dormouse. It is hoped that this can be submitted together with the dormouse from Merlin's Cave sample Q (see above), to provide reliable evidence for the history of the species in this country, as well as direct proof of the presence of such a reliable environmental indicator.

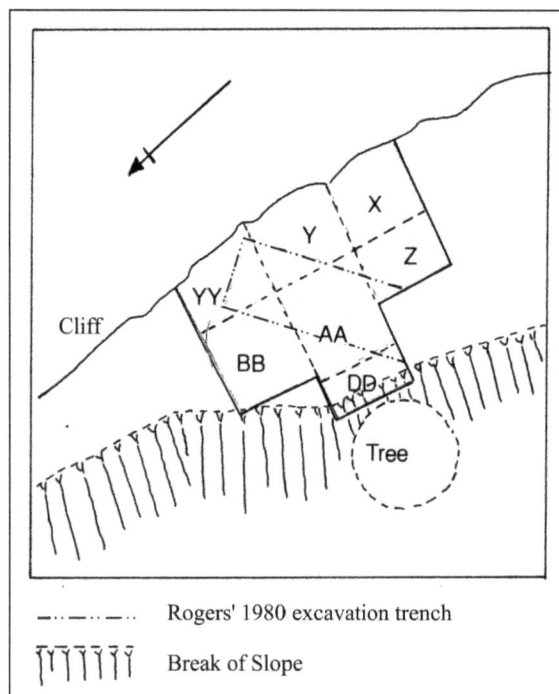

—·—·—·— Rogers' 1980 excavation trench

͡Ί͡Ί͡Ί͡Ί͡Ί͡Ί Break of Slope

Fig. 8.13 – Symonds Yat East Cave area 2

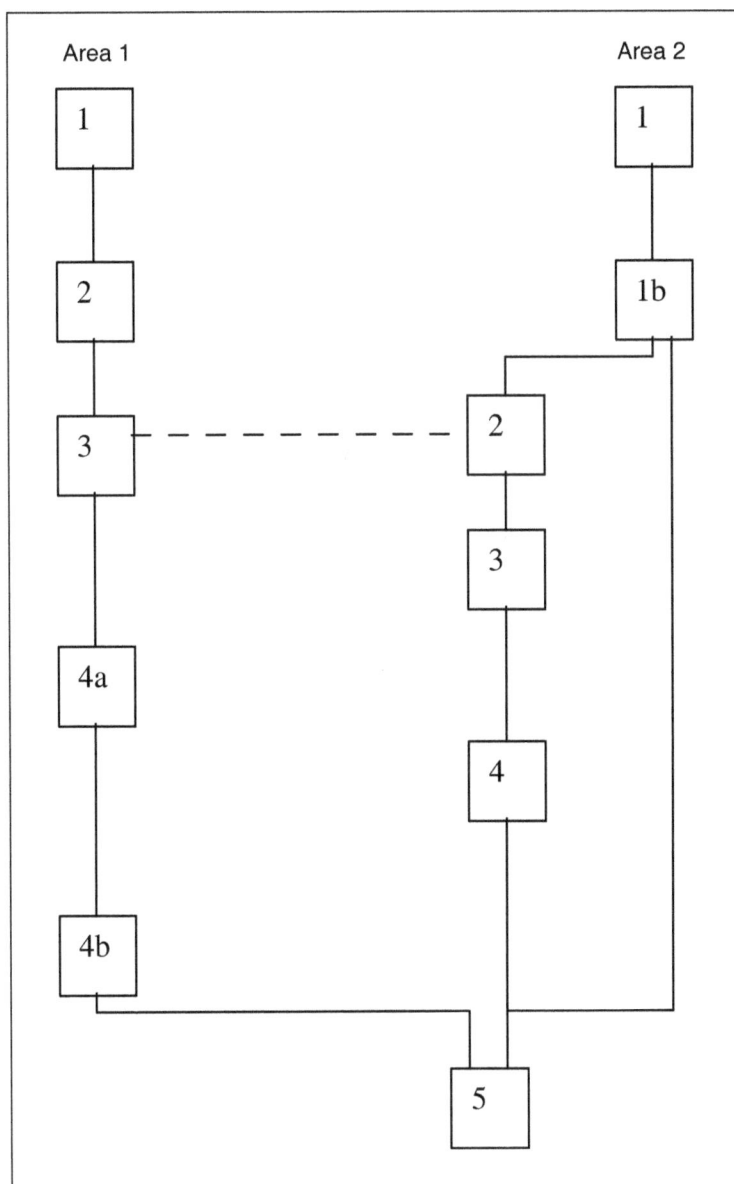

Fig. 8.14 – Provisional matrix showing relationships between contexts,
Symonds Yat East Cave areas 1 & 2.

Chapter 9
Results and analysis (South Wales)

1. Cathole Cave, Gower

A collection of small mammal bone from Campbell's 1968 excavation was examined at the University of Oxford Quaternary Research Centre. The material from McBurney's excavations (1958-9) was not studied, as Campbell's refinement of the stratigraphy of the Lateglacial deposits was considered necessary for environmental reconstruction. McBurney recognised a single 'yellow thermoclastic scree'

(McBurney 1959, p.266), which was subdivided by Campbell into five different contexts, namely the Lower Sandy Thermoclastic Scree (LSB), Lower Open Thermoclastic Scree (LOB), Middle Sandy Thermoclastic Scree (MSB), Upper Open Thermoclastic Scree (UOB) and Upper Sandy Thermoclastic Scree (USB). Of these, he found the LOB and MSB to contain Late Upper Palaeolithic artefacts. The overlying context C, a 'Sandy Thermoclastic and Weathered Scree' contained Mesolithic artefacts near its base, as did context D, a 'Sandy Weathered Scree'

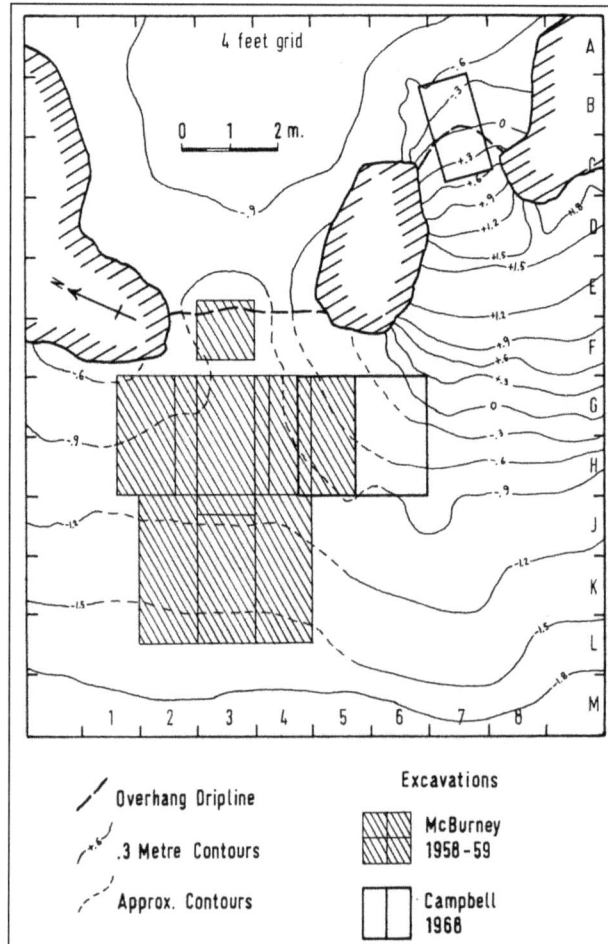

Fig 9.1 – Plan of Cathole Cave, showing excavated areas (Campbell 1977).

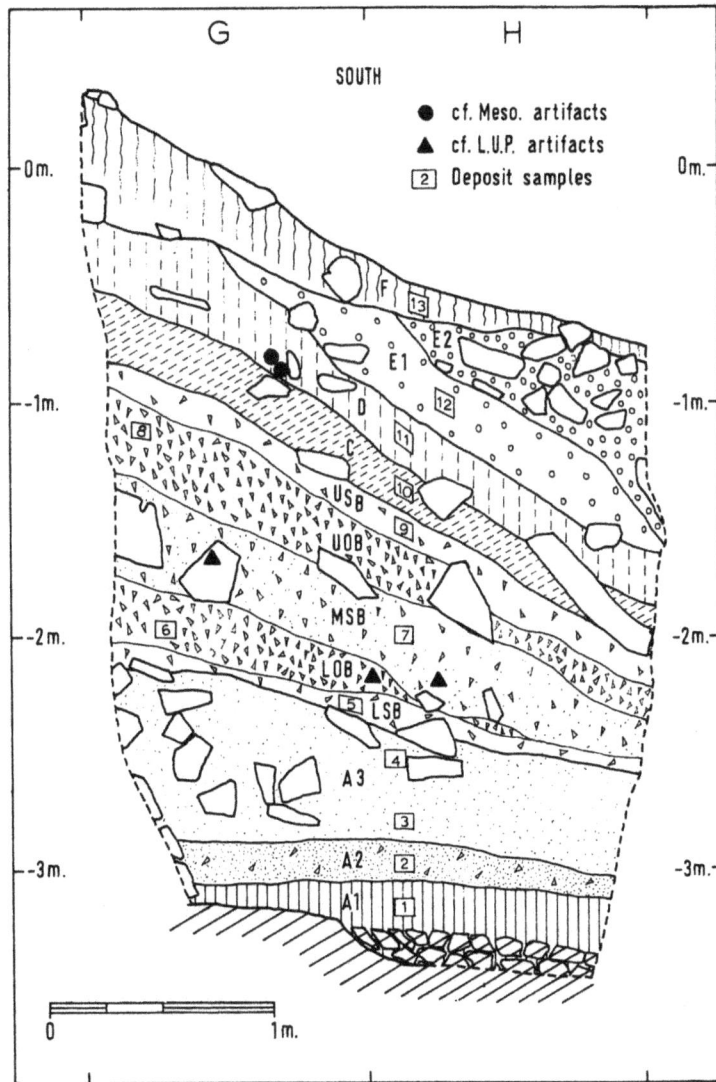

Fig 9.2 – Section through excavated sediments, Cathole Cave1968 (Campbell 1977).

(Campbell 1977, p.57). Context E, a weathered scree with humic content, was divided into three facies by McBurney and two by Campbell. The lower, E1, contained 'some scattered human remains and a sherd of impressed ware identified as of Early to Middle Bronze Age type' (McBurney 1959, p.266), and the middle, E2, was 'adequately dated by sherds of medieval glazed-ware' (McBurney, *ibid*). The third of McBurney's subdivisions, E3, was identified as the spoil from Col. Wood's 1860s excavation. Context F is the modern topsoil. The basal deposits, context A, are sandy with some scree clasts.

a. Environmental reconstruction

The collared lemming mandibles from A2 indicates cold, open conditions at the time of deposition, but the lack of any other species of either large or small mammal except for common shrew means that no further conclusion may be drawn about the contemporary environment. The common shrew has a modern distribution covering western Europe from the Arctic coast to the Mediterranean, and eastwards to Lake Baikal and the River Yenesei, excluding only dry steppe and desert

areas (Corbet 1978). It occurs in a very wide variety of ecological conditions, and so is a poor indicator of specific environment. Contexts A1 and A3 were sterile.

The various facies of context B contain a generally cold fauna. The LSB, with arctic hare, collared lemming and probable narrow-skulled vole, indicates cold, open conditions. A slight amelioration of climate is demonstrated by the increase in proportion of voles over lemmings in context LOB, and there is a possible indication of areas of shrub developing in the area in the presence of one specimen each of bank vole and wood mouse. These seem to be the only indication of the warmer Lateglacial Interstadial conditions normally associated with human habitation. The single fragment of Norway lemming mandible indicates a damper biome in the area, perhaps in the lower lying valley floor, persisting into and through the cold Lateglacial, indicated by both Norway lemming and northern vole in the MSB, UOB and USB. The few specimens recovered from the MSB or UOB indicate little change in the local environment, which remains cold and open. The total absence of any temperate species from the USB indicates a return to a very cold climate.

Table 9.1 – Species representation, Cathole Cave.

	Oldest				LUP							
	A1	**A2**	**A3**	**LSB**	**LOB**	**MSB**	**UOB**	**USB**	**C**	**D**	**E**	**F**
Lepus timidus				1				1				
Lemmus lemmus					1		3	1				
Dicrostonyx torquatus		2		24	15	4		3				
Arvicola terrestris					1					1	1	
Microtus oeconomus					1	1	1					
Microtus gregalis							1	1				
Microtus gregalis/agrestis				4	5				3			
Microtus agrestis										12	30	92
Microtus sp.					2				1	6		
Clethrionomys glareolus					1	1				1	1	
Apodemus sylvaticus					1		1		3	5	22	68
Micromys minutus										1		
Rattus sp.											3	2
Sorex araneus		2		1	1					4	20	8
Neomys fodiens										2		2
Talpa europaea										1		2
Oryctolagus cuniculus											1	1
Total identified specimens	0	4	0	30	27	6	6	7	7	33	78	175

A marked change is seen with the fauna from context C. Once again, the number of specimens is low, but no cold climate indicators are included, and near-equal numbers of wood mouse and *Microtus* vole were recovered. It is tempting to see this as an indication of an increase in cover but short of actual woodland, as would be expected in the Pre-boreal period. However, the small size of the bone assemblage makes it in truth inadequate to prove this. Context D yielded a larger assemblage, which does allow more detailed environmental reconstuction. The *Microtus* specimens include one maxilla, positively identified as *Microtus agrestis* (field vole), and the mandibles all fall into the range of M_1 morphologies for that species. It is probable that all are field vole, and that those of context C are the same. The relatively low numbers of wood mouse and single specimen of bank vole indicate the area supported scrub or open woodland rather than fully developed forest. The single mandible of harvest mouse indicates stands of tall grass, reeds or sedge, possibly in the damper valley floor that is indicated by the presence of water shrew.

Contexts E and F show the valley to have retained a similar ecological composition throughout the subsequent periods of deposition. There is no indication that dense climax woodland ever developed here.

b. Taphonomy

The material from the Campbell excavation includes no specimens smaller or less complete than a mandible fragment. It is likely that the samples were not wet-sieved,

and that smaller specimens were therefore not collected. In consequence, discussion of the bone condition would be based on samples so biased as to render it meaningless. There are large numbers of complete mandibles in the collection, but only one cranium, that of a common shrew, from context F (topsoil). The large number of complete or near-complete mandibles indicates the primary accumulator throughout the period of deposition to have been an owl or owls. A single barn owl (*Tyto alba*) bone from layer E was identified by Bramwell (Campbell 1977), but as the modern breeding distribution of this species is at its northernmost in Britain, it is not expected to have been present here in the Lateglacial. Numerous bird bones of other species are listed, some of which might have been humanly imported, for example, the goose (*Anser* cf. *anser*) in layer LOB and the grouse (*Lagopus* cf. *lagopus*) in context MSB. Others are small or medium sized species, including pipits, tits, warblers and goldcrest, various waders and several duck species. It is likely that these fragmentary remains are the feeding debris of a falcon, probably peregrine (*Falco peregrinus*) or gyr (*Falco rusticolus*), perching on a ledge above the site. As falcons of this type feed almost exclusively on birds taken in flight (Mullarney *et al.*, 1999), the small mammal bone in the same deposits must have accumulated by a different means. An owl resident on the cliff face above the cave might have been in some danger from falcons using the same cliff, as indeed a falcon might be from one of the larger species of owl. Interspecific predation among the owls and diurnal raptors is well-documented (Mikkola 1983), and it is possible that the barn owl from context E was not a resident, but a lunch. It is most probable that the cliff was used by different species at different times, and that the bone assemblage is the result of sporadic occupation by a variety of avian predators.

2. Priory Farm Cave, Pembroke

A short excavation was carried out at Priory Farm Cave in July-August 1999, directed by Dr R.N.E. Barton of Brookes University, Oxford, and the author. Excavations at the site in 1906-7 by Dr A. Hurrell Style and Mr E.E.L. Dixon recovered evidence for human use of the cave in various different periods: late mediaeval pottery, a shell midden, a small hoard of Middle to Late Bronze Age metalwork, human remains possibly associated with the hoard, and Mesolithic and Upper Palaeolithic flint artefacts (Grimes 1933). The 1999 excavation was instigated to provide information about the stratigraphic relationships of any surviving cultural deposits, as well as to research the Upper Palaeolithic industries and

environments of this westernmost location. The temporal range of the finds recorded from the cave offered the possibility of a column of environmental samples covering the Late Glacial and early Holocene through to at least the Bronze Age.

a. Cave exterior - environmental reconstruction

Three trenches were opened on the platform outside the cave entrance (see fig.9.3), locating in trench 2 'apparently undisturbed sediments … beneath [Hurrell Style's] spoil tip' (Barton & Price 1999, p.5). These were described as unit 4, 'angular stony red silts', and 'the most likely candidate for the "gravel" layer in which Mesolithic and Upper Palaeolithic finds were reported by Grimes 1933, p.94, although no *in situ* artefacts were recovered' (*ibid*). A column of environmental samples was taken from a section through unit 4, providing a stratified sequence through the deposit for processing by the author in the laboratory. Several samples from the excavation of the deposit were also retained for wet-sieving, and the remainder of the spoil dry-sieved on site. Samples processed in the laboratory all received the same treatment.

None of the cold climate indicator species typical of the Late Glacial were recovered from unit 4, except a small fragment of broken molar which is possibly collared lemming. The environmental column does show an increase, from bottom to top, in indicators of a more wooded environment. 21 of the 36 identifiable specimens in the top 20cm spit are bank vole, compared with 11 specimens of *Microtus*. No M^2 was present, making definite identification to species impossible, but all M_1s and M_1 fragments were of *Microtus agrestis* (field vole) morphology. Given the nature of the rest of the fauna, it is reasonable to assume field vole, rather than narrow-skulled vole, was present. The second spit shows a marked decline in bank vole, indicating a less wooded or shrubby environment in the area. No firm indicator of woodland is found below this level, and in spit 4 an upper second molar of either narrow-skulled or northern vole was found, together with a first lower molar of typical narrow-skulled vole morphology.

Spit 5, at the base of the section, yielded only a single fragment of vole molar. Unfortunately, the poor condition of the majority of teeth throughout the column makes firm identifications difficult. Environmental reconstruction is therefore limited. Trench 1, on the north-west side of the cave entrance (see fig.9.3), quickly reached bedrock, and provided no environmental evidence.

Trench 3, running across the cave entrance from trench 2, exposed 'a more complex sequence of sediments … against part of the sloping bedrock floor and within the vadose trench' (Barton & Price *op.cit*, p.5), including the loessic light brown fine silts (unit 5) which had been observed in a small area between the large rocks at the base of trench 2. Only small samples of this sediment were obtainable, and proved sterile. The red clayey silt (unit 7) from beneath unit 5 was found to contain 'heavily altered and mineralised bone fragments' (*ibid*), but no identifiable specimens.

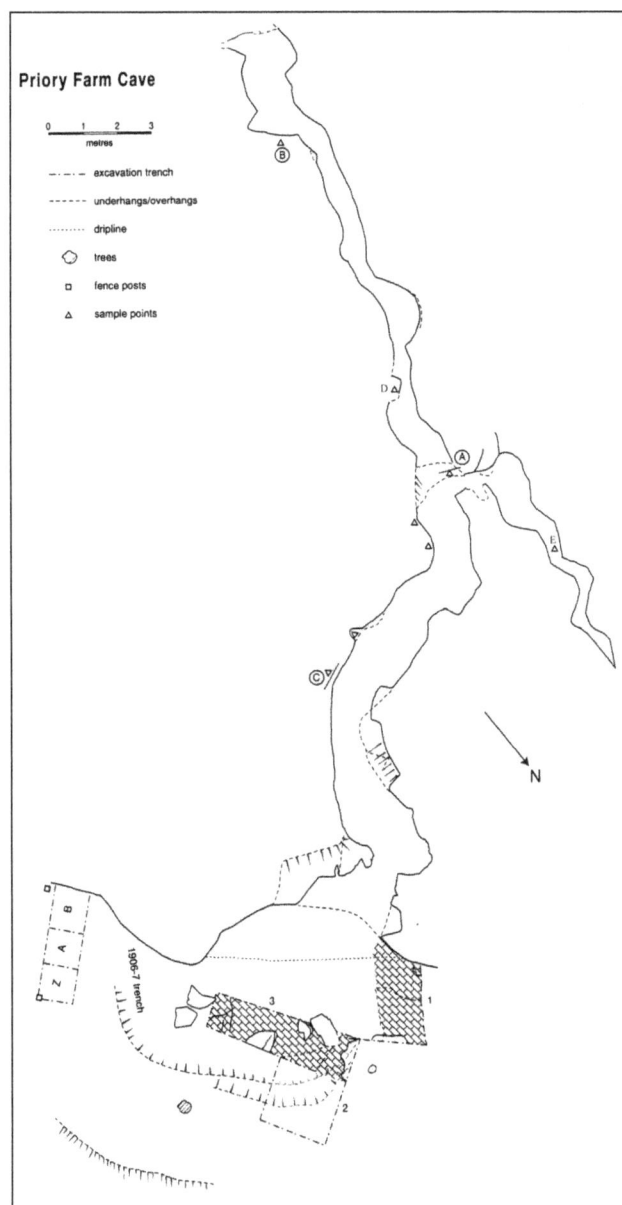

Fig. 9.3 – Plan of Priory Farm Cave, showing excavated areas and sample points (after Barton & Price 1999).

Plate 11 – Priory Farm Cave 1999.

Table 9.2 – Species representation & bone condition, trench 2.

Context	4	4 spit 1	4 spit 2	4 spit 3	4 spit 4	4 spit 5
		Environmental column				
Dicrostonyx torquatus	?					
Arvicola terrestris	20		1			
Microtus oeconomus	1					
Microtus gregalis					1	
Microtus oeconomus/gregalis	1				1	
Microtus gregalis/agrestis	6				3	
Microtus cf. agrestis	88			1		
Microtus sp.	123	11	13	19	37	1
Clethrionomys glareolus	146	21	4			
Apodemus sylvaticus	49	3			1	
Sorex araneus	9	1				
Sorex minutus	1					
Talpa europaea	2					
Chiroptera sp.	3					
Mustela erminea	4					
Condition of bone	B	B/C	D	D/E	D	E
Total identified specimens	453	36	18	20	43	1
Total samples analysed	7	1	1	1	1	1

A fourth trench was excavated on the eastern side of the platform (squares Z, A & B – see fig.9.3) outside the area of the 1906-7 excavations, locating undisturbed deposits. The sequence is as follows (Barton & Price 1999):

– Unit 1: stony brown silt, with a midden of mainly edible marine shellfish remains. Few stratified artefacts.

– Unit 1b: brown to pinkish grey silt, less stony. No artefacts.
– Unit 2: clean, white tufaceous deposit with no limestone fragments. Rich in terrestrial mollusc remains, but no artefacts or large bones.
– Unit 2b: diffuse boundary with 2. Pinker tufaceous sediment with broken limestone fragments and some bedding visible. No faunal remains or artefacts.

Table 9.3 – Species representation & bone condition, squares Z, A & B.

Context	Base 3	2	1b	Top 1
Arvicola terrestris	1?			
Microtus agrestis		1		
Microtus sp.	18	1		
Clethrionomys glareolus			1	
Apodemus sylvaticus	3		3	
Rattus rattus				2
Condition of bone	D	C	D	A
Total identified specimens	22	2	4	2
Total samples analysed	3	2	1	1

– Unit 3: yellowish to brown-red silt with some sharp stones. Stratified struck flint flakes and microdebitage.
– Unit 5: light brown fine silts. Sterile.

Samples were collected during excavation for laboratory analysis.

The two black rat mandibles from context 1 are a matching pair in excellent complete condition, recovered from a pit-fill. The species is now uncommon in the British Isles. It is thought to have been introduced to this country during the Roman period, as no well stratified remains of the species pre-date the 3rd-5th century AD specimens from London, York and Wroxeter (Corbet & Harris 1991; Yalden 1999). The black rat is only associated with human activity, and so is not a useful environmental indicator. No other small mammal bone was recovered from unit 1.

The wood mouse and bank vole teeth from unit 1b indicate good vegetation cover, whether actual woodland or a shrubby environment. Units 2 and 3 show more open conditions, with the shorter grass more suited to field voles. The one diagnostic artefact from unit 3, a broken retouched blade, is of Final Upper Palaeolithic type (Barton & Price 1999), indicating the deposit to have accumulated during the latter part of the Lateglacial Interstadial. The presence of wood mouse, and absence of lemmings, confirms the temperate climate of the time, but there are insufficient small mammal remains to judge whether there was any development of open woodland in the area. There is no indication in the small mammal assemblage of the colder conditions of the Younger Dryas, as there appears to be a hiatus in the stratigraphy where deposits of that period would be expected.

b. Cave exterior – taphonomy

The small mammal bone from trench 2, unit 4, is in reasonable condition, with many complete or near-complete mandibles, and one complete cranium from the deepest level (see below). It is likely that there is some mixing in this deposit, as the column of samples taken from the definitely *in situ* sediment contained complete mandibles only in the top two spits, and

the isolated teeth from these spits are broken and abraded. The hypsodont molars from the lower spits are frequently fragmented, split along the joints of the prisms, and with damaged outer angles. Very little complete bone was recovered, with only the smallest skeletal parts such as phalanges and caudal vertebrae surviving. The remainder of the assemblage is trampled or crushed. The complete cranium of a field vole was recovered from the deep sounding on the north side of trench 2, together with three complete mandibles of bank vole and three of probable field vole, which suggests possible admixing from the backfilling of Hurrell Style's excavation. Analysis has therefore been restricted to the samples from the environmental column which are known to be uncontaminated,. The condition of the small mammal material from the environmental column suggests a minimal accumulation from mammalian carnivore scats, subsequently dried out, and scattered by trampling. There is possibly some later input from owl pellets in the topmost spit of the column, where two complete vole mandibles and one with the teeth missing were found. The rest of the specimens from this sample were in similar condition to the material from lower in the column, with worn and broken isolated teeth and only the smallest bones unbroken.

Bone from the eastern trench, squares Z-B, appears to be trampled and crushed rather than digested or abraded. The complete rat mandibles are exceptional, and must have been protected by their deposition in a pit or burrow. The condition of the remainder of the assemblage is consistent with the concentrated human activity suggested by the other finds from the trench (see above). The bones do not appear to be digested, but their fragmentation renders it difficult to be definite about this, or to suggest by what means they were originally deposited.

c. Cave interior – results and taphonomy

The interior of the cave was surveyed to provide a complete plan of all accessible parts. This included a careful examination of any areas with potential *in situ* deposits, as the cave was thought to have been virtually emptied by earlier excavations. All bone deposits were marked on the plan, with levels extended from the site datum at the cave entrance. Surviving remnants of the deposit considered by Hurrell Style to be a hyaena den (Grimes 1933) were discovered at the entrance of a low side passage at point A (fig.9.3). The bone fragments removed from the buff clay of this deposit are black and mineralised, and include specimens of reindeer (*Rangifer tarandus*) and spotted hyaena (*Crocuta crocuta*) (Barton & Price 1999). The presence of hyaena, extinct in Britain since the last glacial maximum *c*.18,000 BP (Gibbons, pers. comm.) or earlier, shows this deposit, and other bone in the same highly mineralised state found in the cave, to be outside the temporal range of this study. The buff clay was surrounded and overlain by the red-brown clay ubiquitous in the cave, and difficult to differentiate from it under artificial lighting.

Small bone fragments were observed in the deposits adhering to the south-east cave wall near to the cave entrance (point C, fig. 9.3). The sediments were sampled as a 'section', from the base of the wall at c. 99.10m (site datum) to the top of the deposit, c. 99.53m (site datum), above which the wall is bare rock.

The top four samples were of red-brown clay with inclusions of breccia and limestone. Spit 5 was a soft, pale buff breccia or tufa, with little small mammal bone, which formed a layer 2cm thick at site datum 99.15 to 99.13m. A further sample of red-brown clay (spit 6) was taken from below this, from 99.13 to 99.10m. The uniformity of the red-brown clay found throughout the cave, and forming many of the samples here, suggests that it is not an *in situ* deposit, but the product of a mud flow event or events (Collcutt, pers.comm.), which would mix and redistribute any small bones. The samples contain a rather general temperate fauna, with a few specimens of possible Lateglacial origin (collared lemming, narrow-skulled

vole, northern vole). Because of doubts about the integrity of the deposits, no reliable information about past environments can be offered from this material. The only sample not of red-brown clay (5) provided too few identifiable specimens to contribute useful data.

Samples of the red-brown clay were collected from other locations in the cave, in the hope of discovering its origins and the conditions of its deposition. These sample locations are marked on the plan (fig.9.3).

Samples W, X, Y and Z were taken from the upper passage at point D, a continuation of the main chamber separated from it by a vertical step rising c. 1 metre. A thick deposit of the red-brown clay covers the upper passage floor, where it is particularly soft and wet. After a spell of wet weather during the excavation, the sediment in parts of the passage became almost liquid. This demonstrates how easily the sediment, and any inclusions, could be moved in mud flows during periods of prolonged rainfall. It could not be determined whether the water derived from percolation through the limestone or from drainage from the land surface into the back of the cave. A fissure was located in the cave roof, above point B on the plan (fig.9.3), which might lead up to the plateau. Few small mammal specimens were recovered from the samples taken from the upper passage. Their preservation is mixed, with some *Microtus* teeth and the *Dicrostonyx* specimen heavily stained. Samples W and Z yielded a few fish bones, 3 and 8 vertebrae respectively. Anuran (frog or toad) bones were also recovered. The bones from these samples could derive from elsewhere in the cave, or even from the plateau.

Samples U and V, from the lower passage (fig. 9.3, point E), produced quite extensive collections of small mammal bone,

Table 9.4 – Species representation & bone condition, section C, cave interior, Priory Farm Cave

	Top					Base
Spit	1	2	3	4	5	6
Dicrostonyx torquatus						2
Arvicola terrestris	2	6				3
Microtus oeconomus		2				1
Microtus oeconomus/gregalis	1	4		1		2
Microtus gregalis/agrestis		9		2		8
Microtus agrestis		1	2			3
Microtus sp.	4	72	16	16	2	66
Clethrionomys glareolus	1	6	10	2		8
Apodemus sylvaticus	1	7	39	17	1	8
Sorex araneus		7	1			1
Sorex minutus				1		
Neomys fodiens				1		
Chiroptera sp.		1?				
Condition of bone	D	D	C	D	C/D	C
Total identified specimens	9	116	69	40	3	102
Total samples analysed	1	1	1	1	1	1

Table 9.5 – Species representation – other locations inside Priory Farm Cave (see fig.9.3 for locations)

	U	V	X	X	Y	Z
Dicrostonyx torquatus		5				1
Arvicola terrestris	2	2				
Microtus oeconomus	1	2				1
Microtus oeconomus/gregalis	1	1				1
Microtus gregalis/agrestis	6	16				
Microtus agrestis					1	
Microtus sp.	67	65			2	12
Clethrionomys glareolus	1					2
Apodemus sylvaticus	14		1			2
Sorex araneus	2					
Sorex minutus	1					
Chiroptera sp.	1					
Total identified specimens	96	91	1	0	3	7

Table 9.6 – Condition of bone from other locations inside cave (see fig.9.3) – see fig. 6.1 for key.

Sample	Condition
U	C (fish vertebrae in excellent condition)
V	B
W	E
X	
Y	D
Z	D/X Mixed preservation; some dark staining

together with a large amount of fish bone, mostly small vertebrae of salmonids and eels. Herpetofaunal remains were also present. The 96 identified specimens from U, and 91 from V, were extracted from only 0.58 and 0.1 litres of sieved residue respectively. Three additional samples were taken from the lower passage 0.90m north of U and V in July 2000, to investigate the possible accumulation process involved in depositing so many fish remains in this unlikely location. A small quantity of fragmentary small mammal bone (*Microtus* sp., 12 molars; *Apodemus sylvaticus*, 10 molars; *Clethrionomys glareolus*, 6 molars; *Sorex minutus*, 1 mandible fragment) was recovered, but only one fish vertebra. This extremely localised concentration of fish bone suggests a different method of accumulation than the low numbers of bones scattered in the red-brown clay throughout the cave. The small mammal bone from U and V is in similar condition to the common state of specimens from the rest of the red-brown clay, with four complete or near-complete mandibles and many isolated teeth. Again, differential staining separates some *Microtus* and all the collared lemming teeth from the otherwise temperate fauna. It is likely that these black specimens are derived from the deposit containing hyaena, at the entrance to the lower passage. The remainder of the fauna could represent any part of the Holocene.

The fish bones, unlike the small mammal remains, are in excellent condition, with neural spines intact, and many are quite fresh-looking (plate 12). Their condition and accumulation in this inaccessible place seems remarkable. Transport by even a low-energy mud flow would have broken or abraded the delicate spines of the vertebrae. No avian predator would enter the totally dark, extremely cramped space of the 0.6m wide, 0.3m high passage. Comparison with fish remains collected from gull and heron pellets by the author showed the cave specimens to be far more complete. With previous knowledge of the bone modifications resulting from mammalian digestion (see chapter 5), it was a complete surprise to find, on obtaining and disaggregating a small collection of otter spraint, that the fish bone was unaffected by the digestive process, and matched perfectly with the specimens collected from Priory Farm Cave. The fish vertebrae from the otter spraints were considerably smaller than those from the cave, but otters are opportunist feeders, taking whatever prey is most available. 'In a Devon river 74% of salmonid fish taken were under 12cm long; in the coastal marshes of Norfolk during one month, only stickleback remains were found in spraint. Predation on pike and salmon up to *c*. 10kg has been reported' (Corbet & Harris 1991, p.428). The accumulation of the putative otter spraint in the lower passage can be explained by the observation that otters (*Lutra lutra*), though they normally dig their own holts, will sometimes inhabit ready-made caves and tunnels (Kruuk 1995). Close to the sample site in the lower passage, an arched undercut was observed in the east wall. It was thought likely to be the blocked entrance to a small tunnel exiting lower down the slope towards the river. Several small caves were located 10-15m downslope from the main cave entrance, any of which might have provided access for an otter. As spraints are used as territorial markers, it is likely that the otter would deposit them up the passage from its holt area, to communicate its presence there. The fish bone deposit was located towards the main chamber from the possible tunnel entrance in the east wall, where any animal entering the lower passage via the main chamber would pass. A resident otter might also have contributed a proportion of the small mammal bones, though mammals form only a minor part of their diet, and no specimens were recovered from the otter spraints for direct taphonomic comparison.

A further interesting discovery from sample point U is the flint microlith, a microscalene triangle, discovered during sieving. This is a distinctive Late Mesolithic type, and has the white patination seen on the Upper Palaeolithic flints from the eastern platform trench. It is likely to be coincidental that it should be associated with this small, bone-rich deposit, and to have moved, with many of the other inclusions, in a mud flow. It cannot be taken to date the deposit, though an attractive story could be woven around its possible use as the terminal point of a fish spear, and its subsequent arrival in the cave, firmly embedded in 'the one that got away'!

While little firm environmental evidence was recovered from Priory Farm Cave, the relative scarcity of well-preserved small

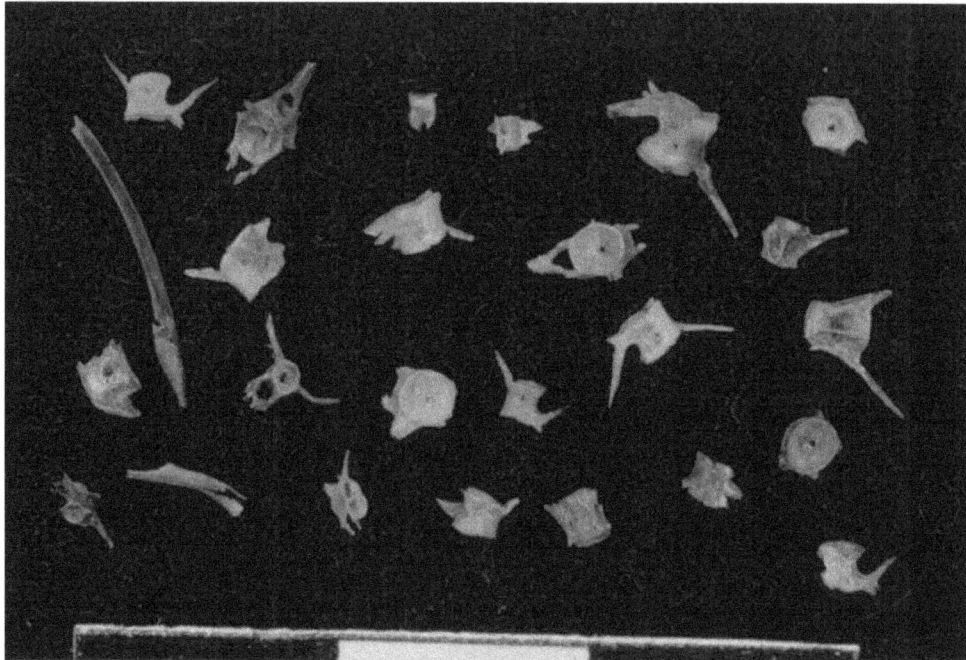

Plate 12 – Fish bones from Priory Farm Cave lower passage (3cm scale)

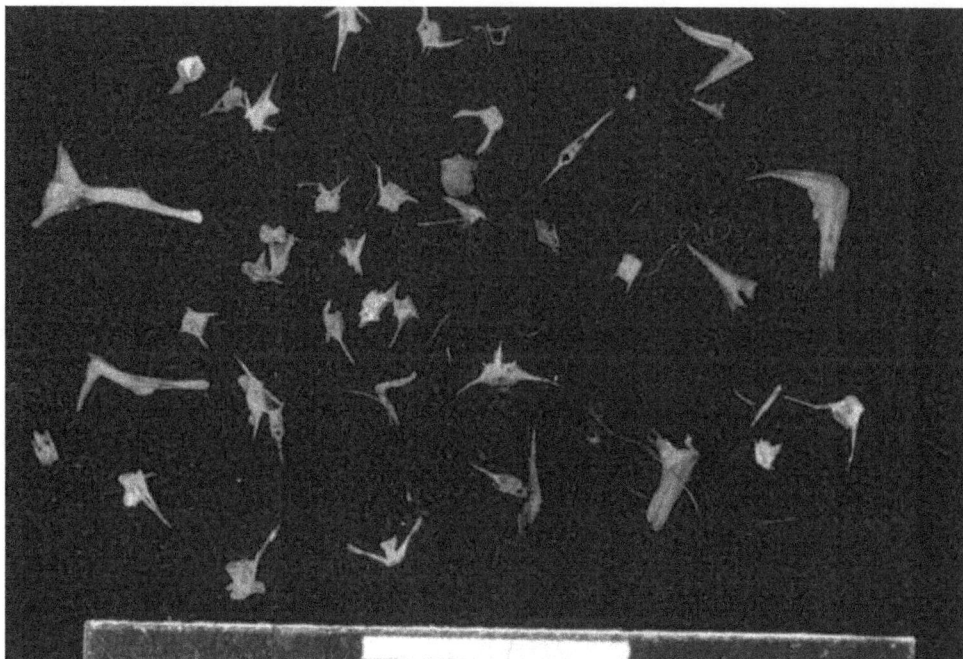

Plate 13 – Fish bones from otter spraint (3cm scale)

mammal bone on the site is a good indication that, at least in the Lateglacial, the cave did not provide a favourable habitat for the owls which are so often the best accumulators of such material (see chapter 4, section 1b). This in itself can be taken as an indication of the conditions experienced by the Upper Palaeolithic human occupants of the site. Damp, rain-bearing westerly winds blowing up the valley into the cliff face and cave mouth would make it unattractive to raptors, but equally to humans. There must have been a strong reason to use the site, such as a local, possibly seasonal, abundance of some particular food resource or strategic importance for hunting methods.

The tufa deposit (unit 2) exposed by the trenches on the external cave platform (see above) offers another factor to consider in analysing the microfaunal evidence. 'Preliminary observations suggest that [the tufa] covered a wide area of the platform, extending beyond the edge of the present dripline, and this would imply the existence of a much greater projecting overhang during the period of its deposition' (Barton & Price 1999, p.8). Its position above the *in situ* Final Upper Palaeolithic sediments implies that they were deposited inside the cave, as was the tufa (Collcutt, pers.comm.), and that at some point since there has been a major roof collapse. It is unusual to find owl accumulations inside low-roofed caves. In most caves similar in shape to Priory Farm Cave, any owl pellet deposit is found around the dripline, produced by birds roosting or nesting on ledges on the cliff rather than inside the cave (for example, Three Holes Cave, King Arthur's Cave). If the shape of the cave roof was similar before its collapse to its present form, it is possible that any useful owl assemblage that may once have accumulated at Priory Farm Cave has been lost to quarrying, erosion of the slope, or the 1906-7 excavations.

Chapter 10
Conclusions

1. Small mammal populations & ecology – a chronological overview

a. Lateglacial Interstadial

The samples from King Arthur's Cave context 4 offer the most extensive collection of Lateglacial Interstadial material studied here. 53 sediment samples were processed, averaging 2 litres each before sieving. 179 identifiable specimens were recovered. Allowing for a certain amount of contamination from the downward movement of small bones within the stratigraphy, it is still possible to conclude that the fauna of this period does not match that of modern temperate regions. It is clear that there is a continuing presence of species now restricted to colder climates; collared lemming (*Dicrostonyx torquatus*), Norway lemming (*Lemmus lemmus*) and narrow-skulled vole (*Microtus gregalis*). The coexistence of such apparent indicators of near-polar conditions with what are now perceived as woodland indicators - bank voles (*Clethrionomys glareolus*) and wood mice (*Apodemus sylvaticus*) - initially suggests the assemblage to be mixed. However, when the site is considered within the landscape, the range of species seems more plausible. The topography of the Wye Valley offers the potential for wide ecological diversity within the catchment area. A similar situation is found in the Mendip region and to a lesser extent in South Devon.

The survival of a species in less than ideal conditions is dependent on the availability of an ecological niche in which it is not threatened by intense competition from a different member of the same ecological 'guild' better adapted to the prevailing conditions. In this instance, the guild of small grazers includes the two species of lemming, water voles (*Arvicola terrestris*), three *Microtus* voles (northern, narrow-skulled and field vole), and two species of *Clethrionomys* (bank and grey-sided vole). The current distribution of these

species (see chapter 3) shows that there is nowhere that they all occur together, some having a more north-easterly distribution (collared lemming, narrow-skulled vole) while others are confined to the north-western parts of Europe (Norway lemming, field vole, bank vole). This suggests that for some, the main factor in their preferred ecology is not temperature, but moisture. Collared lemmings and narrow-skulled voles are restricted to cold, dry areas such as the Siberian tundra, while Norway lemmings populate the damper cold environment of Scandinavia. Bank voles occur throughout Scandinavia except the far north, their range overlapping that of the Norway lemming and grey-sided vole. The grey-sided vole is found in Norway, northern Sweden and Finland, and in a patchy distribution across Siberia. The water vole is widespread throughout much of the former U.S.S.R. and Europe, except in France and Spain, where it is replaced by the southern water vole (*Arvicola sapidus*), suggesting a tolerance to a wide range of conditions. Field voles also have a wide distribution, inhabiting all of Scandinavia and central Europe, but excluded from the far north of Siberia. Clearly the species can thrive in the cold damp conditions of Lapland, but drier conditions at a similar temperature are untenable. The conditions available in the Wye Valley during the Lateglacial Interstadial must have offered a range of environments suitable for each of these species, allowing their coexistence. This will be considered more fully below (section 2, this chapter).

As the modern world can provide no analogous small mammal fauna to that of the Lateglacial Interstadial, it is likely that no similar environment exists now. 'The Late Glacial Interstadial was marked by so unique a combination of environmental parameters that it permitted the temporary coexistence of otherwise unlikely combinations of mammalian species' (Currant 1991, p.48). The rapidly changing conditions, from deglaciation, through temperate, and back to sub-polar in three thousand years, meant that the environment had insufficient time to achieve a state of equilibrium, and this is reflected by the small mammal population. If the Lateglacial Interstadial had not been followed so closely by the Younger Dryas Stadial, the development of the wooded environment would have continued as it later did in the early Holocene. The open colonising woodland which had become established on the newly developed soils would have been invaded by secondary colonisers once the primary colonisers had enriched the soil with leaf litter and stabilised it with their roots. The small mammal species such as collared lemmings, which had flourished in the cold, dry, open environment of the Younger Dryas (Dimlington Stadial), were joined first by species tolerant of the damper conditions which resulted from the melting of glaciers, and then by successive invasions of those requiring the richer vegetation encouraged by the increasing warmth. Gradually, the more specialist cold-climate species would have been out-competed by the more adaptable generalists such as field voles, and creatures adapted to a woodland existence, such as bank voles. The climatic reversal to the colder conditions of the Younger Dryas effectively halted the ecological development before a new balance was reached. The fauna of the Lateglacial Interstadial can therefore be seen to be the product of a continually shifting state of biological flux, with survivors and invaders competing for the changing resources.

Voles and lemmings are particularly adept at colonising new territories. The population dynamics leading to the cyclic 'boom and bust' of individual species in specific areas allow their rapid spread into previously unpopulated areas. Vole plagues and apparent mass-suicides of lemmings are the result of local populations of a species expanding rapidly after good grazing and winter breeding. The density of animals reaches 'critical mass', when the pressure on resources (food, burrows, mates) becomes too great, and large sections of the population disperse. Access to territory where no animals of the same species are already established would allow a very rapid colonisation, and avoid the population collapse usually witnessed after rapid increase. The arrival of new species, and the resultant pressure on existing species, is a natural result of changing environments. With easy access to Britain from the continent via the landbridge to the south and east, and a lowland corridor along the south coast (Gleed-Owen 1998), the fast-breeding small mammals had an excellent opportunity to colonise South-West England and South Wales as the vegetation developed into suitable habitats.

The discovery of *Clethrionomys rufocanus* (grey-sided vole), a new species record for Britain, from King Arthur's Cave and probably from Gough's Cave, is an interesting addition to the Lateglacial Interstadial fauna. Its modern distribution overlaps with the northernmost populations of bank vole (*Clethrionomys glareolus*), and also with the most southerly populations of collared lemming (*Dicrostonyx torquatus*) (Corbet 1978). Its preferred habitat of 'stony (rocky) places with many natural holes' (Mitchell-Jones *et al*.1999, p. 214), both in open birch or pine forest and above the timberline, suggests that the environment of the Lateglacial Interstadial in rocky areas such as the Wye Valley and Mendip would

have been near-perfect. A second new species, *Myopus schisticolor* (wood lemming), may also be present. Several very small lemming molars recovered from King Arthur's Cave context 4 were compared with wood lemming specimens from Yakursk, Russia, held at the Natural History Museum. Unfortunately, the division of this species from *Lemmus lemmus* is almost entirely dependent on size. The length of the cheek tooth row in *Myopus* is 6.4 -6.8mm, and in *Lemmus*, 7.4 – 8.2mm. The tooth morphology is identical in the upper molars, and with only a minor difference in the lower third molar, which in *Myopus* has straighter edges on the buccal side (Hillson 1986). As definite specimens of *Lemmus lemmus* were present in the context, the smaller putative *Myopus* specimens cannot be separated, despite their being a perfect match in size and form. No lower third molar was recovered. Examination and measurement of a large number of specimens, preferably complete mandibles, would be necessary to prove the incontrovertible existence of both species in Britain. Given the similarity of dentition between the two species, it seems illogical that they should not be the same genus. Both grey-sided voles and wood lemmings experience the cyclic population explosions cited as a factor in the rapid dispersal of small grazing rodents (Elton 1942).

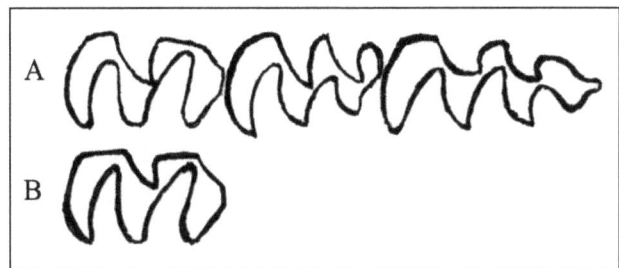

Figure 10.1 – Morphological differences in *Lemmus lemmus* & *Myopus schisticolor*
A – *Lemmus lemmus*, lower left dentary
B – *Myopus schisticolor*, lower left M$_3$ (after Hillson, 1986).

b. Lateglacial Stadial (Younger Dryas)

The small mammal faunas from Lateglacial Stadial contexts show the return of cold conditions with the proportional increase of collared and Norway lemmings, and the disappearance of the more temperate species, bank vole and wood mouse. This can best be seen in the material from Merlin's Cave west wall (table 8.6), as the consolidation of the samples means that there is less danger of contamination from higher deposits. No bank vole remains, and only a single wood mouse specimen, were recovered from the breccias. It must be remembered, though, that the consolidated samples from Merlin's Cave represent only the latter part of the Younger Dryas. Younger Dryas material from Cathole Cave layers MSB to USB (table 9.1) and Bridged Pot context B (tables 7.5 and 7.6) also show very low frequencies of these two species.

The *Microtus* species continue to contribute the majority of specimens, with the greatest number of those identified to species being *Microtus gregalis* (narrow-skulled vole). This is likely to be due to the hunting behaviour of the predators responsible for these assemblages concentrating on the higher ground, where hunting would be easier. The higher, drier ground would offer a more desirable habitat for the narrow-skulled vole, while the lower, damper terrain would favour the northern vole (*Microtus oeconomus*) which is also found throughout the period. A higher proportion of northern vole was recovered from the Late Pleistocene deposits at Broken Cavern, where a greater proportion of low-lying ground is available locally than in the Wye Valley or Mendip areas. The examination of morphological change in *Microtus gregalis* and *M. oeconomus* from Merlin's Cave shows that the size of narrow-skulled vole individuals tends to increase through the latter part of the Younger Dryas, while that of northern vole is stable in the later phase of deposition. However, it would be impossible to estimate the date of individual specimens on size alone, as a considerable size range is present in all phases of deposition. Only the most generalised conclusions can be drawn; for example, that particularly large specimens of narrow-skulled vole are likely to come from deposits dating to the end of the Younger Dryas.

The appearance of *Ochotona pusilla* (steppe pika) in the Lateglacial Stadial provides a marker species for the period. Very few examples of the species have been attributed to other periods, and none of them are directly dated. Yalden lists records of steppe pika in Britain, from sites including 'Westbury-sub-Mendip - Anglian Glacial?' and Pontnewydd, Denbigh - Wolstonian Glacial?' (Yalden 1999, p.51 – his question marks). The establishment of populations of this rather specialist animal, a member of a genus mostly restricted today to rich steppe grasslands in eastern Asia with the exception of two species in North America, is an important environmental indicator. It appears to have a spatially as well as temporally limited distribution, with the great majority of examples coming from the south-west of England and the Wye Valley. Other Lateglacial specimens are known from Nazeing, Essex, and Robin Hood's Cave, Derbyshire (Yalden 1999). It is interesting, and perhaps significant, that no other specimens have been recovered from caves in Derbyshire, despite extensive excavation and research in the area (Jacobi, pers. comm.). It is possible that the limited period during which the conditions in Britain were favourable to the species was too small a 'window of opportunity' to allow a wider distribution, and that the scattered population was unable to spread into the upland areas where suitable vegetation for them survived after the Lateglacial Stadial ended. The absence of the species from Cathole Cave, where deposits of an appropriate age contained good samples of small mammal remains, suggests that pikas did not spread this far west in South Wales, possibly due to environmental conditions. This will be discussed below. The population structure of steppe pikas may limit their effectiveness as colonisers as they are reported to be gregarious, and 'most juveniles remain in their natal home range throughout the summer and eventually settle within 50 meters of the centre of the area' (Nowak 1999, p.1719). Their preference for rocky scree areas might also have limited their spread.

There is no record of cyclic population growth and decline in this species.

Yalden also lists sousliks (*Spermophilus superciliosus/S. citellus*) as coexistant with steppe pika in 'various Mendip sites' (Yalden 1999, p.50). No direct dates are available for this species, and it does not appear in any of the assemblages examined here. The species is characteristic of the Middle Devensian (Sutcliffe & Kowalski 1976), or more specifically, the 'mammoth steppe' of OIS 3, 60,000 – 25,000 BP (Currant, pers. comm).

Small numbers of common shrew (*Sorex araneus*) are present in the Merlin's Cave west wall samples, though absent from the Cathole Cave and Bridged Pot assemblages of Younger Dryas age, and from the cleanest samples from King Arthur's Cave context 3. Their presence in consolidated sediments implies that they are not intrusive, but did in fact survive the Lateglacial Stadial, at least in sheltered areas, and perhaps in reduced numbers. Their current distribution (see chapter 3, map 13) shows them to inhabit tundra and sub-polar regions, and survive wherever sufficient invertebrate prey is available to sustain their demanding energy requirement.

c. Early Holocene

Evidence from the Greenland ice cores for the end of the Lateglacial Stadial and beginning of the Holocene at around

Table 10.1 – Identified specimens from Sample F, Merlin's Cave west wall.

	n	%
Lepus timidus	6	1.3
Ochotona pusilla	23	5.1
Lemmus lemmus	26	5.7
Dicrostonyx torquatus	44	9.7
Arvicola terrestris	8	1.8
Microtus oeconomus	35	7.7
Microtus gregalis	82	18.1
Microtus oeconomus/gregalis	66	14.5
Microtus sp.	162	35.7
Sorex araneus	1	0.2

10,000 BP shows a rapid rise in temperature, with most of Britain achieving a temperate climate by around 9,925 BP (Adams 1997, Taylor *et al* 1997). Two specimens from the small mammal assemblage from Merlin's Cave west wall sample F (see fig.8.4) are directly dated at 9915 ± 60 (OxA-8073) and 9685 ± 60 (OxA-8072). It should be remembered that radiocarbon dates around 10,000 BP can be unreliable due to compression in the radiocarbon record, which produces age reversals and plateau effects in the dating sequence (Barton, pers. comm.). While the dates of this sample appear to be Pre-boreal Holocene, it could equally well be Late Glacial. The identified specimens recovered from the sample include 23 of pika, 26 of Norway lemming and 44 of collared lemming. No definite field vole was found amongst the 66 maxillae and second upper molars examined.

Expressed as percentages, the fauna is not radically different from that of samples dated well before the climatic improvement (see table 8.7). This shows that the small mammals, and by inference the vegetation, did not respond rapidly to the increased temperatures, and that pikas and lemmings continued to thrive despite the warmer conditions. No temperate woodland species are present at this early stage of the Holocene.

Without consolidated deposits, it is difficult to be certain whether apparently transitional faunas including both cold climate and temperate species are a genuine representation of the small mammal population or the product of post-depositional mixing. Context DB2 from Madawg Cave (see chapter 8, section 3a) furnished a date of 8710 ± 70 BP (OxA-6081) from a charred sloe stone, and no cold climate indicators were found amongst the 144 identified small mammal specimens from the 35 samples of this context. The fauna has a strongly woodland character, with 91 bank vole specimens, 42 of wood mouse, two of red squirrel and only five of field vole. The Grey-Black (GB) context below the DB2 yielded only a small microfaunal assemblage; of 41 identified specimens from 15 samples, only three were field vole while thirty-one were bank vole and eight wood mouse.

Context LBST from Three Holes Cave (chapter 6, section 1) appears to offer a transitional fauna, with a low number

of collared lemming specimens, a few definite northern voles, narrow-skulled voles and field voles but a large number of *Microtus* remains identified only to genus, and a reasonable collection of bank vole and wood mouse (table 10.2). However, the context is an *in situ* Later Mesolithic occupation horizon, and 'radiocarbon dates on red deer from the predated fauna suggests that the site was occupied during the early Atlantic (OxA 4491, 6330 ± 75 BP; OxA 4492, 6120 ± 75 BP)' (Roberts *et al*, 1996). It is probable that the human activity on the site has caused compaction and mixing. Unfortunately, the condition of the small mammal bone is poor, and no identifiable specimen of sufficient size for AMS dating was recovered. The available dates are too late for this to be considered a transitional fauna. By considering a single 1m square of the excavated area of Three Holes Cave, a degree of biostratigraphy is discernible, with the number of bank voles (woodland indicators) increasing from bottom (spit 4) to top, and the number of *Microtus* species (open grassland indicators) decreasing. Evidence of narrow-skulled vole is very uncommon in early Holocene contexts, though the difficulty of certain identification of the species may contribute to this. The two specimens from Three Holes Cave LBST are its only representation found in this study in deposits post-dating the Younger Dryas. Modern distributions and habitat preferences suggest that collared lemming and narrow-skulled vole would vanish before Norway lemming and northern vole, as is the case at King Arthur's Cave, but in the Torbryan Valley the Norway lemming disappears before the collared lemming.

The Early Neolithic contexts of Three Holes Cave, DBST and BCST, yielded large numbers of bank vole and wood mouse remains, but few of *Microtus* species. At this site, northern vole and narrow-skulled vole have completely disappeared by this time, though examples of northern vole were recovered from the Neolithic deposits at the nearby Broken Cavern. The appearance of dormouse (*Muscardinus avellanarius*) in context BCST, together with mole, water shrew and bat, completes the temperate small mammal fauna which is much the same as in the area today.

It is necessary, in the light of the current research, to review the type faunas given in chapter 3.

Table 10.2 – LBST biostratigraphy, square 7, Three Holes Cave

Species Spit	4	3	2	1
Arvicola terrestris	2	1		
M. gregalis/agrestis	1	3		
M. oeconomus/gregalis	1		1	
M. agrestis		1		2
Microtus sp.	13	17	3	3
Clethrionomys glareolus		1	4	5
Apodemus sylvaticus		1	1	
Sorex araneus				1

Glacial	Dicrostonyx torquatus	Collared lemming
	Lemmus lemmus	Norway lemming
	Microtus gregalis	Narrow-skulled vole
	Microtus oeconomus	Northern vole
	Lepus timidus	Mountain hare
Lateglacial Interstadial	Dicrostonyx torquatus	Collared lemming
	Lemmus lemmus	Norway lemming
	?Myopus schisticolor	Wood lemming
	Microtus gregalis	Narrow-skulled vole
	Microtus oeconomus	Northern vole
	Microtus agrestis	Field vole
	Arvicola terrestris	Water vole
	Clethrionomys glareolus	Bank vole
	Clethrionomys rufocanus	Grey-sided vole
	Apodemus sylvaticus	Wood mouse
	?Muscardinus avellanarius	Dormouse
	Sorex araneus	Common shrew
	Sorex minutus	Pygmy shrew
Lateglacial Stadial	Dicrostonyx torquatus	Collared lemming
& Pre-boreal	Lemmus lemmus	Norway lemming
	Arvicola terrestris	Water vole
	Microtus gregalis	Narrow-skulled vole
	Microtus oeconomus	Northern vole
	Lepus timidus	Mountain hare
	Ochotona pusilla	Steppe pika
	Sorex araneus	Common shrew
Boreal & Atlantic	Arvicola terrestris	Water vole
	Microtus oeconomus	Northern vole
	Microtus agrestis	Field vole
	Clethrionomys glareolus	Bank vole
	Apodemus sylvaticus	Wood mouse
	Muscardinus avellanarius	Dormouse
	Scuirus vulgaris	Red squirrel
	Sorex araneus	Common shrew
	Sorex minutus	Pygmy shrew
	Neomys fodiens	Water shrew
	Talpa europaea	Mole
	Erinaceus europaeus	Hedgehog
	Chiroptera sp.	Bat

2. Environmental implications of small mammal record

Local topography would play a major part in the distribution of different vegetation types, and so of the small mammals dependent on them. The limestone areas studied in this research are all relatively steep-sided valleys, which would encourage a gradation of vegetation from the low, sheltered valley bottoms to the dry, exposed uplands. This is demonstrated by the small mammal assemblages recovered from the caves. While it is improbable that the range of species found, for example, in King Arthur's Cave Allerød context 4 could have survived in exactly the same environment, the collared lemmings and narrow-skulled voles would have exploited the treeless, drier, upland areas while the bank voles, grey-sided voles and wood mice populated the open birch woodland of the lower slopes. This dependence on the

ecological mosaic is seen throughout the prehistoric periods examined, and continues to the present day. With reference to the scale profile of the Wye Valley (fig.10.2), it is possible to reconstruct hypothetical vegetation divisions likely to have existed during the different periods covered, with reference to available pollen diagrams (see chapter 2). The profile is divided into four zones by altitude, with a small allowance for the difference of aspect. This is to demonstrate the possibilities for environmental differences within a restricted area, and the range of small mammals this would encourage, rather than a definite reconstruction.

a. Early part of Lateglacial Interstadial

The small mammal faunas examined from the early part of the Lateglacial Interstadial are dominated by Microtus voles, with collared lemming, water vole and arctic hare. The hares,

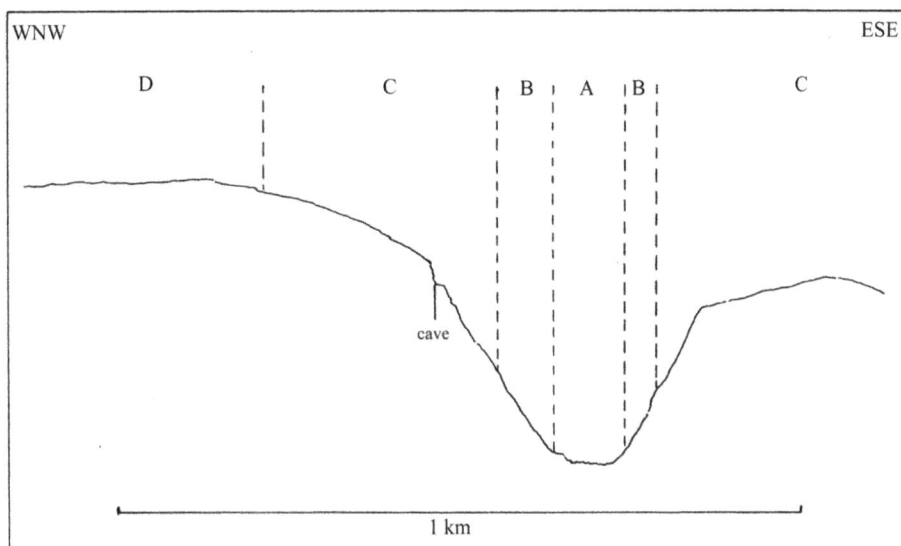

Fig 10.2 – Profile of the Wye Valley at Merlin's Cave showing ecological zones

Table 10.3 - Vegetation and small mammals by ecological zone – early Lateglacial Interstadial.

Zone	Vegetation	Small Mammals
A	Sedges & grasses	Norway lemming Northern vole Water vole
B	Juniper scrub	Narrow-skulled vole
C & D	Juniper, Crowberry etc., Dwarf Birch, short grasses	Narrow-skulled vole, Collared lemming, Mountain Hare
E	Mosses, short grass, lichen	Collared lemming

narrow-skulled voles and collared lemmings indicate an open grassland vegetation, consistent with the pollen evidence available. Although their present distribution implies cold conditions, these species appear to have survived through the interstadial temperate period. The central factor in their continuing presence is the availability of suitable habitat, rather than temperature. As soils developed and birch woodland spread across Britain, sufficient open landscape must have remained for these small grazers to retain a toe-hold in what was, for them, an increasingly unfavourable environment. Other small mammals - bank voles, grey-sided voles and wood mice - spread into the area, taking advantage of the newly suitable habitats, but did not populate the adjacent zones where open conditions persisted. Interspecific competition was therefore limited, and a wide range of small mammal species could coexist in the mosaic of different ecological niches and the ecotones between them.

b. Later part of Lateglacial Interstadial (Allerød)

The degree of woodland development achieved in the Lateglacial Interstadial was limited by the speed at which soils could develop and trees could colonise, and terminated by the return to cold stadial conditions. There is no evidence that fully developed woodland, with the mixture of tree species and shrubby understorey plants indicating climax vegetation,

was reached in this period. However, if sufficient hazel was able to establish itself in the lower lying areas, a relatively thick cover would have been possible, as the species naturally coppices when the leading shoot is removed or broken. This could occur naturally if a sapling was damaged by deer or bitten off by a hare, as is seen in modern forest regeneration. Corridors of hazel scrub along river and stream valleys may have been sufficiently extensive to allow the spread of dormouse into western Britain during the Allerød, as is suggested by the well-stratified specimen from Symonds Yat East Cave (see chapter 8, section 4). If it is possible to obtain a direct date on this specimen, the implications for the understanding of the vegetation of the latter part of the Lateglacial Stadial would be profound.

My own observation of the vegetation succession from the river valley to the fjäll tops around Hemaven, in Västerbottens, Sweden, shows a similar community of plant species as suggested by pollen evidence for the Lateglacial Interstadial in south-west Britain. Hemaven, at around 450m above sea level, is situated on the Umeälven, a large river with frequent lakes. The vegetation along the river is birch, alder and willow carr, with sedges, reeds and tall herbs including meadowsweet (plate 14). Birch woodland with low-growing juniper and dwarf willow dominates the lower slopes of the fjäll (plate 15), gradually becoming open and then patchy. At around 800m, tree birches are scarce, and by 1135m, at

Table 10.4 - Vegetation and small mammals by ecological zone – Allerød

Zone	Vegetation	Small Mammals
A	Sedges, downy birch, hazel, alder carr	Water vole, Northern vole
B	Silver birch, hazel, tall herbs (nettle, meadowsweet etc)	Bank vole, Grey-sided vole, Wood mouse. ?Dormouse
C	Scrubby birch, juniper, crowberry, blaeberry etc.	?Wood lemming Norway lemming Northern vole Field vole
D	Juniper, crowberry, blaeberry, grasses	Field vole Narrow-skulled vole Collared lemming
E	Dwarf shrubs, mosses, lichen	Collared lemming Narrow-skulled vole

Plate 14 – Birch/willow carr vegetation, Sweden.

Storkittelhobben, the vegetation is a low carpet of dwarf birch, crowberry, short grass, mosses and lichens (plate 16). While a direct comparison between this area and South-west Britain cannot be entirely valid, as there are many major differences, such as elevation and latitude, it serves as an example of how the plants indicated in the pollen diagrams available for Britain in the Lateglacial Interstadial might be distributed in the landscape to produce the kind of habitat mosaic suggested by the small mammal fauna. In the Västerbotten and Norrbotten areas of Sweden, where vegetation of this kind is widespread, the distribution of small mammals is similar to that suggested in tables 10.3 and 10.4 (Bjärnvall & Ullström

1985). Collared lemmings do not exist in the area, and so Norway lemmings use the habitats they would dominate if they were present. Similarly, the absence of narrow-skulled voles allows field voles to occupy a wider range.

In periods of rapidly changing climate, the difference altitude makes to the distribution of different ecosystems is more marked than when the environment has reached equilibrium. It is not, therefore, unreasonable to suggest that the distribution of vegetation zones in the Wye Valley should be similar to that in modern Sweden, despite the lower altitude and smaller altitude range.

Plate 15 - Birch/juniper woodland, Sweden.

Plate 16 – Dwarf shrub vegetation, Sweden (*Betula nana* & *Vaccinium vitis-idaea*)

Table 10.5 - Vegetation and small mammals by ecological zone – Lateglacial Stadial

Zone	Vegetation	Small Mammals
A	Sedges, possibly shrubby birch, tall herbs including meadowsweet	Water vole Northern vole
B	Juniper, dwarf shrub community	Northern vole Narrow-skulled vole Norway lemming
C	Grasses	Narrow-skulled vole Mountain hare Steppe pika
D	Grasses, alpine herbs eg. Norwegian mugwort	Steppe pika Mountain hare Narrow-skulled vole Collared lemming
E	Grasses, alpine herbs eg. Mountain avens	Collared lemming Narrow-skulled Vole

d. Younger Dryas

The effect of the Younger Dryas climatic deterioration seems to have been varied across the region studied. In the sheltered areas of South Devon and the Wye Valley, the small mammal assemblages indicate that the environment supported abundant life, and that the vegetation was varied. The presence of steppe pikas indicates a rich grass and herb community, and dry conditions. Damper areas would have supported sedges and mosses, offering ideal conditions for Norway lemmings and northern voles. The persistence of microtine voles as the dominant element of the small mammal fauna suggests that the conditions were not severe, though in more exposed locations, such as the more westerly Cathole Cave, lemmings are relatively more numerous and voles scarcer. The absence of pikas from areas west of the Wye Valley is possibly because of damper climatic conditions there. An east-west gradient of severity affected the environment, and relative exposure to weather coming from the west was an important factor in controlling the local environment. While the hilltops surrounding the Wye Valley and the deep gorges of the Mendips would have been exposed to cold winds, the sheltered valley bottom might have had a relatively mild microclimate.

e. Pre-boreal Holocene

Sample F from Merlin's Cave provides the only definite sample of this period, and shows that it would be difficult to distinguish from the Younger Dryas without the availability of direct dates. It is probable that, if a remnant of scrubby woodland persisted in sheltered areas through the Younger Dryas, it was isolated. This would mean that woodland mammals would only return to the area when trees had spread far enough to join the isolated copses and carrs, and formed corridors of suitable environment along which they could travel. As the climate became warmer, the vegetation would gradually alter, with invaders gradually colonising the valley bottoms, and the relict vegetation from the colder period reacting to competition by moving up the hill slopes. Plant

communities are resistant to sudden change. During the approximate five hundred year period of the Pre-boreal, there would have been a gradual alteration in favour of the more thermophilous species, and a gradual isolation of the sub-polar species on high ground until the encroaching trees and shrubs finally clothed even these last retreats and shaded out the survivors of the ice-age. This is shown by the small mammals, which remained in their preferred environments while they still existed, and were eventually replaced by woodland species as the open country was swallowed up by the forest. In terms of vegetation and mammalian faunas, absolute dates for the beginnings or ends of periods are meaningless, as ecosystems form a continuum rather than a series of disjointed states.

f. Boreal/Atlantic Holocene

The terms 'Boreal' and 'Atlantic' in the British succession are used to describe the period of maximum forest cover. 'Boreal' in this sense does not necessarily equate with the modern ecological use of the word. 'The distinctive vegetation of the Boreal region [western Norway, eastern Sweden, Finland, Poland and northern Russia] is the evergreen coniferous forest, commonly called the *taiga*' (Polunin & Walters 1985). In the British pollen record, there is a distinctive rise in pine pollen, but this is not a country-wide phenomena, and the spruces typical of the taiga were never a native species in this country. A variety of woodland communities developed throughout Britain, according to the soil type and aspect of different sites. As few native small mammal species are specifically dependent on particular woodland types, the faunas tend not to vary according to actual woodland composition, but rather according to the degree of openness and ground cover in the forest. The Wye Valley and Torbryan sites yielded faunas showing the local woodlands were dense, with a thick understorey during these periods. The presence of dormouse is a particular indicator of such conditions. High numbers of bank vole and wood mouse, and very low counts of field vole, suggest that only small areas of open grassland were to be found. At Cathole Cave, few bank

Table 10.6 - Vegetation and small mammals by ecological zone – Boreal/Atlantic Holocene

Zone	Vegetation	Small Mammals
A	Sedges, reeds, alder/hazel/birch carr, tall herbs and grasses	Water vole Northern vole Water shrew
B & C	Mixed deciduous woodland, with shrub layer (blackthorn etc), ivy, honeysuckle.	Bank vole Wood mouse Dormouse Red squirrel Mole Hedgehog
D & E	Open birch & hazel or pine woodland	Bank vole Wood mouse Field vole

vole specimens but large numbers of both wood mouse and field vole were recovered from the upper levels. This suggests very different vegetation. More open woodland, perhaps birch and hazel, with grass growing beneath the trees would account for such a fauna. The sides of the valley are well-wooded today, implying that the natural vegetation progression was much slower in the area, but eventually arrived at a similar ecological climax.

3. Taphonomy

Of the small mammal assemblages studied, the most complete in terms of faunal representation and in identifiable specimens are from owl pellet accumulations. The collections from Kent's Cavern, Three Holes Cave, Bridged Pot, King Arthur's Cave, Merlin's Cave and Cathole Cave are primarily such accumulations, and Broken Cavern, Gough's Cave and Symonds Yat East Cave contain many specimens which appear to be from a similar source. In general, good evidence is available from Late Pleistocene deposits, but there was a decrease in accumulation after the Pre-boreal phase of the Holocene. I suggest that this was for three reasons. The gradual formation of humic soil in temperate periods does not encourage the rapid burial of deposited owl pellets as well as scree formation does, and so the pellets are more likely to be dispersed. A slower rate of bacterial decomposition is evident in sub-polar environments (Pielou 1994), and so the more fragile bones are more likely to be preserved in cold conditions. Also, the habits of the predators must be taken into consideration. Owls living in wooded environments commonly use trees for roosting and nesting, and of all the modern species inhabiting temperate regions, only the eagle owl (*Bubo bubo*) habitually uses cliff ledges (Mikkola 1983). Consequently, the pellets do not accumulate in a sheltered situation which is likely to be investigated by archaeologists, but are dispersed on the forest floor, where they rapidly decompose and the bones are lost. This became apparent when the author investigated the area around a tree in which an owl nestbox was situated, in spruce forest near Tavelsjö, Sweden. The box had been used by pygmy owls, a species that rarely ejects pellets in the nest, but usually from a branch close to the nest-hole. Despite recent occupation - the nest-box

investigation took place on 24th July after the May-June breeding season (Hipkiss, pers.comm) - few small mammal remains were recovered from beneath the nest. No complete pellets survived, and the only identifiable specimens obtained were four vole mandibles, one shrew mandible and one mouse jaw. The average brood of pygmy owl young in Sweden is 5.9, so seven or eight owls would have been resident for the 30 days from hatching to the young leaving the nest. The fledglings produce regular pellets from three days old (Mikkola 1983). The quantity of debris produced by a single family must be considerable, but within a month there was little evidence.

The accumulation of small mammal remains by mammalian predators is more difficult to determine in circumstances where the deposit has undergone post-deposition alteration. Because of the small size of the bones, the distinctive gnaw marks observed on larger mammal remains are missing. This means that determining the species of the predator is often not possible, especially where similar species of potential predator, such as weasel and stoat, are present. Complete identifiable specimens are unusual in assemblages originating in mammal scats, as is demonstrated by the author's examination by of fresh material of known origin, including polecat, pine marten and weasel scats. This means that collections with the large numbers of identifiable small mammal remains necessary for analysis of the sort undertaken here are unlikely to owe more than a small percentage of their components to input from carnivores. The identification of evidence of carnivore predation through examination of bone surface and breakage patterns has been of most use in explaining the absence of easily identifiable material in samples, such as well-preserved molars or complete mandibles.

Human activity in and around the caves investigated was a major contributing factor in the development of the deposits, and often had a detrimental effect on the small mammal bones. No evidence was found for direct human involvement in bringing small mammal remains to the sites, though various examples are offered for the human exploitation of these species (see chapter 5). The effect of early human activity on bone accumulation and preservation is discussed in chapter 5, and is seen in the results from every cave examined, with the exception of Merlin's Cave and Kent's Cavern. In balance, it should be recognised that the presence of artefacts in a prehistoric deposit may - *inter alia* - provide the basis for preliminary judgement of period and stratigraphic division, and in doing so, render the associated small mammal remains more informative.

4. Archaeology and small mammal studies

The analysis of the small mammal component of faunal assemblages from prehistoric sites is of primary importance in determining the local environment. Where the accumulation can be attributed to owls, the small mammals reflect not only the immediate surroundings of the cave, but also a wider view of the locality. This offers an important insight into the food resources potentially available to human inhabitants of the area, and how they may have used the landscape.

Maximum benefit can be derived from microfaunal investigation when it is incorporated into the research design of the excavation from the outset. The data made available by the Wye Valley and Torbryan excavations is considerably more detailed than, for example, that from Cathole Cave and Bridged Pot. Early consideration of the potential of small mammal analysis allows provision to be made for the retrieval of suitable assemblages, whether this is through the sampling strategy for the site as a whole, or the placing of additional trenches outside the area thought to contain rich archaeological material but in a promising place for small mammal remains. This could be beneath a ledge in the cliff or at the base of a fissure. The Wye Valley project permitted the excavation at Merlin's Cave, where no Lateglacial cultural material was expected, to examine the rich small mammal fauna known to be preserved there.

The investigation of the small mammal fauna is also a key component of muliti-disciplinary palaeoenvironmental reconstruction, providing data for comparison with that obtained by other research methods. The Torbryan and Wye Valley Projects, for example, amongst other environmental analyses, also involved the recovery of land snails for specialist analysis. The results obtained in both cases confirm the broad environmental implications of the small mammals (Seddon, in Roberts *et al*.1996, Evans, pers.comm). The two lines of investigation complement each other, as the molluscan fauna reflects the environment immediately surrounding the cave whilst the small mammal assemblage sets this in a wider ecological background.

The direct dating of small mammal specimens is an important result of the development of Accelerator Mass Spectrometry. Only 200mg – 2g of bone is required, depending on the preservation of collagen in the sample. This means that individual specimens of key species in a deposit can be directly dated, giving direct evidence about flora, fauna and climate which may not be available from bulk samples. A large numbers of samples can be dated from different levels of stratified deposits, giving information on sediment disturbance, possible post-deposition mixing or contamination, and deposition rates (Oxford Radiocarbon Accelerator Unit website). The establishment of a reliable small mammal biostratigraphy is dependent on access to sites with well-defined stratification and confidence in the phasing of the deposits. Direct dating of specimens allows stratigraphic relationships to be checked, and the purity of deposits to be determined. By dating species from the same deposit implying different ecological conditions or perceived age, for example, bank vole and northern vole, it is possible to gain an insight into the site formation processes. This is demonstrated by the dating programme on small mammals from Broken Cavern context Lower 7, where dates on steppe pika, northern vole and bank vole proved the fauna to be a mixture of Younger Dryas and Holocene elements (see chapter 6 section 1a). Research of this type is particularly important when considering putative transitional faunas. It allows specimens of what appear to be 'unsuitable' species for a particular period of deposition to be either confirmed as genuine members of the fauna, or proved to be intrusive, avoiding an unscientific dependence on received knowledge and preconceived theories.

Although others have worked towards an understanding of rodent and insectivore populations in the Lateglacial and early Holocene periods, this is the first attempt to reconstruct a comprehensive model of changing small mammal faunas of the British Isles based on material from well-stratified contexts. The examination of new material from excavations with sampling strategies designed to maximise the recovery of micromammal remains made this possible. It is hoped that the results of the current work will facilitate the analysis of other small mammal collections, demonstrate the value of including such study in new excavation projects, and encourage the re-examination of the extensive assemblages from older excavations.

Appendix

Glossary

Prey species

Rodentia

Collared lemming	*Dicrostonyx torquatus*
Norway lemming	*Lemmus lemmus*
Wood lemming	*Myopus schisticolor*
Water vole	*Arvicola terrestris*
Northern vole (root vole)	*Microtus oeconomus*
Narrow-skulled vole	*Microtus gregalis*
Field vole	*Microtus agrestis*
Common vole	*Microtus arvalis*
Bank vole	*Clethrionomys glareolus*
Grey sided vole	*Clethrionomys rufocanus*
Wood mouse (long-tailed field mouse)	*Apodemus sylvaticus*
Yellow-necked mouse	*Apodemus flavicollis*
Harvest mouse	*Micromys minutus*
House mouse	*Mus musculus*
Black rat	*Rattus rattus*
Common dormouse (Hazel dormouse)	*Muscardinus avellanarius*
Red squirrel	*Scuirus vulgaris*
European souslik	*Spermophilus citellus*

Lagomorpha

Mountain hare (Arctic hare)	*Lepus timidus*
Brown hare	*Lepus europaeus*
Rabbit	*Oryctolagus cuniculus*
Steppe pika	*Ochotona pusilla*

Insectivora

Hedgehog	*Erinaceus europaeus*
Common Mole	*Talpa europaea*
Common shrew	*Sorex araneus*
Pygmy shrew	*Sorex minutus*
Water shrew	*Neomys fodiens*

Mammalian Predators

Canidae

Wolf	*Canis lupus*
Arctic fox	*Alopex lagopus*
Red fox	*Vulpes vulpes*

Ursidae

Brown bear	*Ursus arctos*

Mustelidae

Stoat (ermine)	*Mustela erminea*
Weasel	*Mustela nivalis*
Polecat	*Mustela putorius*
Pine marten	*Martes martes*
Badger	*Meles meles*
Otter	*Lutra lutra*

Felidae

Wild cat	*Felis silvestris*
Lynx	*Lynx lynx*

Avian predators

Owls (*Strigiformes*)

Tawny owl	*Strix aluco*
Eagle owl	*Bubo bubo*
Great grey owl	*Strix nebulosa*
Snowy owl	*Nyctea scandiaca*
Tengmalm's owl	*Aegolius funereus*
Long-eared owl	*Asio otus*
Short-eared owl	*Asio flammeus*
Barn owl	*Tyto alba*

Hawks (*Accipitriformes*)

Golden eagle	*Aquila chrysaetos*
Hen harrier	*Circus cyaneus*
Common buzzard	*Buteo buteo*
Rough-legged buzzard	*Buteo lagopus*
Sparrowhawk	*Accipiter nisus*
Goshawk	*Accipiter gentilis*

Falcons (*Falconidae*)

Kestrel	*Falco tinnunculus*
Peregrine falcon	*Falco peregrinus*
Gyr falcon	*Falco rusticolus*

Crows (*Corvidae*)

Carrion crow	*Corvus corone corone*
Hooded crow	*Corvus corone cornix*
Raven	*Corvus corax*

Gulls & Skuas (*Laridae* & *Stercorariidae*)

Great black-backed gull	*Larus marinus*
Lesser black-backed gull	*Larus fuscus*
Great skua	*Stercorarius skua*
Pomarine skua	*Stercorarius pomarinus*
Long-tailed skua	*Stercorarius longicaudus*

Grey heron	*Ardea cinerea*

Great grey shrike	*Lanius excubitor*

Index

Bibliography

Aaris-Sørensen, K. & Andreasen, T.N. 1983 Small mammals from Danish Mesolithic sites. *Journal of Danish Archaeology* vol.11, 30-38.

Andrews, P. 1990 *Owls, Caves and Fossils*. Natural History Museum Publications, London.

Andrews, P. & Evans, E.M.N. 1983 Small mammal bone accumulations produced by mammalian carnivores. *Palaeobiology* 9 (3), 289-307.

ApSimon, A.M., Smart, P.L., Macphail, R., Scott, K. & Taylor, H. 1992 King Arthur's Cave, Whitchurch, Herefordshire. Reassessment of a Middle and Upper Palaeolithic, Mesolithic and Beaker site. *Proceedings of University of Bristol Spelaeological Society* 19 (2),183-249.

Archer-Thompson, J. & Bunker, F. 1993 *Investigating Skomer*. Field Studies Council Publications, Shrewsbury.

Atkinson, T.C., Briffa, K.R & Coope. G,R. 1987 Seasonal temperatures in Britain during the past 22,000 wears, reconstructed using beetle remains. *Nature* 325, 587-592.

Barton, R.N.E. 1993 Wye Valley Caves Project: an interim report on the survey & excavations in 1993. *Proceedings of the University of Bristol Spelaeological Society* 19 (3), 337-346.

Barton, R.N.E. 1994 Second interim report on the survey and excavations in the Wye Valley 1994. *Proceedings of the University of Bristol Spelaeological Society* 20 (1), 63-73.

Barton, R.N.E. 1996 Fourth interim report on the survey and excavations in the Wye Valley 1996. *Proceedings of the University of Bristol Spelaeological Society* 20 (3), 263-273.

Barton, R.N.E & Collcutt, S.N. !986 A Survey of Palaeolithic Cave Sites and Rockshelters in England and Wales. Unpublished Report commissioned by CADW and English Heritage.

Barton, R.N.E. Price, C. & Proctor, C. 1997 The Wye Valley Caves Project: recent investigations at King Arthur's Cave and Madawg Rockshelter, in Lewis, S.G. & Maddy, D. (eds.) *The Quaternary of the South Midlands & the Welsh Marches: Field Guide*, Quaternary Research Association, London. 63 –73.

Barton, RN.E. & Price, C. 1999 The westernmost Upper Palaeolithic cave site in Britain and probable evidence of a Bronze Age shell midden: new investigations at Priory Farm Cave, Pembrokeshire. *Archaeology in Wales* 39, 3-9.

Barton, N., Roberts, A.J. & Roe, D.A. (eds.) 1991 *The Late Glacial in North-West Europe: human adaptation and environmental change at the end of the Pleistocene*. Council for British Archaeology Research Report 77.

Bate, D.M.A, 1901 A short account of a bone cave in the carboniferous limestone of the Wye Valley. *Geological Magazine*, new series vol. 8, 101-6.

Becker, B. & Kromer, B. 1991 Dendrochronology and radiocarbon calibration of the early Holocene, in Barton, N., Roberts, A.J. & Roe, D.A. (eds.) 1991 *The Late Glacial in North-West Europe: human adaptation and environmental change at the end of the Pleistocene*. Council for British Archaeology Research Report 77. 22-24.

Bilton, D.T., Mirol, P.M., Mascheretti, S., Fredga, K., Zima, J. & Searle, J.B. 1998 Mediterranean Europe as an area of endemism for small mammals rather than a source for northwards postglacial colonization. *Proceedings of the Royal Society of London* B, vol.265, 1219-1226.

Bjärvall, A. & Ullström, S. 1985 *Däggdjur*. Wahlström & Widstrand, Stockholm

Blamey, M. & Grey-Wilson, C. 1989 *The Illustrated Flora of Britain & Northern Europe*. Hodder & Stoughton, London.

Bowen, D.Q., 1980 The Pleistocene scenarios of Palaeolithic Wales, in Taylor, J.A. (ed.) 1980 *Culture & Environment in Prehistoric Wales* B.A.R. British Series 76. 1-14.

Bowen, D.Q. 2000 Calibration & correlation with the GRIP and GISP2 Greenland ice cores of radiocarbon ages from Paviland (Goat's Hole), Gower. Aldhouse-Green, S, *Paviland Cave and the 'Red Lady', a Definitive Report*. WASP, Bristol. 61-63.

Bowman, S.G.E., Ambers, J.C. & Leese, M.N. 1990 Re-evaluation of British Museum radiocarbon dates issued between 1980 and 1984. *Radiocarbon* Vol. 32, no.1. 59-79.

Brown, A.P. 1977 Late Devensian and Flandrian vegetational history of Bodmin Moor, Cornwall. *Philosophical Transactions of the Royal Society of London* B, vol. 276, 251-320.

Campbell, J.B. 1977 *The Upper Palaeolithic in Britain*. Clarendon Press, Oxford.

Campbell, J.B. & Sampson, C.G. 1971 *A New Analysis of Kent's Cavern, Devonshire, England*. University of Oregon Anthropological Papers No 3.

Caseldine, C.J. & Maguire, D.J. 1981 A review of the prehistoric and historic environment on Dartmoor. *Proceedings of the Devon Archaeological Society* 39, 1-16.

Chapman, P. 1993 *Caves and Cave Life*. Harper Collins, London.

Chappell, J. & Shackleton, N.J. 1986 Oxygen isotopes and sea level. *Nature* 324, 137-140.

Chinery, M. 1986 *The Living Garden*. Dorling Kindersley, London.

Clarke, R.H. 1970 Quaternary sediments off South East Devon. *Quaternary Journal of the Geological Society of London* 125, 277-318.

Coles, G. 1986 The palynology of the Little Hoyle sediments:an interim statement. In Green, S. 1986 Excavations at Little Hoyle (Longbury Bank), Wales, in 1984. In D.A. Roe (ed). *Studies in the Upper Palaeolithic of Britain and Northwest Europe*. B.A.R International Series 296. Oxford. 99-119. 277—318.

Coombs, F. 1978 *The Crows*. Batsford, London.

Coope, G.R., Lemdahl, G., Lowe, J.J. & Walkling A. 1998 Temperature gradients in northern Europe during the last glacial-Holocene transition (14-9 ^{14}C kyr BP) interpreted from coleopteran assemblages. *Journal of Quaternary Science* 13 (3), 419-433.

Corbet, G.B. 1978 *The Mammals of the Palaeoarctic Region: a Taxonomic Review*. British Museum (Natural History), London.

Corbet, G.B & Harris, S. 1991 *The Handbook of British Mammals* (3rd Edition). Blackwell, Oxford.

Crowcroft, P. 1957 *The Life of the Shrew*. Reinhardt, London.

Currant, A.P., 1986 Lateglacial mammal fauna of Gough's Cave, Cheddar Gorge, Somerset. *Proceedings of the University of Bristol Spelaeological Society* 17, 286-304.

Currant, A.P. 1991 A Late Glacial Interstadial mammal fauna from Gough's Cave, Somerset, England. In Barton, N., Roberts, A.J. & Roe, D.A. (eds), *The Late Glacial in North-West Europe*. Council for British Archaeology Research Report 77, London. 48-50.

Currant, A.P., Jacobi, R.M. & Stringer C.B. 1989 Excavations at Gough's Cave, Somerset 1986-7. *Antiquity* 63 (no.238), p.131-6.

De Jonge, G. & Dienske, H. 1979 Habitat and interspecific displacement of small mammals in the Netherlands. *Netherlands Journal of Zoology* 29 (2) 177-214.

David, A. 1991 Late Glacial archaeological residues from Wales: a selection, in Barton, N., Roberts, A.J. & Roe, D.A. (eds) *The Late Glacial in North-West Europe*. C.B.A. Research Report 77, Council for British Archaeology, London. 141-159.

Eastham, A. 2000 The Paviland avifauna. In Aldhouse-Green, S. *Paviland Cave and the 'Red Lady': a Definitive Report*. Western Academic & Specialist Press, Bristol. 287-290.

Elton, C. 1942 *Voles, Mice and Lemmings – Problems in Population Dynamics*. Clarendon Press, Oxford.

Evans, J.G., French, C. & Leighton, D. 1978 Habitat change in two Late-glacial and Post-glacial sites in southern Britain: the molluscan evidence. In Limbrey, S. & Evans, J.G. (eds.) *The Effect of Man on the Landscape: the Lowland Zone*. Council for British Archaeology Research Report no.21. 63-75.

Evans, J. & O'Connor, T. 1999 *Environmental Archaeology: Principals & Methods*. Sutton, Stroud.

Fairbanks, R.G. 1989 A 17.000-year glacio-eustatic sea-level record: influence of glacial melting rates on the Younger Dryas event and deep-ocean circulation. *Nature* 342, 637-642.

Fearnley-Whittingstall, H. 1997 *A Cook on the Wild Side*. Boxtree, London.

Fitter, R., Fitter, A. & Farrer, A. 1984 *Grasses, Sedges, Rushes & Ferns of Britain and Northern Europe*. Harper Collins, London.

Freethy, R. 1983 *Man & Beast - the Natural and Unnatural History of British Mammals*. Blandford Press, Dorset.

Gleed-Owen, C.P. 1998 *Quaternary Herpetofaunas of the British Isles: Taxonomic Descriptions, Palaeoenvironmental Reconstructions & Biostratigraphic Implications*. Unpublished PhD thesis, Coventry University.

Glue, D.E. 1974 Food of the Barn Owl in Britain and Ireland. *Bird Study* 21, 200-210.

Godwin, Sir H. 1975 *History of the British Flora: a factual basis for phytogeography* (2nd edition). Cambridge University Press.

Green, S. 1986 Excavations at Little Hoyle (Longbury Bank), Wales, in 1984. In D.A. Roe (ed). *Studies in the Upper Palaeolithic of Britain and Northwest Europe*. B.A.R International Series 296. Oxford. 99-119.

Grimes, W.F. 1933 Priory Farm Cave, Monkton, Pembrokeshire. *Archaeologica Cambrensis* 88. 88-100.

Harrison, C. 1975 *A Field Guide to the Nests, Eggs and Nestlings of British and European Birds*. Collins, London.

Harrison, C.J.O. 1980 A re-examination of British Devensian and Earlier Holocene bird bones in the British Museum (Natural History). *Journal of Archaeological Science* 7, 53-68.

Harrison, C.J.O. 1987 Pleistocene and prehistoric birds of South-West Britain. *Proceedings of the University of Bristol Spelaeological Society* 18 (1), 81-104.

Hewer, T.F. 1925 First report on excavations in the Wye Valley. *Proceedings of the University of Bristol Spelaeological Society* 2 (2), 147-162.

Hillson, S. 1986 *Teeth*. Cambridge University Press.

Housley, R.A. 1991 AMS dates from the Late Glacial and early Postglacial in north-west Europe - a review. In Barton, N., Roberts, A.J. & Roe, D.A. *The Late Glacial in North-West Europe: human adaptation and environmental change at the end of the Pleistocene*. Council for British Archaeology Research Report 77, 25-39.

Isarin, R.F.B., Renssen, H. & Vandenberghe J. 1998 The impact of the North Atlantic Ocean on the Younger Dryas climate in northwestern and central Europe. *Journal of Quaternary Science* 13 (5), 447-453.

Jacobi, R.M. 1980 The Upper Palaeolithic of Britain, with special reference to Wales, in Taylor, J.A. (ed.), *Culture and Environment in Prehistoric Wales*. B.A.R., Oxford. 15-99.

Jacobi, R. 1991 The Creswellian, Creswell and Cheddar. In Barton, N., Roberts, A.J. & Roe D.A.(eds.) *The Late Glacial in North-West Europe: human adaptation and environmental change at the end of the Pleistocene*. Council for British Archaeology Research Report 77, 128-140.

Jones,R.L. & Keen, D.H. 1993 *Pleistocene Environments in the British Isles*. Chapman & Hall, London.

Köppen, W.P. 1933 *Handbuch der Klimatologie*. Berlin.

Kra, R. & Stuiver, M. 1986 *12th International Radiocarbon Conference, Trondheim, Norway 1985*, Proceedings of Radiocarbon, 28, 2A and B.

Kruuk, H. 1995 *Wild Otters*. Oxford University Press.

Lee, R.B & DeVore, I. 1968 *Man the Hunter*. Aldine Publishing Company, New York.

Leroi-Gourhan, A. 1985 Pollen analysis of sediment samples from Gough's Cave, Cheddar. *Proceedings of the University of Bristol Spelaeological Society* 17 (2), pp.141-144.

Lopez, B. 1986 *Arctic Dreams*. Harvill Press, London.

Macdonald, D. & Barrett, P. 1993 *Mammals of Britain & Europe*. HarperCollins, London.

Marsden, W., 1964 *The Lemming Year*, Chatto & Windus, London.

Marshall, S. 1967 *Fenland Chronicle*. Cambridge University Press.

McBurney, C. 1959 Report on the first season's fieldwork on British Upper Palaeolithic cave deposits. *Proceedings of the Prehistoric Society* XXV 260-269.

Meteorological Office 1990 *The Climate of Great Britain: Climatological Memorandum 132; The Midlands*. Bracknell, Berks.

Meteorological Office 1990 *The Climate of Great Britain: Climatological Memorandum 138; Somerset and Avon*. Bracknell, Berks.

Meteorological Office 1990 *The Climate of Great Britain: Climatological Memorandum 139;The South-West Peninsula and the Channel Islands*. Bracknell, Berks.

Mikkola, H. 1983 *Owls of Europe*. Poyser, London.

Mitchell-Jones, A.J., Amori, G., Bogdanowicz, W., Krysufek, B., Reijnders, P., Spitzenberger, F., Stubbe, M., Thissen, J., Vohralik, V. & Zima, J. 1999. *The Atlas of European Mammals*. Poyser, London.

Moore, P.D. 1978 Studies in the vegetational history of Mid-Wales. V. Stratigraphy and pollen analysis of Llyn Mire in the Wye Valley. *New Phytologist* 80. 281-302.

Mullarney, K., Svensson, L., Zetterstrom, D. & Grant, P.J. 1999 *Collins Bird Guide*. Harper Collins, London.

Nadachowski, A. 1982 Late Quaternary Rodents of Poland with Special Reference to *Morphotype Dentition Analysis of Voles*. Polska Akademia Nauk, Warsaw.

Nowak, R.M., 1999 *Walker's Mammals of the World* (sixth edition), Johns Hopkins University Press, Baltimore & London.

Ognev, S.I. 1964 *Mammals of the USSR and Adjacent Countries Vol. VII - Rodents*. Israel Program for Scientific Translations, Jerusalem.

Pennington, W. 1977 The Late Devensian flora and vegetation of Britain. *Philosophical Transactions of the Royal Society of London* B 280, 247-271.

Pernetta, J.C. & Handford, P.T. 1970 Mammalian and avian remains from possible Bronze Age deposits on Nornour, Isles of Scilly, in *Journal of Zoology, London*, vol. 162, 534-540.

Pielou, E.C. 1994 *A Naturalist's Guide to the Arctic*. University of Chicago Press

Polunin, O. & Walters, M. 1985 *A Guide to the Vegetation of Britain and Europe*. Oxford University Press.

Proctor, C.J. 1995 *A British Pleistocene chronology based on U-series & ESR dating of speleothem*. Unpublished PhD thesis, University of Bristol.

Roberts, A.J. (compiler) 1996 Evidence for late Pleistocene and early Holocene human activity and environmental change from the Torbryan Valley, south Devon. In Charman. D.J., Newnham, R.M. & Groot, D.G. (eds) *The Quaternary of Devon & East Cornwall: Field Guide*, Quaternary Research Association, London. 168-224.

Schober, W & Grimmberger, E. 1993 *Bats of Britain and Europe*. Hamlyn, London.

Simmons, I.G. 1975 The ecological setting of Mesolithic man in the Highland zone. In Evans, J.G., Limbrey, S. & Cleere, H. *The Effect of Man on the Landscape: the Highland Zone*. Council for British Archaeology research report no.11, 57-63.

Smith, K., Coppen, J., Wainwright, G.J. & Beckett, S. 1981 The Shaugh Moor project: third report, settlement and environmental investigations. *Proceedings of the Prehistoric Society* 47, 205-273.

Stewart, J.M. 1992 *The Nature of Russia*. Boxtree, London.

Stuart, A.J. 1982 *Pleistocene Vertebrates in the British Isles*. Longman, London

Sparks, B.W. & West, R.G. 1972 *The Ice Age in Britain*. Methuen, London.

Sutcliffe, A.J. & Kowalski, K. 1976 *Pleistocene Rodents of the British Isles*. Bulletin of the British Museum (Natural History) Vol. 27 No.2.

Taylor, I. 1994. *Barn Owls: Predator-Prey Relationships and Conservation*. Cambridge University Press.

Taylor, K.C, Mayewski, P.A, Alley, R.B, Brook, E.J, Gow, A.J, Grootes, P.M, Meese, D.A, Saltzman, E.S, Severinghaus, J.P, Twickler, M.S, White, J.W.C, Whitlow, S. & Zielinski, G.A. 1997 The Holocene – Younger Dryas transition recorded at Summit, Greenland. *Science* 278, 825-827.

Thompson, F. 1945 *Lark Rise to Candleford*. Oxford University Press.

Voisin, C. 1991 *The Herons of Europe*. Poyser, London.

Walker. M.J.C. & Harkness, D.D. 1990 Radiocarbon dating the Devensian Lateglacial in Britain: new evidence from Llanilid, South Wales. *Journal of Quaternary Science* 5 (2), 135-144.

Walker, M.J.C., Griffiths, H.I., Ringwood, V. & Evans, J.G. 1993 An early-Holocene pollen, mollusc and ostracod sequence from lake marl at Llangorse Lake, South Wales, UK. *The Holocene* 3, 138-149.

White, G. 1788-9 *The Natural History of Selbourne*. 1987 Reprint - Penguin, London.

Whitten, D.G.A. with Brooks, J.R.V. 1972 *The Penguin Dictionary of Geology*. Penguin, Harmondsworth, Middlesex.

Yalden, D.W. 1981 The occurrence of the Pigmy shrew *Sorex minutus* on moorland, and the implications for its presence in Ireland, in *Journal of Zoology, London*, vol. 195, 147-156.

Yalden, D.W. 1986 Neolithic bats from Dowel Cave, Derbyshire. *Journal of Zoology* 210, pp.616-619

Yalden, D.W. 1999 *The History of British Mammals*. Poyser, London.

Yalden, D.W & Yalden, P.E. 1985 An experimental investigation of examining kestrel diet by pellet analysis. *Bird Study* 32, 50-55.

Adams, J. 1997 Sudden climate transitions during the Quaternary. http://www.esd.ornl.gov/projects/qen/transit2.html 29/11/99

Adams, J. 1998 Europe during the last 150,000 years. http://www.esd.ornl.gov/projects/qen/nercEurope.html 22/10/98

Meteorological Office 1999 UK Climate Averages. http://www.meto.govt.uk/climate/uk/averages/images. 12/12/00

ORAU website: Radiocarbon Measurements for Environmental Science. http://www.rlaha.ox.ac.uk/orau/02_04.htm 30/10/01

www.ingramcontent.com/pod-product-compliance
Lightning Source LLC
Chambersburg PA
CBHW061007030426
42334CB00033B/3391